Capitalizing
on Conflict

Capitalizing on Conflict

Strategies and Practices for Turning Conflict to Synergy in Organizations

—A MANAGER'S HANDBOOK—

KIRK BLACKARD
JAMES W. GIBSON

DAVIES-BLACK PUBLISHING
Palo Alto, California

Published by Davies-Black Publishing, an imprint of Consulting Psychologists Press, Inc., 3803 East Bayshore Road, Palo Alto, CA 94303; 800-624-1765.

Special discounts on bulk quantities of Davies-Black books are available to corporations, professional associations, and other organizations. For details, contact the Director of Book Sales at Davies-Black Publishing, an imprint of Consulting Psychologists Press, Inc., 3803 East Bayshore Road, Palo Alto, CA 94303; 650-691-9123; fax 650-623-9271.

06 05 04 03 02   10 9 8 7 6 5 4 3 2 1
Printed in the United States of America

Library of Congress Cataloging-in-Publication Data
Blackard, Kirk
  Capitalizing on conflict : strategies and practices for turning conflict into synergy in organizations : a manager's handbook / Kirk Blackard, James W. Gibson.—1st ed.
    p. cm.
  Includes bibliographical references and index.
  ISBN 0-89106-164-9
  1. Conflict management—Handbook, manuals, etc.   I. Gibson, James W. II. Title.

  HD42 .B575 2002
  658.4'053—dc21

2001058255

FIRST EDITION
First printing 2002

Contents

Preface

Enron Corporation was near the top of the Fortune 500 list of companies, considered one of the most innovative, sophisticated, and progressive companies in the world. Then, late in 2001, it imploded, resulting in the biggest corporate bankruptcy in U.S. history. The company owed billions of dollars to creditors. Its stock value was devastated, down 99 percent for the year at one point. Thousands of employees lost their jobs, and many, heavily invested in Enron stock in their retirement accounts, lost most of their life savings. Numerous lawsuits were filed. The SEC, congressional panels, and the Justice and Labor Departments began investigations.

Finger-pointing began almost immediately, and pundits, experts, and would-be experts will no doubt opine for years about what actually happened to topple the giant and why. We are not so presumptuous as to think we have the whole answer. However, reports about this amazing downfall raise classic questions about organizational conflict management and trigger the thought that failure to effectively manage conflict was at the root of many of Enron's problems. This view of Enron's fall from grace provides an important perspective for *Capitalizing on Conflict*.

Published reports[1] suggest that Enron's senior management behaved in ways that seemed to encourage the dark side of conflict rather than capitalize on its potential benefits. Management reportedly implemented performance review and reward processes that all but demanded negative conflict in the form of excessive employee competition, guarded communication, reduced teamwork, protection of self-interest, back stabbing, and other such problematic behavior. At the same time, management stifled positive conflict in the form of dissent, questions, and other interventions that suggested concern about or disagreement with many of the business practices that now appear to have led to Enron's downfall. It appears that the organization's management fostered the culture in which the downfall occurred by implicitly encouraging conflict, which became a major factor in the disaster, and failing to capitalize on what should have provided early warnings and an opportunity to avert the catastrophe.

This perspective on the Enron experience illustrates the basic premise of this book: that conflict within an organization has broad, systemic effects that go well beyond what one can see on the surface, and that effectively managing conflict requires much more than simply resolving disputes. To be effective, management must take action to minimize conflict that is negative and capitalize on conflict that is positive. While most managers will not face issues of the magnitude of those at Enron, they will, on a day-to-day basis, encounter opportunities large and small to improve their organization's performance through the way they manage conflict. The purpose of *Capitalizing on Conflict* is to help them take advantage of these opportunities and avoid their own version of the Enron collapse.

Most books on workplace conflict tend to be one-dimensional, focused only on how to resolve unhappy situations. They define "conflict management" as the handling of troublesome events or cases. And they often suggest conflict can be resolved with a few easy steps or by a single approach, such as adjusting personal styles, communicating effectively, listening actively, or controlling emotions.

This narrow view of conflict management, which addresses only specific disagreements that have become recognized organizational problems, is a little like worrying about a runaway horse after it is already out of the barn. It helps deal with existing problems but is only of marginal value to managers with broad organizational responsibilities. Instead, managers must take a much broader and more multifaceted view of conflict management: one that includes all the things they do or should do to minimize the negative effects of conflict and create an environment that capitalizes on the synergy it offers. They must prevent events of counterproductive conflict whenever feasible as well as deal effectively with those instances that inevitably do occur and need to be resolved.

In this broader context, workplace conflict is one of many issues that must be managed in its entirety, like the investment strategy, the safety program, the environmental effort, or any of the myriad other issues that require management's continuing attention. Managing conflict must be a comprehensive effort, an integral part of the organization's human resource management strategy that includes but goes well beyond resolving specific conflict events. It must foster positive, synergistic differences, avoid many possible causes of counterproductive conflict, and take the right action in many different areas.

> Just as selling a poorly performing asset is only part of an effective investment strategy, resolving conflict events is only part of an effective conflict management strategy.

Capitalizing on Conflict is not about management resolving conflicts. Thinking in such terms presumes conflict is linear, static, and always negative, and that management's actions to deal with it should be reactive rather than purposeful. Such thinking also implies that management's role is fixing other people's problems—a backward-looking view that often discredits the people involved and suggests holding on to the past. But the workplace is not simple, linear, or static. It is an uncertain and continually changing world in which all participants—employees and management alike—are faced with new challenges and different issues every day. Conflict is different today than it was yesterday, and it will be different tomorrow. It will have varying causes, play out in unpredictable ways, and result in new consequences.

Conflictive behavior in the workplace can range from very positive at one extreme to very counterproductive at the other. Properly managed, conflict can enhance creativity through constructive challenge and interchange, improve decisions by introducing more information and perspective, and foster learning through mutual problem solving. It can therefore further the purpose of the organization by improving the performance of its people and systems.

> • Several employees combine their differing views to solve a difficult problem in a way that neither individual had thought of.
>
> • A challenge to an organizational policy leads management to improve that policy.

Counterproductive conflict, however, detracts from the organization's purpose by impairing the performance of its people or systems. It usually tends to prevent employees from working on the right things, obtaining quality results, or being as productive as they can be. This happens in various ways, such as when employees

- Are inattentive and distracted, causing sloppy or slow work and reducing creativity
- Work at cross-purposes with other employees and the organization
- Waste time worrying about conflict or being involved in conflict events
- Unreasonably challenge supervisor direction
- Initiate conflict that interferes with the work of others
- Are intentionally less productive as an exercise of power
- File costly law suits or other actions

Conflict imposes costs on employees as well. It often takes the fun out of even the most interesting work and makes it drudgery. It imposes an emotional drain on employees that can easily spread to co-workers, family, and friends. And of course these costs to employees usually loop back to escalate the negative impact on the organization.

Although positive and counterproductive conflicts have very different organizational impact, the line between them is often fuzzy and fluid. Similar initial conditions can ultimately evolve into different situations and lead to differing behavior. Under some circumstances, a disagreement can create synergy, aid in problem solving, and make the workplace more interesting and fun. But under different circumstances, the same disagreement can create problems such as low morale, a distracted workforce, lawsuits, and other behavior that detracts from the organization's purpose.

> A disagreement between engineers over product design can lead to improvement in the operation and marketability of the product in a healthy organization but can lead to backbiting, low morale, and employee turnover in another.

In spite of their common roots, management all too frequently approaches positive and counterproductive conflict as though they were independent and had nothing in common. With this bifurcated approach, management tries to foster positive conflict through systems that are thoughtfully designed and implemented to enhance performance. Corporate visions and statements of ideology make organizational purpose and expectations of employees clear. Differences are encouraged by diversity in hiring and are acknowledged and valued as long as the resulting behavior contributes to the organization's purpose. Teams, task forces, and other collaborative work groups facilitate the synergy of differing information and ideas. Thoughtful compensation processes provide an incentive for different people to work together. Supervisors make the most of what all employees have to offer. And various management processes are synchronized so that positive conflict becomes an important driver of organizational excellence.

In this model, however, counterproductive conflict is often handled differently. Behavior that detracts from organizational purpose is seen as the ad hoc action of troublemakers, deviants, or marginal employees who do not have the ability, skill, or desire to behave properly. This behavior is addressed after it occurs, on an as-needed basis, with emphasis on sanctions, policies, discipline, remedial training, and other reactive approaches. Unfortunately, such processes for addressing counterproductive conflict are viewed independently of those for managing productive conflict.

Another view of conflict—which is the view adopted in this book—suggests a different model. This alternative approach accepts that troublemakers, deviants, and ignorance may cause some counterproductive conflict in the workplace. More important, however, it acknowledges divergent interests, accepts that some counterproductive conflict is natural and inevitable, and even suggests that management and its systems cause much workplace conflict—both among employees and between employees and management.

- Several employees aspire to the same job, and the competition escalates to bad behavior.

- A zero-sum pay program in which one employee gets less when another gets more causes unhealthy competition and failure to communicate.

- Hours of work expected by management impinge on employees' social life and cause them to try to manipulate the system.

- Investment demands lead to lower levels of pay and employee discontent.

In this model, counterproductive conflict is one end of a continuum of behavior that management must plan for and manage if it is to capitalize on the positive, synergistic aspects of conflict. Although counterproductive behavior differs from positive behavior, it does not require fundamentally different management approaches. Instead of being effectively managed with stand-alone programs or interventions, it must be addressed with management strategies and practices that are an integrated part of the human resource management system of the enterprise. Just as counterproductive conflict is an inevitable and normal part of a continuum of behavior in an organization, approaches for dealing with it must be an integrated part of the continuum of management practices. This model emphasizes a systems approach that integrates management of both positive and counterproductive conflict while recognizing that actual practices for maximizing the first will usually differ from practices for minimizing the second.

- Teaching team skills will help employees resolve work issues but is less likely to prevent or resolve conflict over pay issues.
- Getting the pay system right may provide incentives for creativity and innovation, but it will not address personality clashes.
- Encouraging diversity without providing the right climate may cause rather than reduce counterproductive conflict.

Thus, conflict is neither good nor bad, behavior resulting from it may be either positive or negative, and conflict management should be viewed as a continuum of strategies and practices. This book, however, will not attempt to address all the management practices required for optimizing the full spectrum of conflict. Instead, it will provide managers with a basic understanding of the negative side of conflict and how they can manage their organization to create an environment that allows the positive aspects of conflict to flourish. It views management of counterproductive conflict as a journey in which management's primary roles are to lay out the destination, provide an incentive to employees to take the journey, and expect employees to select the best route and negotiate the potholes they encounter along the way. Such actions effectively leverage the ability and willingness of each individual to minimize the negatives and accentuate the positives of conflict for both employees and the organization.

Capitalizing on Conflict is not a how-to book. Managing counterproductive conflict in our complex world is not that simple. No single approach fits all situations, and solutions to conflict issues cannot be designed with a cookie cutter. Rather, management must acknowledge that although it sets the tone for the organization and initiates most of the actions that determine whether the results of conflict will be positive or negative, it is incapable of imposing simple solutions or legislating away counterproductive conflict. It must work with employees in a good faith journey to figure out and implement ways to manage conflict in the best interest of all concerned. Such a journey has the following phases:

- Minimizing counterproductive conflict in the first instance
- Ensuring that conflict that nevertheless occurs is surfaced so it can be dealt with
- Seeing that conflict is appropriately resolved
- Learning from the process to further minimize conflict in the future

These four phases form a continuing cycle that provides a common frame of reference to help managers at all levels think more deeply about conflict in their organization, assess each situation individually in the context of broader management systems, identify the problems and opportunities that exist, and analyze options for improvement. Managers can then make their own informed decisions about their personal behavior and how they will manage systems under their control.

The book is divided into three parts:

- Part 1 provides a broad perspective on conflict. Chapter 1 discusses what it is and introduces various types of conflict among different parties. It also reviews the systems basis of most conflict and discusses its main causes in the workplace. Chapter 2 addresses the role of managers and management in dealing with conflict, pointing out the often paradoxical nature of their role. This chapter introduces the "minimize, surface, resolve, and learn" cycle that forms the basis of the remainder of the book.

- Part 2 recognizes that management and its systems are key factors in either causing or minimizing counterproductive conflict and presents ideas for managing the organization to minimize its overall conflict level. Chapters 3 through 7 address ways to develop a trusting environment, avoid policy-driven conflict, manage change to minimize conflict, hire and maintain the right workforce, and foster appropriate supervisor behavior.

- Part 3 acknowledges that some counterproductive conflict will occur even in the best-managed organizations and presents the remaining three phases of the conflict management cycle. Chapters 8 through 12 review ideas for surfacing suppressed conflict, dealing effectively with it, learning from the process, and using that learning to capitalize on the synergistic aspects of conflict.

Many experiences have contributed to the writing of this book. We are both longtime conflict management practitioners who have experienced firsthand the frustrations, challenges, and rewards of dealing with conflict. Kirk Blackard spent many years as a manager with Shell Oil Company. In his various management roles, he developed a keen appreciation of the many ways in which management can either cause or minimize conflict, the limited role direct management intervention usually plays in resolving conflict over the long term, and the need to learn from each conflict in order to continually improve the organization's performance. His recent mediation and arbitration work has only confirmed these beliefs. Jim Gibson's many years of experience as a practicing attorney, educator, and mediator provided important insights into the most effective ways of resolving conflict. The synergy of our experiences has allowed us to develop and present ideas that will help managers and supervisors in all types of organizations manage workplace conflict in ways that optimize organizational performance.

Acknowledgments

We have been fortunate to benefit from one of the good aspects of conflict—the opportunity it presents to those involved to learn and grow. This book would not have been possible without our involvement in hundreds of conflicts over the years—either as direct parties, as representatives of management, or as third parties assisting with their resolution. We sincerely thank all those people who allowed us to work with them. The experiences helped us greatly, and hopefully they benefited the others who were involved as well. We also thank our many colleagues in the conflict resolution business. The opportunity to converse, question, listen, and learn from you has been invaluable, and we owe you a debt of gratitude.

Kirk Blackard is especially grateful to have worked for Shell Oil Company, which encouraged many of the ideas expressed in this book and allowed the room for experimentation and learning. Jim Gibson credits all his mediation students for teaching him so much by sharing their backgrounds, cultures, and personal experiences.

We both appreciate the efforts of Dr. Patricia Williams and her staff at Sam Houston State University in the preparation of the manuscript. And finally, we greatly appreciate the encouragement our families have provided for all our efforts. Kirk is especially thankful to wife Marcia and sons Chris and Drew. Jim is especially thankful to wife Betty and daughters Kathryn and Allyson.

About the Authors

Fred K. (Kirk) Blackard

Kirk Blackard was employed by Shell Oil Company from 1968 until 1998. In his early assignments he represented Shell in negotiations, grievances, arbitration cases, and other matters involving the company's relationship with labor unions. From 1975 until 1989 he held several assignments in Shell's mining division, including president, successively, of three subsidiary companies. He subsequently was assigned as General Manager Industrial Relations for Shell Oil, where his responsibilities included initial work leading to Shell Resolve, Shell Oil's internal conflict management system. From 1996 to 1998 Blackard was assigned to London as Shell Oil liaison to Royal Dutch Shell. He currently is a management consultant, arbitrator, and mediator.

Blackard is a member of the State Bar of Texas, the Industrial Relations Research Association, the American Arbitration Association, the Texas Association of Mediators, and the Association for Conflict Resolution. His work has been published in the *Dispute Resolution Journal*, and his book *Managing Change in a Unionized Workplace* was published in April 2000. He holds a B.A. degree in economics from Texas A&M University and a J.D. degree from the University of Texas School of Law.

James W. Gibson

James Gibson is an attorney, mediator, and educator with an extensive background in alternate dispute resolution and conflict management. Since 1994 he has trained mediators through the Sam Houston State University Extended Learning Program, Texas A&M University, Texas Woman's University, and the University of Houston–Clear Lake by conducting seminars in basic mediation, advanced mediation, family mediation, mediation of employer/employee disputes, and advanced communication skills. He also serves as student legal advisor at Sam Houston State, mediates disputes for private clients, and consults with organizations on the development and implementation of alternate dispute resolution systems.

Gibson is a frequent speaker on conflict management at regional and national conferences. He has written or contributed to many training manuals, and his writing has been published in *Texas Trial Lawyer, Alternative Resolutions, Texas Mediator,* and the newsletter of the Texas Court of Criminal Appeals.

Gibson is a member of the State Bar of Texas and was a founder and board member of the Texas Mediator Credentialing Association and the Texas Mediation Trainers Roundtable. A former member of the board of directors of the Texas Association of Mediators and president of the Houston chapter of the Society of Professionals in Dispute Resolution (now the Association for Conflict Resolution), he has been honored for outstanding service to the ADR Section of the State Bar of Texas. Gibson received his B.B.A. degree from the University of Texas and his J. D. degree from Southern Methodist University School of Law.

PART 1

Background

CHAPTER 1

Perspectives

*"What occasions the greater part of the world's quarrels?
Simply this: Two minds meet and do not understand
each other in time enough to prevent any shock of
surprise at the conduct of either party."*

—JOHN KEATS

Managing workplace conflict to optimize organizational performance is not easy. Conflict is ephemeral and dynamic, and cookie-cutter approaches, ad hoc actions, imposed solutions, or other remedial, backward-looking techniques will not do the job. They may settle disputes, but they will not minimize conflict and its effects over the long term. Optimizing organizational performance requires more. Managers must plan for conflict, treat each conflict event as unique, and respond holistically to events when they occur. They must think, learn, analyze, prioritize, and decide.

This thoughtful approach to conflict management will not work in a vacuum. It requires a conceptual framework to guide managers in what to think about, what facts are or are not important, and what criteria should govern their decisions. It also requires a common language that facilitates communication among managers, supervisors, and employees and allows them to develop collaborative approaches.

This chapter provides that framework and language. It defines conflict, reviews the parties typically involved, discusses various types of workplace conflict situations, and summarizes the causes of conflict as a basis for understanding how to manage it effectively.

CONFLICT DEFINITION

Workplace conflict is a dynamic process reflecting the interaction of two or more interdependent parties who have some level of difference or incompatibility between them. Conflict can exist in widely varying workplace situations: in a collaborative meeting of colleagues exploring new ideas about an exciting opportunity, between an employee and supervisor discussing different views of the employee's performance, among several managers in a heated argument about budget issues, between peers when one perceives the other's activities as harassing, or between employees collectively and the employer in the case of a labor strike.

Thus, while conflict envisions differences between parties, its definition changes based on the people involved, the circumstances, and the perceptions of those circumstances. Its intensity often ebbs and flows, and its consequences may vary greatly. Whether conflict even exists is in the eye of the beholder; what one calls an exchange of ideas another calls conflict. Sometimes it is good, and at other times it is not so good.

Some conflict is productive and necessary for an effective organization, as constructive use of differences fosters organizational excellence. An effective organization brings differences together to make the combined contribution of all employees greater than the sum of their individual contributions. Properly managed, conflict

- Enhances creativity through constructive challenge and interchange of ideas
- Improves decisions through thoughtful consideration of different information and different views
- Facilitates implementation through involvement, mutual understanding, and buy-in
- Improves performance of employees and managers through broadened exposure
- Fosters personal and organizational learning through mutual problem solving

Conflict also has its darker side and is often described using negative terms, such as *clash* and *battle*. Counterproductive conflict can

- Cause an unpleasant work environment characterized by employee fear and low morale
- Reduce loyalty and commitment to organizational purpose
- Impair productivity
- Lead to sabotage by employees attempting to cause someone else to lose if they cannot win
- Cause excessive turnover when employees leave because their needs are not being met and they wish to avoid overt conflict
- Create high litigation costs and adverse judgments driven by employees who see no alternative to filing legal action

Counterproductive situations cover the range of employee behavior—from employees just failing to make their best contribution, which translates to the organization's performance not being as good as it could be, to overtly negative behavior that causes problems and imposes unnecessary costs. For organizational excellence, management must deal effectively with the entire range of behavior.

PARTIES TO CONFLICT

Parties to conflict typically have an interdependent relationship that is made difficult by conflicting or incompatible interests. These relationships and interests often define homogeneous groups of employees, such as "supervisors," "management," and "subordinates." Each group has unique interests and goals that cause the people in it to behave in specific, predictable ways when faced with the possibility of conflict.

- Subordinates are likely to be at a power disadvantage to supervisors and react with fear when faced with conflict over their job performance.

- Persons speaking for management have different incentives than individuals speaking for themselves and can be expected to defend the organization's positions.

- Supervisors are likely to behave one way in a conflict with a subordinate and a different way in a conflict with a manager of higher rank.

To effectively manage such incompatible interests, management must identify the potential conflicting parties and the relationships among them:

- *Conflict between individuals.* Individuals may be peers, with similar organizational status, resources, and power base. Conflict may also exist between an individual supervisor and a nonsupervisory employee, or between individuals at different organizational levels when one employee is perceived to have more resources and power than the other.

- *Conflict between an individual and the organization.* While such conflict may appear to be a subordinate-supervisor conflict, the supervisor is in reality an agent of management in the aggregate, responsible for its policies and interests. Since he or she presumably has access to the resources and power of the organization, the real conflict is with the "organization."

- *Conflict between groups of employees.* Similarly situated individuals, who do not represent management, may engage in conflict with other such groups with incompatible interests.

> - Employees in one department have an ongoing dispute with those in another department over a work-related issue.
> - Smokers disagree with nonsmokers on the details of a no-smoking policy.

- *Conflict between groups and the organization.* Groups who are not a part of management are in conflict with the management of the organization.

> - A union is in conflict with management.
> - Members of a particular minority group band together to protest a management decision.

- *Third-party conflict.* Management becomes a party at risk in a dispute in which employees or groups of employees are the primary disputants.

> A sexual harassment case originating as a dispute between two employees ultimately includes management through allegations that management knew or should have known about the problem and didn't do enough to prevent the harassment.

This listing of parties is obviously an oversimplification, as the identity of the real parties to a conflict is often not clear, and each party can have multiple relationships.

- A dispute between departments may be a business issue involving the organization's policy or a personality conflict between department managers as individuals.

- A supervisor involved in a dispute with an employee may represent the interests of the company but does so in ways that create individual personal conflict with the employee.

The essential point is that before management can understand the cause of conflict and possibilities for resolving it, it must be clear about who the parties are and what their relationships are to each other. This information forms the starting point for a more complete understanding of any conflict situation.

WORKPLACE CONFLICT

Management's challenge is to deal effectively with conflict among whichever parties are involved: to foster those situations that are positive and reduce the number and effects of those that are counterproductive. In addressing this challenge, management must recognize that a conflict situation may be composed of different types of conflict and may exist at various levels of severity. The confluence of type and severity describes situations in terms that can help in thinking about causes and options for dealing with conflict.[2]

Types of Conflict

Conflict has its roots in the relationships of the parties and their attitudes toward each other with respect to an issue of consequence to both. Two fundamentally different types arise:

- *Substantive conflict,* often called cognitive conflict, pertains to the conflict of ideas and differences about content related to the work to be done or the interests of the parties. It typically concerns issues such as viewpoints, strategy interpretations, resources, and policies—the question of what was or is to be done.

> - Differing views among engineers about how to design a building
>
> - Differences of opinion between an employee and a supervisor as to whether a policy applies in a particular case
>
> - Differences between a company and a union concerning the appropriate level of medical insurance for employees

Substantive conflict may also concern how something is done. This conflict over process pertains to the power to determine how and when actions or changes are accomplished. It includes timing or the power to convene, displace, or reframe.

> An employee is laid off. He actually wanted to leave with the severance bonus that was offered but was offended and caused a conflict because he first learned of his layoff through the office grapevine rather than directly from his supervisor.

■ *Personal conflict,* often called affective conflict, pertains when personal relationships are characterized by friction, frustration, and personality clashes. It may involve social issues, emotion, personal concerns, norms, or values that cause issues between employees or organizations.

> - Two employees cannot get along because of a love triangle.
>
> - A supervisor and an employee have difficulties because the supervisor is overbearing and unthinking toward the employee.
>
> - Union and management have a long history of adversarial labor relations and individual animosity.

Severity

Regardless of whether a conflict is substantive or personal, the real significance to the organization is often determined by the symptoms and consequences of that conflict as reflected in the behavior of the parties involved. From that perspective, the terms *disagreement* and *dispute* define a severity range of possible behavior.

- *Disagreement* is a state of dissatisfaction, diversity of thought, dissent, or unmet expectations. It may be tangible and obvious but often is ongoing, amorphous, and intangible. Disagreement can exist among parties who are friendly and have common objectives but simply have different perspectives.

> - Co-workers disagree about who is likely to win a football game.
> - A supervisor and his subordinate disagree about whether the employee is performing adequately.
> - Managers disagree about the level of financial support that should be provided to a particular project.

- *Dispute* characterizes a situation that results from unresolved disagreement. It usually is tangible and concrete, with arguments, quarrels, and fights over issues, opposing positions, and expectations for relief. Friendships are usually suspended during disputes, and the parties strive for different objectives.

> - Co-workers are involved in heated arguments or backstabbing.
> - An employee files a grievance or EEO charge against the organization.

Conflict Situations

The confluence of type and severity describes the basic conflict situations that confront management: those situations that must be understood, discussed, and meaningfully dealt with on a daily basis. Figure 1 shows various conflict types and severities as creating four dissimilar situations, each of which generally calls for different management responses. The four situations are described in the paragraphs that follow.

Productive Synergy

When parties to a relationship have differing views (disagreement) about substantive issues, the stage is set for productive synergy. A positive interchange of diverse views and ideas can produce a whole better than the sum of its parts and allow employees to work together to solve problems

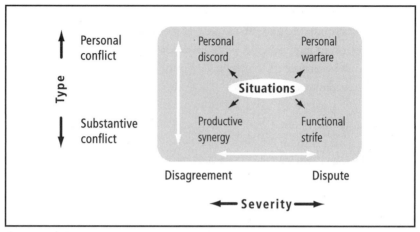

Figure 1 CONFLICT SITUATIONS

or exploit opportunities they could not handle as individuals. Productive synergy can exist in a diverse workforce and in cross-functional teams, employee networks, peer relationships, supervisor-employee relationships, and other forums for dialogue and challenge. It requires individuals to share their differences and learn from them. Management should provide an environment and incentives that foster such sharing and learning, which creates more productive synergy.

- A diverse design team melds differing ideas and expertise to build a breakthrough software system.
- A company-union negotiating team agrees on a difficult work assignment issue that meets employee needs and improves productivity.

Functional Strife

Unresolved substantive disagreement often escalates in severity and becomes a substantive dispute, or functional strife. The parties' previous constructive approaches to their differences dissolve. They engage in heated arguments and fight over the issues. Productive synergy is now functional strife: a quarrel or struggle related to work activities in which personalities or direct personal disagreements are not a significant factor. Parochial vision, poor communication, ineffective problem solving, incompatible interests, and other organizational deficiencies cause unsolved substantive disagreements that negatively affect the way individuals or organizations work together. Differing views and disagreements harden into intractable positions, and heated arguments develop between the individuals or functions that hold the conflicting positions. A win-lose atmosphere follows, in which the interests of the individuals or functions win out over broader organizational interests. This negative situation can persist for years if corrective action is not taken. Management's typical response, if any, to functional strife is to initiate a "program," such as increased training, organizational restructuring, or creation of committees or other parallel organizations to avoid the problem. Such responses may or may not address the real issues underlying functional strife.

- Disagreements between the engineering and marketing departments about product design become destructive and delay production.
- A disagreement between employee and supervisor concerning the appropriate level of pay causes the employee to resign.
- A disagreement between management and a union over work assignment procedures gets out of hand, and the union strikes.

Personal Discord

A low-level disagreement over personal issues causes personal discord, which generally has negative organizational consequences because it is a conflict of people rather than ideas. Personal discord can have two sources. It can arise when functional strife is not appropriately resolved. Continuing discussions about a difficult issue over a long period of time can degenerate into personal disputes or become fueled by personal agendas. Resolving such issues through unfair or power-based methods can cause those involved to harbor personal resentment.

Personal discord can also arise from the personalities of the people in the organization. People are not the same, and their personal differences can cause conflict. Sad to say, even today race, gender, religious, ethnic, and other personal differences can be the source of personal discord, as can bad personalities, stress, genuine misunderstandings, and myriad other factors that affect relationships among people.

Whatever the cause, when personal discord exists people do not get along and usually are unwilling or unable to work well together. Unfortunately, in spite of negative effects on organizational performance, these situations are often benign enough that they either are ignored or simply become the topic of organizational gossip.

> • People in the engineering and marketing departments argue so vehemently over product design that they come to dislike each other personally and refuse to communicate.
>
> • In an argument over pay, the supervisor tells the employee to "take it or leave it," and the employee becomes resentful.
>
> • Two individuals previously dated the same person and because of personal jealousy cannot get along.

Personal Warfare

When personal discord escalates in intensity, the result is personal warfare. It exists when individuals engage in behavior such as continuous quarrels, the silent treatment, retaliation, official complaints, or physical violence.

Personal warfare between an individual and the organization exists when the individual's needs or wants are not being met and the representatives of the organization are personally blamed for the result. Poor morale, continuous complaints, sabotage, or legal action are the likely consequences. The impact is similar but exacerbated when individuals join together as interest groups in a dispute with the company and resort to collective action.

Personal warfare is difficult, if not impossible, to ignore but is commonly addressed by attempts to just settle or dispose of the dispute rather than resolve the underlying causes.

> • An employee who resigns because of a supervisor's "take it or leave it" attitude about pay files a lawsuit for constructive discharge.
>
> • Two individuals who dated the same person become involved in a physical altercation.

Range of Conflict Situations

Although workplace conflict can be characterized by productive synergy, functional strife, personal discord, and personal warfare, the distinctions between these situations are not always clear. The point at which a disagreement becomes a dispute may be in the eyes of the beholder. Many conflicts have both substantive and personal dimensions or move back and forth between those aspects as they evolve. Functional strife and personal warfare may exist simultaneously. Further, the occurrence of the various situations is not linear, as personal or substantive disagreements may move from collegial to warlike in one step. Finally, conflict is dynamic. Any situation may fluctuate between positive and negative stages.

It is fair to say, however, that productive synergy is nearly always positive, while the other situations are nearly always counterproductive. Thus, while perhaps an oversimplification of complex issues, this model suggests that to reduce the impact of counterproductive conflict, management must concentrate on understanding and implementing practices to minimize functional strife, personal discord, and personal warfare and deal effectively with that conflict that does occur.

CAUSES OF COUNTERPRODUCTIVE CONFLICT

Dealing effectively with conflict is not as simple as adopting policies that prohibit functional strife, personal discord, and personal warfare. There is no magic bullet. Trying to prevent one problem often causes another. Trying to resolve a problem can escalate it instead. Disputing parties may make peace today but be at war with each other tomorrow. Management changes a policy to help employees and is rewarded with disputes over the details of implementation. People don't behave as we believe they should, and we feel helpless because we don't understand why.

Under these circumstances, one can begin to understand what to do about conflict only by looking at its causes, which are not always clear-cut. Organizations are systems made up of highly interdependent parts and patterns of interaction, each of which affects and is affected by other parts or patterns, and each of which can be the genesis of conflict. Thus, one must consider the organization as a system and use systems thinking as a framework for understanding the behavior of the people and relationships that are involved in a particular conflict event. Using this systemic framework as a foundation, one must then consider various reasons people respond to systems and other people as they do.

A Systems Basis of Conflict

"A system is an entity that maintains its existence and functions as a whole through the interaction of its parts."[3] The behavior of a system depends on the sum of its parts, but it has properties not found in any one of them. Our bodies are an excellent example. They are made up of many different parts. Each part has its separate purpose, yet they all work together and affect and are affected by other parts. All the parts must interrelate harmoniously for a healthy, functional body. Similarly, an organization is a complex whole comprising many parts and relationships among the parts.

A system is also usually composed of many smaller systems, or subsystems, that contribute to the whole. Just as our bodies are composed of our nervous system, coronary system, and many other systems, business organizations are composed of many subsystems that are interrelated in a vast array of relationships and patterns.

> Work assignment processes, pay policies, retirement programs, and grievance procedures are all subsystems of the larger system. Each has its individual purpose, but each also affects other parts. For example, pay policies usually affect retirement income, and work assignment policies affect pay.

In a complex system, the various parts relate to one another in many different ways. Parts change in different ways in response to changes in other parts, and small changes in one part can lead to large changes in other parts or in the whole. Complex systems also have multiple levels of explanation. From the viewpoint of an observer, a happening such as a dispute might be explained on the basis of the facts of the actual event: who did what to whom. At other levels, the observer could consider long-term trends and patterns resulting from an aggregation of similar events or the relationship between key parts of the organization (its structure and its people's mental models).

A sexual harassment case (event) may be one among many over the past several years (pattern) and is the result, at least in part, of the organization's structures or its mental models.

Understanding complex systems means thinking in loops rather than in straight lines, of wholes as well as the parts, of connections and interrelationships in addition to things, and of patterns of change rather than static views. Systems thinking also considers the effect of feedback loops: the process by which change in one part of the system influences other parts, which then change in ways that loop back to influence the original part. The influence may reinforce and escalate the original change and thereby begin a cycle of influence that can continue unabated until a force from a different part intervenes to alter the cycle.

Management might address high rates of absenteeism by assigning more overtime. But the increased overtime may actually loop back to make absenteeism worse because employees are overworked, can afford to be absent, and therefore elect to be absent more.

Systems tend to be messy and difficult to describe with any degree of certainty. In a business organization, many parts and influences are going in too many different directions to describe a model that accurately depicts how all conflict develops. However, a model that demonstrates various levels of the system, relationships among levels, and relationships among example parts within the levels can be helpful in establishing a framework for considering more specific causes of conflict. The model can be represented as three concentric spheres forming a core and two adjoining layers, as illustrated in Figure 2. The core and each adjoining layer are composed of a number of related parts. The various parts comprising the core are largely hidden from view, yet they are necessary to hold the system together. The parts of the outside layer are obvious to all. The middle layer both separates the other two and holds them together. An external environment that affects, and is affected by, the system surrounds them.

The external layer in the model represents the people in the organization: those whose work effort determines the organization's performance.

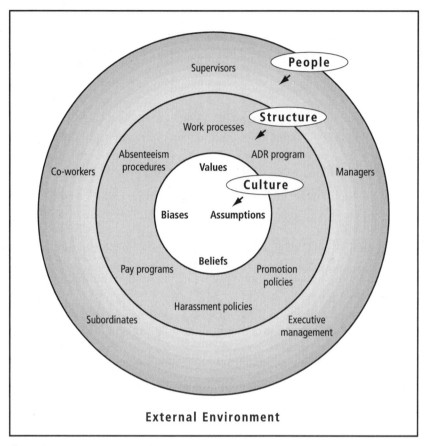

Figure 2 ORGANIZATIONAL SYSTEM

When working together, these people use their diversity and disagreement in a creative synergy that is valuable to the organization and to themselves. When problems develop, however, they often engage in disputes and other counterproductive conflict that impairs organizational effectiveness. Whichever the case, their behavior is typically obvious for all to see, as they are players in events and patterns of behavior that directly affect productivity and get the attention of managers and other interested parties.

The middle layer represents the management processes that make up the organizational structure of the enterprise. This structure includes the many procedures, programs, agreements, decisions, and other initiatives of management that determine how the organization will function. (Figure 2 cites as examples only a few of the many parts that typically make up an organization's structure.) The processes in this layer set the rules and provide the motivations that directly affect people's behavior.

The core of the model represents the organization's culture: the underlying driver of what people do and how they behave, which comprises elements such as values, beliefs, biases, and assumptions. Influences such as these combine to make up mental models, which are deep-seated internal images of the world in which we live and how it works. These images affect what we see and hear in the workplace because they tend to form our concept of reality and confine our thoughts and actions to those that are familiar.

Each level of the model is a subsystem that is closely connected with other subsystems, and each part of each subsystem is related, directly or indirectly, to all the parts of all the subsystems. Actions, influences, and reactions in any part do not stand alone; rather, they are one element of a web of interconnecting relationships that foster multiple causes for most conflict events. These causes may be of three types.

- *Proximate cause* is the direct cause of an event, which in a natural and continuous sequence, unbroken by intervening causes, leads to the conflict in question. The proximate cause is the most likely immediate explanation of a conflict. It usually appears among the people involved and is the obvious trigger of their conflictive behavior. But the proximate cause may be simply a result or manifestation of a more basic problem elsewhere in the organization.

- *Contributing causes* are factors or conditions that surround or influence a conflict and contribute to it, either by helping to bring it about or by escalating it in severity. The concept suggests that most conflicts have several, and not just one, causes. Contributing causes can be conditions that set the climate within which the conflict takes place or intermediate causes in a sequence of events from the root cause to the proximate cause. Contributing causes are usually less obvious and may originate in various places in the organization.

- *Root cause* is the most basic reason for a conflict, which, if eliminated or avoided, would have prevented the conflict from occurring. Like contributing causes, a root cause can originate in any of the organization's subsystems.

A conflict exists between two managers (people subsystem), the symptoms of which are the managers' refusal to communicate, help each other, or cooperate in any meaningful way.

- Proximate cause—the managers don't like each other and seem to have a personality conflict.

- Contributing causes—the two have offices that are in different cities, and the organization does not have effective communication procedures.

- Root cause—the organization has a zero-sum bonus program according to which business units must compete against each other, and if one manager wins the other loses. It is in each party's financial interest to be sure the other loses, so they do not communicate or cooperate.

It is important to note that multiple causes may exist for a particular conflict, and not all conflict has three types of causes. In some simple, straightforward cases the proximate and root causes may be the same, and no contributory causes exist. In addition, in this messy and unpredictable world, people sometimes cause their own disputes without incentives or root causes that relate to the organization's systems. Just as human nature and behavior are influenced by workplace systems, they also are affected by societal pressures and systems external to the workplace that managers are not in a position to change. Thus, while externally caused conflict must be dealt with, management may be forced to deal only with its proximate (internal) cause rather than its root causes.

Fortunately, internal causes are usually available for management to deal with. Its best opportunity to control conflict is usually to look deeper for systemic causes, recognizing that more often than not management will see itself or its systems as a cause. When this happens, management's first step in addressing conflict is to change itself or fix its systems rather than try to extract a pound of flesh from the people involved.

In summary, management cannot over the long term meaningfully control employee behavior by edict or be an ever-present policeman who addresses just the proximate causes of conflict. It cannot dictate to employees that they will not cause conflict. It can, however, control itself and those systems that are proximate causes of conflict, establish conditions that contribute to conflict, or make up the root cause of conflict.

Theories of Causation

Extensive research has developed various theories as to why people react to other people and systems in ways that lead to conflict. To effectively manage conflict, managers must appreciate the various theories and understand that they exist for a reason. Conflict is not homogeneous, but arises in complex systems for many reasons and from many sources. Conflict also has many different symptoms, plays out in many different ways, and has many different consequences. Thus, managers must fashion solutions that fit the real causes rather than try to use generic, one-fits-all programs to deal with various types of workplace conflict.

The following paragraphs summarize a number of potential causes of conflict. *Working Through Conflict* by Folger, Poole, and Stutman[4] was an invaluable source for this information and is recommended for those readers wishing a more complete discussion of the causes of conflict.

Psychic Energy

This somewhat controversial theory holds that the human mind is a reservoir of psychic energy that drives human behavior and provides the basis of conflict. Its energy can be channeled into various activities but must be released one way or another. The human mind attempts to balance the need to discharge the energy at any cost with the need to conform to acceptable, real-world norms, but impulses such as aggression and anxiety that build up over time are often released through aggressive attacks or other conflict. Accordingly, conflict may be dealt with by providing individuals with alternative activities to which aggression can be channeled, or by helping them understand their behavior so they can control it.

Win-Lose Climate

The concept of climate suggests that human behavior is determined by how individuals see the world. A number of factors shape this perception, such as an individual's needs and goals, the atmosphere within which behavior occurs, and the amount of freedom available. In the aggregate, such influences determine the climate, which provides the context for human interaction and for conflict.

The most important aspect of climate is the interdependence between the parties involved. This relationship may be a "mutual-gain" interdependence, wherein the parties perceive that a gain by either will promote gains to the other, and losses will promote losses. Such a climate promotes mutual interests, trusting and friendly attitudes, similar goals, open and honest communication, and minimal counterproductive conflict. Climate may also be seen as a zero-sum or win-lose interdependence, where one's gain will be another's loss. A zero-sum climate promotes unhealthy competition, win-lose behavior, and counterproductive conflict.

Under this theory, organizational climate and individual behavior have a close systemic relationship in which each affects and is affected by the other; the climate drives the behavior, yet the specifics of personal behavior rebound to affect how the individual perceives the climate. More specifically, how employees react to others will be largely determined by their expectations as to how they will be treated, the best predictor of which is the organizational climate. How they react will, in turn, also tend to cause incremental change in the climate.

> Management implements an unpopular change that employees perceive as harmful to them. In a win-lose climate of fear and distrust, affected employees resist the change and escalate conflict to protect their interests. This behavior becomes a part of how things are done in the organization—a part of the organization's climate—and causes management to implement more unpopular changes in order to "stay in control." The cycle continues until one party acts counter to the influence of the other.

Social Exchange

The social exchange theory suggests that conflicts involve calculation of rewards and costs by people who are interdependent and able to influence each other's behavior. The driving force behind behavior is self-interest; people try to maximize their rewards and minimize their costs—up to a point. Since they also value interpersonal relationships, they also consider fairness and equity in their transactions and are willing to have perceptions of rewards balanced with perceptions of the potential effect on relationships.

Rewards and costs generally involve participants exchanging resources for the purpose of influencing each other's behavior. Resources exchanged can vary widely, from economic resources to social resources such as liking, status, respect, or information. Conflicts occur when one party feels the resources offered are too low or the costs are too high and the other party resists efforts to improve its offer.

- Supervisors and employees negotiate salary or job status as an exchange for effort or other employee contributions. If each party feels the other is offering resources that are acceptable, conflict is minimized. If not, it escalates.

- A namby-pamby supervisor attempts to buy personal popularity by giving in to employee requests that are otherwise not justified. The implicit deal is "I will give you this if you will like me." This unjustified concession for a shot at popularity minimizes conflict in the short run because both parties are satisfied with the immediate results. When, however, the popularity wears thin or the employees come back for more, the cost to the supervisor becomes too high, and counterproductive conflict results.

Ineffective Human Relations

Conflict can also be caused by ineffective human relations, particularly in the supervisor-subordinate relationship. Such relationships are determined by individual conflict styles, which have different effects in different situations. The idea of style suggests a specific, consistent orientation that governs personal behavior in conflict situations and that may be seen as part of the individual's personality. Two components of behavior determine style: assertiveness, or behavior intended to satisfy one's own concerns, and cooperativeness, or that which is intended to also satisfy the other's concern. How these components are combined can result in any of five styles: competing, accommodating, avoiding, collaborating, or compromising. And each style raises different conflict possibilities. Competing is likely to cause conflict, avoiding is likely to prolong it, and collaboration is likely to minimize it.

- An arrogant, overbearing supervisor predictably wants his way, and his attitude causes a negative reaction regardless of the substance of a discussion.

- A competitive individual predictably wants to win at all costs, and her behavior tends to cause reciprocal behavior and resulting conflict.

- An individual encourages collaboration by eliciting divergent, conflicting views and then works to meld them in a synergy that avoids counterproductive conflict and makes the whole greater than the sum of its parts.

Seeing Things Differently

Often people who view the same event or conversation reach widely differing conclusions. Frequently we don't believe what we see; instead, we see what we believe. Our beliefs are affected by many influences, such as the cultural patterns that form our views of the world, our own self-concept and expectations, how we view a particular relationship, and the type and quality of communication between the parties. We decide what something means by interpreting events or messages. How we interpret them affects what we see and often determines whether conflict will result.

- A supervisor tries to demonstrate a caring and helpful attitude by asking an employee questions. The subordinate, reacting from a different culture and personal identity and having a different view of the relationship, sees the questions as micromanagement and a lack of trust.

- A subordinate views "talking back" as constructive criticism, while his supervisor views it as insubordination.

- Individuals of different races view the same incident and remember the facts differently because of their different cultural backgrounds.

Social Confrontation

Social confrontation occurs when one person signals to another that his or her behavior is violating a rule or expectation that governs the relationship. In the workplace, this typically happens when a manager or supervisor notifies an employee that a job expectation is not being met or that a policy is being violated. If the employee disagrees, a conflict exists. The conflict can result from disagreement on any of several different issues: whether the employee's behavior happened as alleged, whether it actually violated the expectation or policy, whether there was reasonable justification for the violation because of special circumstances or other excuse, or whether the expectation or policy was legitimate in the first place.

An employee is charged with violating the attendance policy. Conflict might result when he questions the accuracy of the company's absence records, argues that he hasn't had as many absences as the policy prohibits, contends that the absence was justified because he was sick, or argues that the company's policy is unreasonably harsh and therefore not legitimate.

Reciprocity

Reciprocity exists when one person responds in kind to another party's behavior. Negative actions are met with negative actions, threats are met with threats, and use of power is met with power. Initial actions set the tone, and unless one party or the other breaks the sequence, conflict escalates through cycles of reciprocity involving increasingly serious behavior. Reciprocity also works in positive behavior. Logic is met with logic, help with help, and benefit with benefit.

- One employee helps another, who responds by returning the favor at a future time.

- A supervisor lashes out at an employee, who responds with an aggressive counterattack.

- Management tries to coerce a change in work conditions, and employees respond by striking.

Intergroup Differences

Intergroup conflict may be the original cause of conflict or contribute to its persistence and intensity. Its roots lie in the basic human need for self-identity. People tend to define themselves by identifying the groups they belong to and those to which they do not belong; a person might be an employee but not a supervisor, a member of management and not of the union, or a member of one particular minority and not of another.

Once their identity is established, the groups can become polarized, which in turn triggers conflict. Polarization may arise in the workplace from differences in organizational structure, realistic economic opportunity, demographics, seniority, or other factors that put groups into opposition. When polarization occurs, individuals develop a loyalty and commitment to their own group and stereotype others. Both similarity within the in-group and differences with other groups are maximized, uniting one group against another. Once conflict exists, each group begins to develop beliefs that describe the in-group favorably and justify the conflict from its perspective. The combination of group identity, polarization, and beliefs that support the in-group create a we-they context that, at a minimum, produces longer and more intense conflict.

- Minority groups based on race, ethnicity, gender, disability, or sexual preference develop an internal loyalty and commitment, which in turn leads to conflicts with other groups.

- We-they attitudes develop between "workers" as a group and "management," or between unionized and nonunion employees.

KEY POINTS

1. Conflict is a dynamic process that is inherently neither good nor bad. Conflict is sometimes positive and sometimes counterproductive.

2. Conflict typically involves two or more parties with an interdependent relationship and incompatible interests.

3. Different types of conflict and levels of severity combine to create a range of conflict situations with varying organizational impact.

4. Conflict developing within an organizational system is likely to have a proximate cause, contributing causes, and a root cause.

5. There are many different theories about what causes conflict.

6. Understanding the causes of a conflict is essential to dealing with it effectively.

Management's Role

*"An ability to embrace new ideas, routinely challenge
old ones, and live with paradox will be the
effective leader's primary trait."*
—TOM PETERS, *Thriving on Chaos*

Managing conflict can be a little like herding cats. You focus on one, and several others break out. The cats seem more influenced by things you don't understand than by those you do. You try something, and it does more harm than good. There is no obvious way to get the job done. Fixing one problem often causes others. Intervening in a conflict expands the problem when conflicting parties turn on the person who intervened. An intervention that works in one situation is inappropriate in another.

Effective conflict management is more than just solving problems. It is a complex management undertaking that requires disciplined actions based on holistic, systemic thinking. This chapter provides a framework for such thinking. It discusses some conflict management paradoxes, suggests what management's primary conflict management role should be, and outlines some important ethical considerations to guide management's actions.

CONFLICT MANAGEMENT PARADOXES

Dealing with conflict is an important management function in the workplace. However, what managers should actually *do* about conflict is not always obvious. People frequently do not respond as they are expected to, and efforts to minimize or resolve conflict may escalate the problem instead. Thus, managers often must view conflict in terms of paradoxes rather than apparent logic.

Paradoxes are propositions that seem self-contradictory or absurd but in reality contain more than a grain of truth. To deal with them, managers must continually question conventional wisdom and think beyond old solutions to old problems. They must view old problems from new perspectives and consider fresh alternatives for addressing newly defined problems. Thinking about several paradoxes can challenge old ways of thinking and help us see new perspectives as a starting point for defining management's role in dealing with conflict.

Paradox 1: Management Often Must Create Conflict

A key management function is to champion a synergy of diverse information and ideas that allows the sum of the knowledge of individuals to be greater than its parts. To attain such synergy, managers must encourage disagreement by bringing together people with different perspectives and ideas and providing a climate that encourages those ideas to surface. This generally accepted management function can hardly be construed as paradoxical.

But managers must also knowingly cause conflict that is counterproductive, at least in the short term. Management is accountable to different stakeholders—shareholders, governments, environmental groups, employees, the public at large—whose interests may be in conflict. Many of these interests cannot be addressed without negatively affecting others, so management must balance them, which inevitably causes some conflict. Management must make difficult decisions that run counter to the short-term interests of some employees. Doing so is necessary to respond to the balanced best interests of all stakeholders.

- Operating a business often has some negative effect on the environment.
- Optimizing shareholder return may mean laying off redundant employees.

Thus, while management's overall objective may be to reduce counter-productive conflict, it must bite the bullet with actions that disadvantage certain stakeholders and cause counterproductive conflict, at least in the short term. Management actions that create conflict include

- Forcing change that interferes with the status quo and challenges the traditions, practices, customs, status, power, or influence of employees
- Establishing and articulating corporate values that require actions that conflict with the interests of some employees

---

- Management values diversity, but affirmative actions to further that value and promote more minorities and women may cause conflict with a white male who feels threatened.
- Management values empowering employees and giving them more autonomy, but this causes conflict with supervisors who want to maximize their control.

- Communicating performance expectations that foster continuous improvement but also ask employees to do more or different things than they are accustomed to doing
- Establishing workplace policies that conflict with the behavior of some employees when they disagree or do not meet established standards

---

- Sending jokes by e-mail becomes a problem only after a constrictive e-mail policy is established.
- Sloppy dress becomes unacceptable only after there is an established dress code.

- Making distinctions among employees that cause one employee to win and another to lose.

Performance ratings or rankings and pay for performance, promotions, and other such personnel actions involving subjective judgments about employees frequently cause conflict with management or among employees.

- Firing employees, which often is an admission of failure on the part of both the employee and management, but which nevertheless may be the best alternative

Actions such as these may be necessary to ensure performance, profit, growth, survival, and other organizational necessities that, over the long term, are good for most employees and other stakeholders. Conflict that results from such actions is usually a small price to pay for the longer-term advantages they provide. The fact remains, however, that even appropriate decisions often cause counterproductive conflict.

Paradox 2: Management Resolving Conflict Does More Harm Than Good

Aggressive managers find it difficult to allow any counterproductive situation to exist without their intervention. If something is broken, they want to fix it—and the sooner the better. This is especially true when conflict is perceived as hindering workplace performance. When conflict is between employees, and management is not a party, managers can choose to intervene and attempt to resolve the matter. The paradox is that if they intervene, they may do more harm than good.

When managers try to resolve disputes between employees, two things can happen: the conflict can continue, perhaps in a different or escalated state, or it can end. If it continues or escalates, management's intervention was an obvious failure. Time and effort were wasted. Management credibility probably suffered because those involved saw the intervening manager as incompetent at best and perhaps biased in favor of one party. And—in the worst-case scenario—the manager can become an adversary in the dispute. When management intervenes and these things happen, matters often end up worse than they were before the intervention.

> Employee A and employee B are office mates. A plays loud music on his radio. B objects and complains to his supervisor. The supervisor has A get rid of his radio. Now B is satisfied, but A is mad at both B and the supervisor, and the conflict continues, albeit in a different form.

Even when a manager is successful in resolving a conflict among employees, the broader employment relationship may be worsened. A manager who feels successful when she resolves a conflict may, upon reflection, lose confidence in the employees because of her perception that they were unable to solve their own problem. This loss of confidence can cause the manager to intervene even earlier in any subsequent conflict and, more important, to lower her expectations and refuse to allow the employees to contribute all they can to workplace success.

Unfortunately, a manager's loss of confidence may be justified because having someone else resolve their problems causes employees to become more dependent and need more help in the future. In this way they are taught that they cannot resolve their own problems, and they learn their lesson well.

> In a conflict involving differences in power between two employees, where one feels some level of powerlessness as compared to the other, management intervention only confirms the employee's powerlessness and his need for help now and in the future.

Furthermore, management's resolving employee conflicts can lead to an escalating cycle of dependency: management resolves a conflict, which makes the employees involved more dependent, which makes management trust employees less, which leads to earlier management intervention in future cases, and on and on, as indicated in Figure 3. When such a situation develops, management's apparent early success in resolving a conflict is a pyrrhic victory that really isn't worth the effort involved.

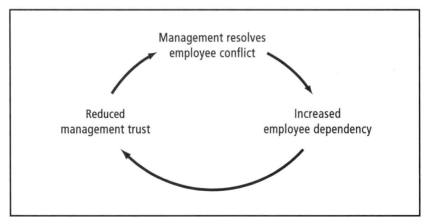

Figure 3 CONFLICT RESOLUTION DEPENDENCY CYCLE

Paradox 3: The Best Way to Resolve
Conflict Fast Is to Go Slow

Even though resolving conflict may have unintended consequences, management must be involved in the resolution of some conflicts. It should intervene when management itself is a party, when there is a conflict between employees and they don't know how or don't have the motivation to resolve it, or when other circumstances make resolution without management intervention unlikely.

When resolving conflict, management often just tries to make the problem go away as quickly as possible. This addresses the symptoms, like taking an aspirin for a headache, and may provide immediate relief. But getting rid of the problem usually does not resolve the conflict. It simply covers it up or sends it underground to resurface another day, perhaps in a different form or place, and likely in a more serious and costly fashion.

> - Two people can't get along, so one is transferred to another department. Now they cause conflict in two departments.
>
> - An employee objects that he wasn't promoted and is "bought off" with a pay increase. Now his pay is out of line and future pay increases must be smaller—giving rise to continuing conflict.
>
> - An employee is fired for misbehaving. She files a lawsuit alleging discrimination.

Resolving conflict usually takes time. Employees who are part of the problem must help resolve it, and involving them takes more time than unilaterally dictating a management decision. Investigating and considering the systems implications and all possible causes, rather than just the symptoms, take additional effort and time. But a high-involvement, systemic process for resolving conflict is necessary for the long-term improvement that really resolves the underlying issues and minimizes the chances of their reoccurrence. Ultimately, the fastest way to resolve conflict is to go slow.

Paradox 4: Resolving Conflict Causes New Conflict

Much of the conflict between employees and management is about employee needs and expectations: how employees will be treated, how much they will be paid, or other issues important to both parties. When employee expectations or desires are not met, conflict often results. Paradoxically, employer actions that address such issues may cause more conflict.

Abraham Maslow's hierarchy of needs—ranging from lower-order subsistence needs such as a wage employees can live on to higher-order self-actualization needs such as challenging work—helps explain this paradox. The point is that addressing lower-order needs doesn't make conflict go away. It merely shifts it to a higher-order need or expectation.

This paradox is seen in the difference between conflict in poorly managed and high-performing organizations. High-performing organizations often do not have fewer complaints and conflicts than poorly managed organizations; however, the subjects of the conflicts are different. In poorly managed organizations, employees may complain about fairness in pay, working conditions, or other areas in which management fails to meet their basic subsistence needs. In high-performing organizations, employees may complain about issues such as ineffective communication, not being involved in various situations, or their talents not being used effectively. Paradoxically, management's emphasizing practices such as communication and involvement encourages employees to complain about deficiencies in them.

At the individual level, this paradox suggests that "no good deed goes unpunished." Improving a situation affecting employees often leads to more, albeit different and narrower, complaints. Sometimes management may wish it had allowed the original concern or conflict to persist. A simple "no" would have been easier, although probably not better in the long run.

- In response to employee complaints, management relaxes the dress code and allows "business casual" dress. This leads to complaints that jeans and T-shirts are not permitted.

- Management adopts flex hours to address commuting problems. Conflicts result about how early employees can start and other details of the new procedures.

Resolving conflict may also lead to new and entirely different conflict. When parties make peace and learn to work together, they tend to communicate, collaborate, and optimize their effectiveness, which can lead to new conflicts.

- Resolving conflict and working together lead to improved communication, which means employees now surface their underlying biases and prejudices, causing additional conflict.

- Working well together breeds success, which leads to conflict over who gets the next promotion or who is the first to be laid off because all are no longer needed.

Paradox 5: Management Can Best Manage Conflict in Others by Managing Itself

Managing conflict is more than resolving conflicts. *Resolving* a conflict is a reactive, backward-looking effort to address a particular event. *Managing* conflict is a purposeful, holistic journey that considers both the past and the future and attempts to minimize conflict and its negative effects. It requires managers to influence employee behavior in order to minimize counterproductive conflict and improve organizational performance.

Management typically uses practices such as active listening, rewarding desired behavior, and management by walking around to influence the thinking and behavior of others. Such practices may work initially, but they lose their power when they are seen as mere techniques. While not inherently bad or wrong, they often are undone by the deep-seated, contradictory beliefs and values of the managers using them, or by the managers' incongruous actions. Such incongruities give mixed messages and the appearance of manipulation, and any initial success is likely to be diminished by a subsequent lack of trust in management.

- A manager asks for employee input and goes through the motions of listening but doesn't respond to expressed concerns. Employees react positively at first but then become disillusioned and confused and attempt to get their questions answered by filing a lawsuit.

- A pay system claims to reward performance but is administered by managers who refuse to give employees the freedom to act. Accordingly, they become frustrated and their performance declines.

Managing conflict requires managers to manage themselves and walk their talk. They must change their inner selves and modify their behavior as necessary to mirror the behavior they are seeking from employees and to be consistent with the practices and techniques they are using. Managers' managing themselves works for three reasons.

Clarifies Expectations

Most employees want to do a good job and perform their assigned duties as expected. But often they don't know what doing a good job looks like; they don't know what management expects because what it says is inconsistent with what it does. Employees can be sure of what is expected only when managers' attitudes and behavior are clear and consistent with stated expectations.

> - When management establishes teams ostensibly to gain synergy from differences, it must encourage real discussion of those differences.
>
> - If management touts communication, it must listen effectively and provide feedback.
>
> - A management with a formal open-door policy must not allow supervisors to defer all complaints to the human resources department.

Provides a Role Model

Knowing what to do is one thing, but knowing how to do it is another. Even when expectations are clear, employees are not likely to know how to meet those expectations until they are taught, and there is no better teaching method than role modeling. Employees watch how managers relate to others and tend to relate in similar ways. When managers respond to complaints with a closed, antagonistic reaction, they teach employees that this is the preferred approach. And when managers deal openly and aboveboard with conflict, employees are likely to follow their example.

Similarly, how managers act when employees complain or protest a management action sets a standard of behavior that employees are likely to emulate. A manager's meeting an employee complaint with goodwill, openness, and a sincere attempt to solve the problem teaches employees to act the same way—not only in disputes with management but also in conflicts with other employees.

Encourages Positive Reciprocity

We may accept as a given that almost any action by management will be met with a corresponding, though not necessarily equal, employee reaction. This is the notion of reciprocity—something is given to another in response to the other's initiative.

Reciprocity is a major factor in conflict between employees and management. It may involve employee reaction to the substance of management initiatives—such as resistance when jobs are changed, protest against new policies, or negative response to individual disciplinary actions. It also may involve reaction to the process management uses to take such initiatives. High-handed, power-based implementation creates resistance and conflict that is similarly high-handed and power-based, while thoughtful, considerate implementation fosters a similar response. And when an employee presents a concern, how management reacts sets the stage for the employee's subsequent actions. Management's relying on its power to force its way encourages employees to use whatever power is available—perhaps to seek redress in the courts. Management's attempting to negotiate a solution causes employees to exaggerate their complaint as a red herring for negotiation. But management acting in good faith to address employees' concerns in resolving a complaint encourages a similar approach from those involved.

CONFLICT MANAGEMENT ACTIONS

These paradoxes seem to suggest that management's only role in managing workplace conflict is to manage itself. Its actions cause problems and frequently do more harm than good. Resolving disputes often leads to new and different conflict. This, perhaps, presents the final paradox: in spite of the paradoxical nature of workplace conflict, there are many actions management can and should take to manage workplace conflict effectively and limit its counterproductive effects.

Management should, therefore, accept the limits to what it can do and yet actively manage conflict to improve employee well-being and productivity. What actions are appropriate will vary from case to case, so management must consider each situation on its own merits and make thoughtful decisions within the context of a broad conflict management strategy. This broad perspective requires the following fundamental roles:

- Minimizing the overall level of counterproductive conflict
- Causing suppressed conflict to be surfaced
- Ensuring effective resolution of counterproductive conflict

- Learning from the resolution process and applying that learning to further minimize conflict

These actions will be briefly introduced in the sections that follow and developed in the remainder of the book.

Minimizing Counterproductive Conflict

Conflict does not just happen. Instead, it typically occurs in predictable ways as a result of the people or circumstances within an organization. This means that management can affect the type and level of conflict by how it manages the organization.

Physicists have developed the notion of "sensitive dependence on initial conditions," best demonstrated by the "butterfly effect"—the idea that a butterfly stirring the air today in the Amazon can cause a tornado next month in Texas. This notion suggests that small differences in input can quickly become large differences in output, and that with a working knowledge of a system's initial conditions and a basic understanding of the laws that govern it, one can reasonably predict behavior of the system and many of its parts.

As in the physical world, the behavior of organizational systems and the people who work within them varies in predictable ways, depending on the system's initial conditions.

- Football players who are well trained and conditioned perform better than those who aren't.

- A car driven on a slick road is more likely to be wrecked than one driven on a dry road.

- Employees who work under conditions that harbor conflict are more likely to be involved in disputes than those who work in a better environment.

Fortunately, management is in a position to influence the system within which employees work. While it cannot prevent all counterproductive conflict nor make good employees out of all people, management can set the initial conditions. Management represents the owners of capital and is responsible for the decisions that allow an employer-employee relationship to exist. It holds and is accountable for the resources and information that are most important to the employment relationship and to relationships among employees. In dealing with employees, management acts and employees react. Therefore, management can decide on the type of employee behavior it desires, the type of relationship it wants with employees, and the type of relationship it wants employees to have with one another. If management wants relationships that minimize counterproductive conflict, it can operate its business to achieve that objective.

To minimize conflict, management must set the right initial conditions—those conditions that determine the environment within which employees work and that tend to cause or minimize conflict. It must develop, implement, and administer systems that (1) provide all employees an incentive and the ability to do their jobs with a minimum of counterproductive conflict, and (2) do not themselves cause or escalate counterproductive conflict. Accomplishing these objectives requires action in the following key areas:

- Maintaining a trusting environment
- Avoiding policy-driven conflict
- Managing change effectively
- Hiring and maintaining the right workforce
- Fostering appropriate supervisor behavior

These areas of action will be discussed in Part 2 as they relate to management's fulfilling its role of minimizing the level of counterproductive conflict in the first place.

Surfacing Suppressed Conflict

Even with management's best efforts to minimize it, some counterproductive conflict exists in all organizations. A management that claims conflict doesn't exist is either fooling itself or doing a commendable job of covering it up.

Not all conflict, however, is disclosed in public disputes that attract the attention of employees, managers, and external parties. It is suppressed below management's radar screen when one party does not acknowledge to another (another employee or the employer) a perceived grievance or when employees are involved in a conflict without management's being aware of it. Suppressed conflict percolates below the surface and often plays out in the form of bitching, failing to communicate, ignoring requests, veiled insults, unfriendly glances, jokes at each other's expense, passive resistance, or other negative forms of behavior. People typically deal with suppressed conflict by tolerating it, taking actions to accommodate the other party, or engaging in private self-help.

Suppressed conflict detracts from employee morale, commitment, and energy (and reduces effectiveness and efficiency) as much as or more than that which is public. At a minimum, when employees spend time on it, they are distracted from accomplishing the organizational purpose. In more problematic cases, employees may intentionally reduce their own level of effort, hinder other employees, engage in acts of sabotage, or intentionally do other things that are contrary to the organization's best interest. Further, suppressed conflict may persist for long periods of time without any public manifestation or management knowledge of it. If not addressed, it usually festers, grows to involve more people and issues, and pervades the entire work atmosphere.

> A supervisor assigns employees to rotate through several job assignments on a periodic basis. Employees believe they cannot handle all the jobs safely, but are reluctant to publicly protest. Therefore, they try to avoid the issue by dragging their feet in learning all the jobs. They also use self-help by withholding effort so the rotation procedure will not work and by bidding out of the department when they can.

To minimize its negative consequences, management must cause suppressed conflict to surface so that it can be dealt with. Surfacing conflict does not mean that all conflict is made public, brought to the attention of management, or dealt with by management through its formal, institutionalized systems of conflict resolution. Rather, it means that conflict is acknowledged and brought into the open as appropriate from the viewpoint of those who are able and willing to address it.

Much conflict can be surfaced and handled through processes such as information-sharing discussions, emotional release, and negotiation. However, whether employees will surface conflict and use such informal processes to resolve it depends largely on what management expects and the work environment it creates. Thus, management must convey its expectations, foster an open, receptive environment, and learn about suppressed conflict so it can intervene with timely resolution in appropriate cases. If it does not, employees will deep-six their conflict, positions will harden, minor conflict will evolve into troublesome disputes that materially affect performance, and resolution will become almost impossible. Ideas to help management surface conflict so it can be dealt with are discussed in Chapter 8.

Providing Dispute Resolution Processes

When it knows conflict exists, management is faced with the often difficult decision of whether to intervene and, if so, how to do so. One option, unless management is one of the parties, is not to become involved. As the paradoxes suggest, much conflict is better left to the parties. In other situations, however, it is in everyone's best interest for management to be involved. In deciding whether to intervene, managers should thoughtfully consider issues such as whether workplace issues are present; whether the parties have the information, ability, and willingness to fairly resolve their own conflict; and whether the potential effects and downside risks of the parties' own resolution are acceptable.

When management is involved in resolving a conflict, it should provide a process that, to the extent possible, accomplishes the following objectives:

- *Corrects negative behavior.* Not all conflicts can be resolved to everyone's satisfaction, but offending behavior must be stopped.

- *Provides satisfactory outcomes.* A solution that does not satisfy the parties simply changes the locus of the conflict. For effective, productive resolution that the parties will accept, all must feel the resolution meets their needs.

- *Produces durable resolutions.* Resolving issues today and having them reoccur tomorrow is of little, if any, value. The resolution of an individual conflict event must endure over time.

- *Fosters effective long-term relationships.* People in an organization must continue to work together on a day-to-day basis and resolve conflict in ways that enhance rather than detract from their relationships.

- *Is cost effective.* The resolution process must be efficient in terms of resources. Employee and management time and out-of-pocket expenses must be minimized so that the cost of resolving conflict does not exceed the cost of the conflict itself.

These conflict resolution objectives should apply regardless of the type of conflict or the stage in which it is being addressed. They are more readily attained, however, when issues are addressed at the early, disagreement stage, before positions are polarized and personal antagonisms take over. At this stage management can use informal, collaborative problem solving to resolve conflict.

The fact is, however, that some disagreements cannot be resolved early and will escalate to difficult disputes, while others are more problematic from the start. In these situations, management must provide more formal processes and often must insist that they be used. In some cases, management must become an advocate that protects the organization's interests while also seeking a resolution that is fair and equitable for employees.

Further details on management's role in providing conflict resolution processes and ideas for establishing effective dispute resolution systems are discussed in Part 3.

Fostering Individual and Organizational Learning

Déjà vu is not a pleasant feeling in conflict situations, as resolving a conflict is of little value if the same conflict or similar ones continue to occur over time. The relief is short-term, and the cost of the problem itself and of resolving similar conflict time and again continues. Thus, conflict management strategies should include a continuous-improvement element that minimizes reoccurrence of similar conflict. Two types of learning are necessary for continuous improvement to occur: individual and organizational learning.

Individual learning occurs when people increase their store of knowledge and are able to act on it. Such learning might be accomplished through work experience, training, or feedback from a formal dispute resolution process.

- Employees discuss a conflict with their open, helpful supervisor and learn that it is safe to surface conflict.

- Employees attend a training class and learn new concepts and practices that enable them to handle potential conflict situations better in the future than they have in the past.

Organizations learn when employee groups develop collective intelligence and ability greater than the sum of the individuals, and their learning is embedded in the organization. Learning becomes embedded when individuals learn and pass their knowledge on to a critical mass of others, and when the organization's policies, procedures, practices, and values are improved to better reflect current reality.

When managers and employees resolve disputes, they inevitably learn new information and develop new understandings. This learning is used to resolve the dispute in question, but its value can be much broader. Individual learning can be consolidated to provide a picture of part of the organization, and that picture can be used to improve future decisions relating to policies and processes that affect the level of conflict. When this happens, the organization itself learns and continuous improvement is possible in those systems that have the potential for either causing or minimizing conflict.

> An organization has a formal dispute resolution process that includes an ombudsperson. The ombudsperson collects nonconfidential information over a period of time, reports to management concerning an evolving problem in a particular department, and uses the information to develop new policies for the department.

Chapter 12 further develops ideas for fostering both individual and organizational learning.

CONFLICT MANAGEMENT CYCLE

Management's four roles in conflict management do not stand alone, but instead are part of a continuing cycle, as illustrated by Figure 4.

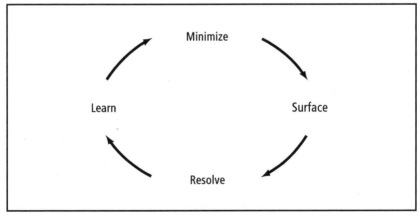

Figure 4 CONFLICT MANAGEMENT CYCLE

This cycle suggests that management should minimize potential or actual conflict, cause conflict that nonetheless exists to be surfaced, ensure that it is effectively resolved, and learn from the process to improve the organization's ability to further minimize the level and impact of conflict in the future. It is a never-ending process of minimizing, surfacing, resolving, and learning that fosters organizational improvement through conflict management.

But conflict management is not as static or sequential as Figure 4 suggests. Instead, it is a system of interrelated processes in which there is no beginning or end and actions intended to change one process may change several. It is a messy, circular world that is continually changing and evolving and that requires intervention whenever and wherever it can be of benefit. Further, conflict management processes cannot be segregated from other management systems. Conflict management, pay systems, job assignment processes, and many other management actions are all parts of a larger, integrated system. Therefore, management must think holistically and build effective conflict management thinking into all its systems and practices without regard to where they fit in the conflict management cycle.

CONFLICT MANAGEMENT ETHICS

When management is involved in conflict, it is nearly always responsible for taking the initiative in making decisions and taking actions. As previously discussed, it has the most information and resources. It, for the most part, has the right to initiate changes in the employment relationship and the responsibility to do so when appropriate. Management also is positioned to make and enforce decisions that cause or minimize conflict, affect the conflict resolution process, and create advantages or disadvantages for employees. Such decisions often present difficult issues of right and wrong. Properly handling them is the foundation that underlies the "minimize, surface, resolve, and learn" cycle of conflict management. To ensure this foundation is solid, management must have a system of moral principles that ensures it does the right thing with regard to all affected by its actions. These ethical principles must apply from two perspectives.[5]

First, managers must be effective in "management of ethics" regarding matters that have ethical dimensions for employees generally: in maintaining appropriate values, rules, procedures, and other processes that guide employee behavior. If such processes are not handled effectively, employees are allowed—or even encouraged—to behave unethically. And their unethical behavior causes conflict rather than minimizes it. If such processes are effectively managed, however, they can be important elements in minimizing conflict, the first of management's roles in the conflict management cycle.

> - A poorly designed bonus plan may encourage an employee to unethically try to take credit for sales that someone else actually made.
>
> - An effective drug policy encourages employees to be honest about their problems and seek help.

Second, managers must themselves act ethically by doing the right thing when faced with difficult situations. Hopefully such behavior will be driven by altruism. Even if it is not, however, such "ethical management" is, as a practical matter, critical for managing conflict. If management does not do the right thing, the entire cycle of conflict is likely to boomerang. Employees will see through unethical actions intended to minimize conflict and it will escalate instead. Fear of further unethical behavior will drive conflict farther underground. Employees will refuse to cooperate, and resolving conflict will become difficult or impossible because employees believe they will not be treated right. And learning will be distorted because the system is dishonest and the input is unreliable. The cycle works only when ethical management does the right thing at every opportunity.

Fortunately, ethicists have suggested ideas for dealing with such issues and for fostering both management of ethics and ethical management. The following simple guidelines for addressing ethical issues in conflict management can be gleaned from them:

- Following the law is not enough. Everything that is unethical is not illegal. Some issues, such as interpersonal relationships at work, are impossible to regulate by law. Even where matters lend themselves to legislative regulation, the law often falls behind and fails to address issues that need to be addressed. Finally, the law itself is often ambiguous, requiring moral or ethical judgments for its administration.

- Decisions must be supported by reasons. The decision process for an action must include consideration of reasons that embody moral arguments we believe in and that are persuasive to others.

- Decisions must fairly, honestly, and impartially address the interests of everyone, including ourselves, related to the case.

A simple but very good test of whether these guidelines are being met is to ask whether the decision maker would be comfortable reading about all aspects of a decision on the front page of tomorrow's newspaper. Would the decision maker willingly discuss all the details and defend his actions with family, friends, colleagues, and other employees? If a decision can withstand this level of openness and scrutiny it probably is ethical.

Conflict management, as broadly envisioned in this book, presents several situations that raise such issues.

The Manager's Role

Managers and supervisors have certain rights and responsibilities above and beyond those of everyday life. The problem is that these rights and responsibilities often conflict with each other or with other obligations.

- A manager's responsibility to stockholders to maximize profits may conflict with her responsibility to ensure employees competitive pay.
- A manager may be obligated to terminate an employee for the good of the organization even though the action will hurt the employee.

When a manager is faced with a decision involving a rule or policy, it may be easier to attend to the "squeaky wheel" than to maintain a balanced, fair approach to administration. Or when faced with an apparent conflict between an individual employee and the organization, it often is easier to favor the individual employee because this will avoid conflict, at least in the short term. But avoiding conflict in such situations is not necessarily the ethical thing to do. Managers have responsibilities to many different stakeholders, and the interests of all must be considered. Managers must make such decisions as though all the stakeholders, including those with an indirect interest, will read about the details in tomorrow's newspaper.

The Employer's Power

Employers are generally presumed to have the right to hire employees; set their wages, hours, and conditions of work; and terminate them when deemed appropriate. Many local and federal laws encroach on the substance of these rights, but management almost always has the right to initiate actions it deems appropriate with respect to employees. The employees' only recourse, except in rare cases, is to do what management says and protest after the fact. Management's broad substantive rights, combined with its right to require action even when subject to employee objection, gives it broad power over employees. Exercise of such rights can raise ethical dilemmas.

> An unreasonable management insists that a single parent work extensive overtime on a long-term basis. The employee's only recourse for ensuring adequate child care is to resign and seek other employment.

The appropriate balance of these powers is a continuing controversy at both the organizational and societal levels, and we make no pretense of resolving it here. Management is obligated, however, to be aware of the power disparity, to avoid arbitrary use of its power, and to apply standards such as those discussed above in good faith when making employment decisions.

Confidentiality

Management obtains a great deal of personal information about employees in the normal course of its business. Additional information of a personal nature is usually obtained when management is involved in resolving conflicts with or among employees. Management's acquiring such information invades the employee's privacy to some extent, justified or not, and raises two primary ethical issues: what information may management appropriately elicit from employees and how must such information be handled? Some general guidelines can be helpful in addressing these issues.

With regard to the first issue, employers are normally justified in eliciting information from employees if it is necessary to fulfill legitimate organizational purposes. When resolving a dispute, management generally has a right to elicit information that is reasonably necessary to make an informed decision about the dispute and how it should be resolved. Going beyond that and inquiring into matters that have no bearing on the dispute would in most cases cross the line.

> In an accusation of sexual harassment, facts that speak to the work environment, language, and employee work actions would be reasonable to ascertain, but facts that speak to the employee's life after work would not be reasonably necessary.

The second issue, concerning disclosure of information to others, also requires exercise of good judgment. If an employee consents to disclosure of certain information, management generally may disclose it consistent with that consent. Without consent, however, management generally should avoid disclosure to other parties except as is necessary to accomplish the purpose for which it was obtained. Information obtained in the process of resolving a dispute can generally be divulged to others if necessary to resolve that dispute. (Formal mediation with a third party may be an exception. Local rules should be understood prior to engaging in formal mediation.) However, management should carefully consider possible damage to the employee involved if the information is divulged and balance that damage against the value of using it to resolve the dispute in question.

> An employer and employee have a disagreement over a possible accommodation under the Americans with Disability Act. Disclosure of the employee's medical condition to others would need to be limited to those necessary to review the situation and arrange an appropriate accommodation.

Favoritism

Favoritism is a form of discrimination, but the legal and ethical issues of discrimination as commonly understood—on the basis of race, color, religion, sex, national origin, and sexual preference—are best discussed in other books. Favoritism in the conflict management process is generally not specifically proscribed by law, but it may nevertheless raise ethical questions, as it violates the principle of equality in dealing with employees and is likely to be for a morally unjustified purpose.

> • A supervisor grants a favor to one employee that is not generally available to others in order to avoid a conflict's escalating and becoming public.
>
> • When helping resolve a dispute, an ombudsperson favors a supervisor over an employee in order to avoid embarrassing a colleague.

Aristotle's principle of justice as proportional equality—that "like cases should be treated alike, and unlike cases should be treated differently in proportion to the relevant differences"[6]—provides basic guidance for addressing issues of possible favoritism. In this context, management must make a judgment as to whether the purpose of the differing treatment is justified by any relevant differences between the individuals involved. If there are no relevant differences, are there any justifiable reasons for favoritism? And would management like to read about its decision on the front page of tomorrow's paper?

KEY POINTS

1. Conflict management in the workplace is frequently paradoxical, and things don't always work as it seems they should. Managers must continually question conventional wisdom and think beyond old solutions to old problems.

2. Management has four fundamental roles in managing workplace conflict:

   • Minimizing the level of counterproductive conflict

   • Causing suppressed conflict to be surfaced

   • Ensuring effective resolution of counterproductive conflict

   • Learning from dispute resolution and applying that learning to further minimize conflict

3. The four roles do not stand alone but rather work in a continuing cycle of conflict management processes that are related to each other and to other management processes.

4. Management's responsibility to take the initiative in conflict resolution raises several important ethical considerations. Management should always make decisions as though they would be reported on the front page of tomorrow's newspaper.

PART 2

Minimizing Conflict

Maintaining a Trusting Environment

"Trust men and they will be true to you."

—RALPH WALDO EMERSON

T rust is the unwritten and usually unspoken contract that allows each of the parties to a transaction to believe in the honesty, integrity, reliability, and justice of the others. Trust is based largely on perceptions, beliefs, and feelings. It is demonstrated through the parties' behavior toward each other but at the same time provides a common, enduring experience that influences that behavior.

When employees don't trust management or other employees, they feel a need to protect themselves and win all they can. This leads to a work climate in which employees are concerned primarily about themselves to the detriment of others and the organization as a whole. Employees in this situation are likely to exhibit behavior such as the following:

- Always seeing the worst in management or other employee actions

- Predictably resisting management or employee initiatives, almost regardless of their substance

- Refusing to collaborate with management or other employees
- Refusing to share information
- Engaging in unhealthy competition with other employees
- Refusing to surface conflict so that it can be resolved
- Frequently using formal, win-lose dispute resolution processes such as grievance procedures and litigation

Since management is not likely to trust employees in such an environment, it compensates by limiting employees' freedom and controlling as many of their activities as possible. Where trust is deficient, management behavior is likely to include the following:

- Extensive policies and rules to cover every imaginable eventuality
- Micromanagement and excessively close supervision
- Inappropriate use of employees to obtain information about other employees
- Frequent, punitive employee discipline
- Refusal to share information except on a narrowly defined "need to know" basis

Such behavior by employees and management leads inevitably to counterproductive conflict, as each party places its own needs above the interests of others and takes action to protect itself. The result is a win-lose climate in which there are frequent disagreements, extensive rules, arguments over whether the rules have been violated, and other conflictive behavior. To meaningfully improve such behavior, the parties must first learn to trust each other.

Building trust presents a chicken-egg dilemma, as it is both cause and effect; distrust begets distrust, and, fortunately, trust begets trust. Changing the level of trust must therefore be driven by the concept of reciprocity, the idea that if one person does something for or to another, the second person will then feel grateful (or exploited) and seek to respond in a similar manner. Reciprocal actions can create a spiral that builds a trusting work environment and minimizes counterproductive conflict. Conversely, when employees demonstrate distrust, their actions lead to reciprocal actions by other employees or management that are defensive, controlling, and often punitive. These reactions then circle back to escalate employee resistance, self-serving attitudes, conflict, and further deterioration of trust. The climate becomes one in which everyone claims to trust but also wants to "cut the cards."

Systems thinking, as discussed in Chapter 1, helps explain how the spiral of trust or distrust works and how management can build a trusting environment through its behavior and actions. Systems thinking suggests that reality is not made of straight lines but rather is composed of feedback loops reflecting reciprocal flows of influence that are both cause and effect. All parties in an organization are part of this process. Each influences and is influenced by what happens, and each is at least partially responsible for the actions of other parties. These loops of influence can cause a spiral in the level of trust—either up or down, depending on the behavior of the parties in the loop. The cycle can begin anywhere and works generally as indicated in Figure 5 for the relationship between management and employees.

The cycle builds over time, with individual cases of bad behavior on the part of one party leading to conflict or bad or worse behavior by the other, and cases of good behavior by one party leading to good behavior and increased trust by the other. The cycle is perpetuated when both parties continue to respond as suggested by the influences on them; both employees and management reciprocate to trusting (or distrusting) actions of the other with their own trusting (or distrusting) actions. A cycle of distrust can be reversed only if one party breaks the cycle by acting counter to the distrusting influence it is receiving and takes action that the other will respond to positively.

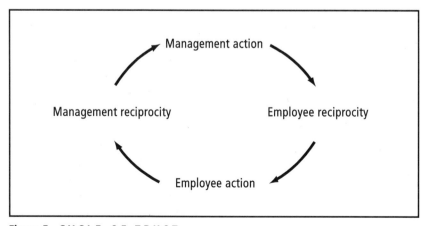

Figure 5 CYCLE OF TRUST

- One employee refuses to share information with another because she doesn't trust him. He gets even by misleading her about the true facts of a situation.

- An employee has been abusing the organization's e-mail system through excessive personal use and exchange of sexually suggestive messages. Rather than escalate the conflict by punishing the employee with time off without pay and a written reprimand, the supervisor explains the rule and asks him to reach his own decision about whether he can continue to work within the terms of employment. Because there is no punishment and the employee is treated like an adult, he has no incentive to punish the employer by further abusing the system.

A cycle of distrust can be reversed, or a cycle of trust perpetuated, only when the work environment encourages positive actions in specific cases regardless of the influence being received. Fortunately, management is positioned to establish such an environment because it has the resources and has a great deal to gain with few risks. Its challenge is to (1) be more trustworthy so employees will trust management and react positively to its actions, and (2) cause or allow employees to be more trustworthy so that managers, supervisors, and other employees will react positively to them. Through such actions, management can create a trusting work environment that provides the continuity, coherence, and predictability that foster compatibility between management and employees, and among employees themselves. The following sections offer ideas for building this trusting environment.

BUILDING MANAGEMENT TRUSTWORTHINESS

Employees decide whether management is trustworthy on the basis of what they hear it say and what they see it do. Interestingly, management often takes actions that teach employees it is not trustworthy and then is surprised when employees get the message! To instead teach employees it is trustworthy, management must engage in a broad range of positive behavior that is based on the following:

- Ensuring its words and actions are based on clearly communicated core values
- Being truthful in all it says and does

- Using its power fairly
- Providing effective processes for resolving conflicts

These minimum standards for building management trustworthiness, and thereby reducing conflict, are discussed below.

Core Values

For management to be trusted, its actions must reflect generally accepted community standards and be reasonably consistent and predictable. And for trust to exist over time, management must be guided by core values— that set of shared moral and ethical standards that create a continuing expectation of regular and honest behavior. Core values provide enduring guidelines for the behavior of all people in the organization. They guide the choices people make, suggest what issues should be given most attention, and allow each to reasonably predict what the other will do.

The organization's core values may be formally stated and communicated or simply part of the stories and myths that define it. To effectively engender trust, however, they must be seen by employees as guiding management. Managers must speak and act with a common voice that consistently validates the organization's values and allows employees to predict how management will act in particular situations.

Consistency must be maintained over time, even when difficult business situations, process changes, or the need to resolve immediate disputes brings pressure to compromise the organization's values. If management compromises a value, it causes employees to expect another compromise; soon employees don't know what to expect, and trust is gone. On the other hand, sticking by the organization's values, particularly in tough times, reinforces management's credibility and predictability and builds trust even when a management action is unfavorable from an employee perspective. Most employees understand that decisions based on strong core values are not negotiable and are willing to credit management for sticking to its guns.

As important as core values are, management must avoid two potential dark sides. First, inappropriate values destroy trust rather than build it. From one perspective, core values provide predictability and a type of trust regardless of their substance. Whether they are liked or disliked by employees, whether they are good or bad from the business viewpoint, or even whether they are in conformance with reasonable ethical standards, clear values nevertheless engender a clear understanding of the rules and the consequences of violating them. But if their substance is objectionable to employees or otherwise inappropriate, they will not build trust that is of use to the organization and its employees and instead will foster conflict from right-thinking individuals. Therefore, to build legitimate, positive trust, an organization's values must include concepts such as loyalty, merit, equal opportunity, freedom, honesty, openness, and integrity—concepts that not only allow employees to know what to expect, but also convince them that their interests will be fairly considered.

Second, without careful management, the predictability arising from nonnegotiable values—even positive ones—can have negative consequences. When carried to extremes, predictability means that management tells employees what the rules are, doesn't change them, and enforces them rigidly over time. This approach allows employees to know what to expect, but it also prevents change, stifles initiative, and leads to conflict between old rules and contemporary needs and interests. Thus, management must value change, flexibility, and experimentation while acknowledging that some values evolve over time and that implementation and detail often must be changed to fit current needs. With thoughtful management, such flexibility can be maintained in an environment based on core values where employees reasonably know what to expect on matters of importance.

> Management places a high value on professionalism. This value doesn't change, but management does change its policy to allow business casual dress in order to stay apace of contemporary norms and enhance its recruitment program.

Truthfulness

Truth within an organization is the mutual version of reality that allows management and employees to get things done with minimal conflict. It must have its basis in facts, but its real force results from the parties involved being able to rely on each other and the mutual understandings necessary to make the organization function effectively with minimum conflict. This reliability, based on a common understanding of what makes up the truth and each party's belief that the other will tell it as it is commonly understood, is a necessary ingredient for mutual trust.

Being truthful requires more than a moral and ethical management accurately reciting necessary facts and avoiding false testimony. Such a black-and-white view of truth might work if our workplaces were static, closed, machinelike, and backward looking. But in fact our workplaces are based largely on relationships rather than facts and are open, living, continually changing, and interconnected. There are few eternal, unchanging, or absolute truths, and most issues of truthfulness do not arise from concern about misstatements of fact. Instead, issues of truthfulness usually arise from differing views of reality. Therefore, management must not only be accurate in statements of facts but also cause the parties involved to have a common view of reality. This can be done in three fundamental ways.

Do Not Withhold Information

If we believe others are sharing all the information they have on issues of importance to us, we are likely to trust them and their motives. But when management tells only part of a story or withholds relevant information, employees tend to become suspicious, have doubts about what was not said, and believe what was said is bunk.

Employees may have several reasons for believing management is withholding information—the first and most important of which is that it is! Management may not trust employees and therefore communicate only on a "need to know" basis, with management unilaterally deciding what information employees need. Or managers may negligently withhold information because they pay too little attention to employee needs and desires.

Even when management intends to communicate fully, employees may infer from the way it is handled that information is being withheld. Communicating via formal and highly disciplined processes such as written memorandums or canned presentations, although necessary at times, can cause such inferences to occur and may make management appear to be quibbling over issues such as "what the meaning of 'is' is." Formal communication often places tight parameters on what is said, limits opportunity for tough questions, and minimizes accessibility of the individual with the best information. Rigid requirements that all personal communication be through supervisors in the chain of command, rather than with others in the organization who have more or better information, may also suggest that management is not completely forthcoming. Whatever the case, the appearance of withholding information can cause employees to doubt the veracity of management even when what it says is true.

To build trust in the truthfulness of management and individual managers, management must be as pure as Caesar's wife. It must provide employees not only with the information it believes they need, but also with the information they want and believe they need. Management must encourage open, unrestrained discussion of issues and direct access, to the extent feasible, to the best sources of information and expertise available. This creates a self-correcting environment, in which management takes extra precautions to fully and truthfully represent the facts because it is faced with the discipline of having to tell the whole story. And employees are more prone to believe in management's truthfulness because they have the information to validate the facts for themselves and understand the entire picture.

> An employee questions the meaning of a confusing vacation policy, which his supervisor doesn't really understand either. Limiting the conversation to the supervisor gives the appearance of withholding information because the supervisor cannot commit to what the meaning really is. Arranging a full discussion with a human resources representative who deals daily with vacation matters, however, puts everything on the table and increases management's credibility, thereby minimizing the likelihood of continuing conflict.

At times it may be appropriate for management to withhold certain information for legal, confidential, or business reasons. Before withholding information for purely business reasons, or to protect its legal position, management's decision process should balance the potential cost of withholding the information with the potential value of sharing it. It may have fewer options where confidentiality is an issue, as certain information should, of course, be protected. Whichever the case, when sharing information is inappropriate, management should not pretend the information does not exist. Instead, it normally should divulge the fact that it has the information and also discuss why it cannot be shared. Employees usually accept legitimate, understandable reasons for nondisclosure.

Do Not Predict the Future

Situations often arise where management wishes to address employee concerns by advising them of what it believes, but doesn't know, will happen in the future. But statements about the future are dangerous and may constitute a high cost for resolving a short-term problem. If circumstances change and management needs to go in a different direction, it could be limited to costly inaction or face charges of lying to employees.

> If management believes layoffs are unlikely in the future it may wish to say so in order to quell rumors. But what if it loses a major contract and must adjust its workforce? Will management be viewed as truthful?

There are two apparent approaches for dealing with this dilemma. Neither one works very well. Refusing to even discuss an issue only exacerbates the problem, as employees are likely to infer silence as negative. Using qualifying comments with predictions would seem to be the answer, but doing so often does not work either. Qualifying statements that leave room for uncertainty and change are often not heard. If they are, they usually are perceived as hedges to cover the complete truth, casting doubt on the main points being made.

While there are no surefire solutions to this dilemma, several guidelines can be helpful.

■ Willingly discuss all relevant, nonconfidential issues. Refusing to do so can be perceived as withholding relevant information even if none actually exists.

■ Be willing to say "I don't know" if that is truthful. Employees appreciate the honesty, sincerity, and vulnerability conveyed by such an admission.

■ Discuss facts, not predictions. Presenting predictions for the future can be dangerous. However, discussing the past and present as facts may be sufficient to allow others to draw their own conclusions or make their own judgments.

■ If sharing predictions about the future cannot be avoided, articulate appropriate qualifications so that they are clear, unequivocal, and easily understood.

Communicate Consistently

To build and maintain trust among employees, management must speak with one voice and be perceived to be consistent. However, managers may be seen as inconsistent—and actually be inconsistent—even when they all are being truthful from their perspective. This can happen under several circumstances: when managers speak from different time frames or perspectives, when one presents details and the other generalizations, when managers reach different conclusions from the same facts, and when one or more managers honestly do not understand the true facts.

Such circumstances are most likely to exist between managers at different levels in the pecking order, who have different roles and responsibilities and therefore need and dispense different types of information. More senior managers are often distant from where the action takes place, so they need information that is objective and abstract and can be tracked and compared over time. Similarly, they tend to dispense information that is general, conceptual, strategic, and long-term. More junior managers and supervisors, on the other hand, need information that is concrete and subjective and that can be used for immediate decisions, and they dispense information that tends to be concrete, specific, and short-term. Managers with these varying perspectives on information, using the logic that meets their needs, can create misunderstandings with their audience by presenting different information, even when they are telling the truth as they know it. And employees are likely to hear different information as an inconsistency that is not wholly credible.

Regardless of the circumstances under which it exists, inconsistency hurts trust and therefore needs to be minimized. One approach to maintaining consistency is to communicate broadly in writing whenever feasible. This ensures that, at a minimum, all employees are presented with the same basic information. Written communication is usually inefficient and impersonal, however, and may fail to address the background and details necessary for full understanding and commitment. Therefore, when written communications are used, they are best used in conjunction with more engaging communication processes.

Individual managers should also avoid meddling in areas that are the responsibility of others. Although senior managers may see great value in management by walking around and engaging in meaningful conversation with employees, they must balance its value against the possibility that what they say will be compared in great detail with what more junior, directly responsible managers are saying. If senior managers do elect to communicate directly with employees, they should do so very carefully. They should usually resist the temptation to respond to hypothetical questions, avoid discussing issues for which inconsistencies are particularly likely, and be willing to state that certain issues have been delegated to more junior managers, who are the ones who should discuss those issues.

More importantly, when managers, regardless of their level, do talk to employees, they should engage them in the give-and-take of dialogue rather than just talk to them. Effective dialogue, whether one-on-one, in small meetings, or through electronic channels, provides opportunities for questions, reactions, and full understanding of the type that can surface possible perceptions of inconsistency and provide an opportunity to address them. It must be recognized, of course, that electronic communication has its limits, as it has no inflection or tonality, which increases the likelihood of misinterpretation and miscommunication.

Fair Use of Power

Power is the ability to make things happen. Three types of power can be used to make things happen in the employment relationship.

- *Coercive power* requires or forces one's cooperation without willing agreement.
- *Utility power* buys what one wants.
- *Collaborative power* uses the hearts and minds of all parties to accomplish common objectives.

All parties in the employment relationship—management, managers, supervisors, and subordinates—have some level of power. All have some ability to make things happen. But from an individual perspective, management and managers have power that far exceeds that of their subordinates. Management has the coercive power derived from its legal right to direct the workforce and discipline employees; the utility power of its resources and capacity to buy much of what it wants and bestow rewards to influence behavior; and the collaborative power derived from its acknowledged leadership role as well as the information and expertise available to it.

Employees, on the other hand, have relatively little coercive or utility power in the workplace. Their only legitimate coercive power is the right to use their legal rights, such as those proscribing discrimination or setting certain employment standards, to resist actions of management or to elect a union and collectively exercise their power. They may also exercise illegitimate coercive power through sabotage or other illegal job actions. Even where they do have some coercive power, however, employees generally are required to comply first and resist after the fact.

Employees also have relatively little utility power. A reasonable contribution of their time and effort in conformance with appropriate workplace rules is an implicit aspect of their employment contract. Beyond that, they rarely have the resources to buy what they want in the workplace.

Employees do, however, have significant collaborative power. They have the information, skills, knowledge, and capacity to get things done, and the ability to work with others as necessary to accomplish the organization's goals. Employees' collaborative power often exceeds managment's.

Generally speaking, management's use of its power advantage over employees destroys trust, while its recognition of employee power builds trust. More specifically, using coercive power nearly always destroys trust, using utility power has negative or neutral effects, and using its collaborative power along with that of employees builds trust. Each of these will be discussed in more detail.

Coercive Power

Almost any use of coercive power to try to force employees to do what management wants will induce an opposing, though perhaps unequal, reciprocal use of coercive power, along with the negative behavior associated with a power struggle. While use of coercive power may at times be necessary, it typically reduces communication and causes defiance and conflict in the short run. In the long run it poisons relationships, subverts learning, breaks spirits, and destroys trust. The most that can be expected is submission and conformity rather than support and commitment.

The best approach to avoiding the negatives associated with use of coercive power is, of course, to not use it. But this is not always possible. Management is accountable to many stakeholders other than employees and from time to time may find it necessary to impose very unpopular or even hurtful decisions on employees. Use of coercion may be the only way.

> Management is not likely to accomplish a termination for poor performance with collaboration, or even by buying agreement for a reasonable sum.

Further, many intractable or emotional conflicts simply cannot be resolved with goodwill or collaboration alone. Unless management takes a stand, such conflicts will linger without any prospect of closure. In such cases management cannot avoid the likelihood of some negative impact on trust and the employment relationship. But it can do things to minimize it, such as the following:

- Use coercion only as a last resort. Use collaboration first, then utility power.

- Be sure affected employees understand from the beginning the seriousness of a situation and management's intention to use force as a last resort if necessary.

- Convince employees that the reason for using force is valid, that the organization really needs what management is trying to get.

- Don't let the disagreement become personal.

- Don't surprise employees, either with the substance of a decision or with management's use of coercion as a last resort.

- Even when the basic decision must be made unilaterally by management, collaborate with affected employees to the extent feasible on other issues, such as the implementation process.

- Do not compromise management's values.

- Whenever feasible, have the person who holds the power exercise it. Hearing bad news from the person who actually made the decision is important.

Utility Power

Using utility power to buy agreement or avoid a conflict is different from paying wages, benefits, and other rewards for service to the organization. The latter is an accepted and necessary business practice. The former often is a cop-out. Although using utility power in this way generally does not cause a negative reaction like that caused by coercion, it also has its problems. Buying cooperation may get management what it wants, but it is conditional and temporary. When the situation changes, the power evaporates, everything is up for grabs, and employees are likely to ask, "What have you done for me lately?" Ironically, employees may trust management less if it gives in and tries to buy its way out of a conflict than if it exhibits backbone and stands by its values.

However, as with coercion, use of utility power may at times be necessary. When it is, consideration of the following will help minimize the negative impact:

- Offer money to respond to interests and balance equities, not to buy agreement or avoid conflict.

- If money is to be offered, the amount should be fair and should meaningfully address the issue. Being too stingy suggests trying to buy one's way out rather that responding to a legitimate interest.

- Anticipate the conflict, and offer money or something of utility before being asked for it.

- Openly and candidly discuss all aspects of the issue, including the appropriateness of the money offer.

Collaborative Power

Collaboration means working together. It presumes the employment relationship is not a zero-sum game and that the parties can work together to resolve their problems to their mutual advantage. They can complement each other through a synergy that results in the combination being greater than the sum of its parts.

Collaboration requires openness, honesty, sharing, respect—and trust. But it also builds trust in two ways. Where collaboration does resolve a conflict, the substance of the resolution is likely to be the best possible for all parties, avoiding the negative impacts of coercive and utility power. More important, collaboration requires the very traits that best build trust—openness, honesty, sharing, respect, and trust. And exhibiting such behavior encourages the reciprocity that escalates the cycle of trust.

Effective Dispute Resolution Processes

Like many other workplace processes, formal dispute resolution processes (discussed in more detail in Part 3) are often both cause and effect. They are put in place to resolve conflicts, but they can also build trust that reduces the very conflict they were established to resolve. To build trust, conflict management processes must

- Assure employees that they can safely and effectively challenge management

- Contribute to personal growth

The mere presence of a formal dispute resolution procedure conveys the notion that management is willing to put up or shut up. It signals that management feels strongly enough about resolving conflict among employees to incur the cost necessary to make it happen effectively. More importantly, a formal process signals that management is willing to have its own actions challenged. Being subject to easy challenge exposes management's vulnerability and puts pressure on it to ensure that employees' trust is not violated. The knowledge that this vulnerability and pressure exist then helps reinforce the idea that management will deliver on its promises.

Dispute resolution procedures also provide employees with a fallback that makes absolute trust less necessary. People are rarely so cynical as to completely mistrust, but they also are rarely so naïve as to completely trust. A gap will always exist. Effective conflict resolution helps fill that gap by assuring employees that if management violates their trust, it can be called to account. The availability of this recourse can make employees more willing to take management on faith and go with the flow in areas where it has not yet had an opportunity to demonstrate its trustworthiness.

But the objectives and substantive provisions of formal dispute resolution processes can vary widely, and not all are effective in building trust. Some aim to just make disputes go away. Such processes may provide some short-term relief, but they do not address the real issues, so the conflict is likely to return with a vengeance and cause even greater problems and distrust. Others help solve the fundamental problems and also often help in building trust. Still others aim to make the people involved better people, and these almost always build trust.

Dispute resolution processes that focus on solving problems help build trust, particularly where systems are the cause of conflict. The process of solving problems usually gets the facts on the table, considers causes of conflict, explores options for change, and otherwise addresses issues important to how the parties view each other. Where organizational systems are causing mistrust, such dispute resolution processes can make this clear and help develop opportunities for improving them. In addition, as will be discussed in Part 3, the organization as a whole can learn to be more trusting.

Processes for resolving disputes that go beyond resolving the immediate problem and focus on making people better can do even more to build mutual trust. Much conflict is more about perceptions of broken trust than about substantive differences. And focusing on the individuals involved can be a key vehicle for mending broken trust.

The best example of this approach is "transformative" mediation, as discussed by Bush and Folger in *The Promise of Mediation*.[7] They present mediation, a form of dispute resolution, as an opportunity to foster moral growth and make the participants better human beings by helping them work through difficult situations and bridge human differences. The essence of transformative mediation is "empowerment," which enhances a party's awareness of self-worth and ability to deal with problems encountered, and "recognition," which contemplates an improved capacity to acknowledge and respond to other parties and their circumstances. The integration of the two—improved self and improved relations with others—captures the moral growth being sought. And moral growth among individuals over time spreads to the organization and the broader society.

Importantly, a key beneficiary of moral growth is the organization's trust level. With improved self-worth comes adherence to legitimate values, greater likelihood of sticking to the truth, fairer use of power, and other behavior that is trustworthy. And with improved relations with others comes an increased capacity to see and understand others' views and engage in reciprocal behaviors that build trust. The combination of the two can lead to positive cycles of trust that reduce the level of conflict in the organization.

Regardless of the purpose of a dispute resolution system, to build trust it must be trustworthy, and to be trustworthy it must

- Be publicized to the extent that all employees know about it and how to use it

- Be fair on its face, so employees can trust that their challenges will be dealt with fairly

- Allow participants to become personally empowered

- Help participants develop the capacity to recognize and credit the other party

- Contain provisions for processes such as mediation or arbitration that tend to reduce the power imbalance between management and employees

- Convince employees that there will be no retaliation for using the system

- Protect employee confidentiality

BUILDING EMPLOYEE TRUSTWORTHINESS

Trust must work in all directions if conflict is to be minimized. Not only must employees trust management, but management must trust employees, and employees must trust one another. Two conditions are important for employees to be seen as trustworthy. First, each employee must act with honesty, integrity, and fundamental fairness, which means not intentionally behaving in an untrustworthy manner. And each employee must be willing and able to meet his job requirements. If either is missing, conflict is likely to result.

Management cannot be fully responsible for the trustworthiness of its employees. Whether a result of genes or the environment in which they grew up, a few employees bring negative patterns of behavior to the workplace that are beyond the scope of management's ability or responsibility to deal with. No reasonable effort will cause them to change. Management can, however, through behavior and actions such as those discussed below, create a climate that fosters trustworthiness among most employees.

Changing Its Own Behavior

Trust typically begins and ends with the actions of the organization's leaders. Incompetent or unethical management can quickly erode whatever trust exists and cause employees to become untrustworthy, while actions of trustworthy management tend to cause employees to become more trustworthy.

The previous section discussed what management can do to be more trustworthy. To build on this and provide leadership in improving the trustworthiness of its employees, management must look at itself through its employees' eyes, identify its own untrustworthy behavior, and change its own attitudes and behavior in a highly credible manner. This will work because of the concept of reciprocity and the cycle of trust. Fortunately, just as bad behavior begets bad behavior, good behavior begets good behavior, and exhibiting trust builds trustworthiness.

To build trustworthiness, management cannot wait for employees to go first, but instead must take the first step. If it has been behaving badly, it must correct its behavior. Even when its behavior has been an apparently reasonable response to untrustworthy employee behavior, it often must begin to act counter to the influences it is receiving and demonstrate trust in employees even when it may question whether trust is justified. Doing this may require a leap of faith, but management can initially take small steps commensurate with the risks involved, monitor the response, and take larger steps when appropriate. Over time, employees will begin to respond to trusting actions of management with behavior that warrants that trust, and the trust improvement cycle takes over, as illustrated in Figure 6.

Improving Its Management Processes

Just as poor behavior on the part of leaders can rebound to cause subordinates to be untrustworthy, management's organizational structures and

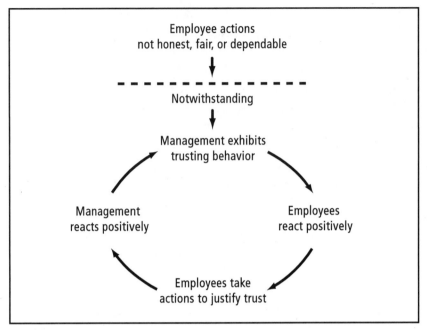

Figure 6 TRUST IMPROVEMENT CYCLE

processes can either promote or destroy trustworthy employee behavior over time. Poor or ineffective policies and processes can erode employee trustworthiness in two ways. First, management's processes may imply that employees are not expected to be trustworthy. Excessive rules, use of monitoring devices, and other such practices convey a lack of trust and often invite efforts to get around them. When employees do try to avoid the intrusive management processes, they become less trustworthy in the eyes of management.

Second, management processes may pit employees against each other or provide them with easy opportunities to take advantage of others. While processes of this type may not alone cause initial distrust, they can exacerbate existing situations and provide opportunities for mistrust to play out.

- Use of traditional time clocks may be seen as proof that management does not trust its employees, while having employees keep their own time demonstrates trust.
- 360-degree peer review performance assessments provide opportunities for employees to take unfair advantage of each other if they wish.

All management processes presumably are established for a reason and no doubt serve a legitimate purpose. Management's challenge is to hit the right balance—to ensure its objective is accomplished with a minimum impact on employee trustworthiness. Ideas for processes and policies that hit this balance, foster trust, and minimize conflict are discussed more fully in Chapter 4.

Setting Clear Standards

Establishing clear expectations of employees is important because people make assumptions; and when people make different assumptions about whether employees are contributing or behaving as they should, suspicion and mistrust result. Conversely, employees tend to respond to what they understand is expected of them. When they know how they are expected to behave and what they are expected to deliver, they usually will meet those expectations. When other employees and management see this, they learn to trust them.

Where trust concerns matters of honesty and integrity, commonly accepted moral standards of the community usually provide general guidelines for behavior. It is important, however, for organizations to have published core values or codes of conduct that reiterate and reinforce generally accepted standards, add or clarify any areas where the organization's standards are higher, and perhaps indicate the consequences of violating them. Where employees understand such standards they are likely to measure up, and when they do, they become incrementally more trustworthy in the eyes of management and other employees.

Employees can also violate management's trust by failing to do what needs to be done in their jobs. This can happen because they don't know what is expected of them or because they don't know how to do it. Unclear expectations can be remedied, not by detailed job descriptions and micromanagement, but by being clear about the organization's purpose, vision, values, and business plans, by establishing clear and measurable performance targets, and by empowering employees to use their judgment and expertise to accomplish them. Mistakes will be made with such an approach, but in most cases they will be more than offset by situations in which employees exceed normal expectations. When this happens, both management and other employees trust them more.

Establishing clear expectations is often a management balancing act: an overly legalistic approach that covers all situations or has too much detail leaves people with no freedom or incentive, while standards with too little detail don't accomplish their purpose or cause confusion and mistrust. To hit the right balance, management must usually collaborate with employees to set clear standards about what is expected but also leave employees considerable room to determine how such standards will be accomplished.

Offering Training and Help

When employees don't do their jobs, or don't do them well, management and fellow employees are disappointed. If the disappointment reoccurs or continues, the parties no longer are willing or able to depend on each other. Lack of dependability causes mistrust, while dependability builds trust.

Employees frequently fail to do what needs to be done because they don't have the ability or the know-how; either they don't have the underlying education and talent or they don't have the current knowledge and skills required for the specific tasks. While employees themselves must take responsibility for their own performance, management nevertheless has an important role to play. It must hire people with the ability to do the work and then offer appropriate training, development, and placement to ensure employees have a reasonable opportunity to deliver. Ideas for accomplishing this are discussed in Chapter 6.

Sometimes employees also fail to be honest or to do the morally correct thing because they do not know how to do so in a way that limits damage to themselves and others at a level they believe is acceptable.

- An employee hides his mistake because of fear of unfair discipline.

- A woman employee fails to report cases of sexual harassment because she believes nothing will be done.

- An employee refuses to report an ethical violation by a manager for fear of retaliation.

To address such situations, management must have processes and procedures in place that allow employees to safely do the right thing. Of equal importance, it must ensure that employees understand that such processes exist and how to use them. This essentially requires effective communication and significant supervisory and employee training. With such training, employees are more likely to know how to do the things that cause others to trust them.

KEY POINTS

1. Trust allows people to believe in the honesty, integrity, reliability, and justice of those with whom they interact.

2. Changes in trust are usually driven by reciprocity: the idea that if one person does something for or to another, the other will respond in a similar manner.

3. Management can become more trustworthy by

   • Basing its actions on core values

   • Being truthful in ways that communicate a common view of reality

   • Using its power fairly

   • Maintaining effective dispute resolution processes

4. Management can help cause employees to be more trustworthy by

   • Changing its own behavior

   • Improving its management processes

   • Establishing clear standards

   • Offering training and help

CHAPTER 4

Avoiding
Policy-Driven Conflict

"The more laws, the more offenders."

—THOMAS FULLER, M.D., *Gnomologia*

Most employment policies cover a wide range of issues affecting the employer-employee relationship. As a general rule, these policies, often accompanied by more detailed administrative procedures, lay down rules of behavior for managers and employees. They may be formal and written, or informal and unwritten. Formal policies usually appear in manuals, employee handbooks, operating procedures, or labor contracts (although dealing with those appearing in labor contracts requires considerations not covered here). Unwritten policies are reflected in the stories, myths, and precedents that guide the actions of those who know about them.

Effective policies are part of the glue that holds an organization together: necessary and positive guides for management and employee action. They encourage optimum use of resources by providing managers and supervisors with investment, operating, and other guidelines that fit with the overall business strategy. They also provide a level of consistency that tends to reduce unfair actions or favoritism by managers and supervisors, gives employees something they can rely on, and builds trust in management. All this amounts to a form of industrial justice that helps ensure that employees are treated fairly and impartially by establishing appropriate behavior and setting standards that guide management decisions and employee expectations.

What is deemed appropriate and fair, however, often means a variety of contradictory things that are defined on the basis of each person's point of reference and expectations. What is the right balance between fairness to an employee and to the organization? Does impartiality mean equality? If not, what differences justify unequal treatment? Does fairness mean giving employees what they deserve, what they need, or what they want? And once this is determined, who decides and how do they make their decision? And if one party doesn't like the decision, how can he reverse or get around it?

Issues such as these present a paradox. Policies intended to ensure workplace effectiveness, justice, and peace often instead cause counterproductive conflict and present essentially irreconcilable dilemmas. They provide centralized management control when employee initiative and empowerment are what is really needed. They foster nondiscrimination and equality when people want to be acknowledged and treated as individuals. They encourage stability when flexibility and change are needed. So instead of preventing conflict, policies often just recast it into another form.

Naturally, all policy conflict cannot be prevented. But policies can be managed to accomplish their purpose with a minimum of resulting conflict. This chapter presents ideas for attaining this objective.

PERSPECTIVES ON POLICY-BASED CONFLICT

Managing policies to minimize negative conflict requires an understanding of the basic types of policies and how they cause conflict.

Types of Policies

Policies fall generally into three broad categories based on their purpose. Allocation policies guide the distribution of scarce resources and rewards and advise employees what they can expect from the organization. They help divide available resources between the organization and its employees in situations where organizations often want the most work for the least cost, while employees often want the most rewards for the least work. A workable balance must be struck. Allocation policies also address employee demands for fair and nondiscriminatory treatment in relation to that of other employees.

> • Pay policies help set the overall level of employee compensation and decide how scarce dollars are divided among employees.
>
> • Overtime policies attempt to fairly divide limited overtime work among many employees who want more overtime pay or to designate which employees will be required to work when there is too much overtime.

Behavior policies establish the organization's expectations and standards of personal conduct and typically outline the consequences of failing to meet expectations or comply with standards. Some are closely tied to generally accepted community standards, while others go further and reflect what the organization needs to remain competitive and accomplish its purpose. They may also establish specific penalties, often up to and including discharge, as the consequence of violation.

> • A policy proscribes harassment in the workplace.
>
> • A policy communicates what personal use of the organization's computers is acceptable and unacceptable.
>
> • A policy spells out in detail the organization's position on issues such as theft, fighting, dishonesty, disloyalty, or other unacceptable behavior and states the penalty for transgression.

Mixed policies attempt to indirectly induce desired behavior with a carrot rather than a stick through the allocation of resources. They offer employees an incentive in the form of money or other resources of value for certain levels of performance or types of behavior. Some policies encourage commitment, collaboration, and mutual gain by offering employees a larger share of any larger pie they help create. Others try to buy desired behavior by rewarding it directly from the organization's existing resource base. And still other policies create a zero-sum situation, where employees are encouraged to compete with each other for limited resources.

- A bonus policy rewards behavior that contributes to improvement in the organization's performance.

- An attendance bonus policy offers money to buy better attendance.

- A merit pay policy allocates scarce pay dollars to those employees whom management rates as better performers.

Causes of Policy Conflict

Unfortunately, each of the three types of policies can have unintended consequences. Instead of causing desired behavior, they can create workplace conflict that detracts from employee feelings of well-being and reduces organizational effectiveness. This does not mean that policies that cause conflict are necessarily bad. When all the needs of the business and employees are balanced, the best choice for all concerned may inevitably sow the seeds of conflict. But to thoughtfully balance such needs and minimize conflict flowing from policies, managers must understand how they frequently lead to conflict.

Policy conflict can be either direct or secondary. Direct conflict occurs when an employee or employees directly object to a policy or its application—typically over questions of applicability, fairness, or consistency. These objections can be based on either the substance or the administration of a policy. Conflict is over substance when it arises from the explicit terms of a policy, without regard to how it is administered. The fundamental disagreement is with the organization and the policy itself. Conflict over administration arises from issues involving management procedures, interpretation, or application of a policy. The objection here is with the acts of the managers who implement and maintain the policy. A direct conflict may challenge the policy itself or its administration, and its apparent focus may be between an employee and a manager or supervisor, but the real dispute is with the organization as a whole as represented by the policy or the individual administrator.

- An employee challenges a disciplinary action for violation of the organization's e-mail policy, claiming the policy is inappropriate because it violates his freedom of speech.

- An employee challenges the size of a pay increase, arguing that the policy was administered incorrectly and he should have received more.

Secondary conflict occurs when policies intended to allocate resources fairly or to encourage certain behavior backfire and cause negative behavior instead. This behavior can take the form of employee attempts to evade, manipulate, or take advantage of a policy to gain additional benefit or avoid adverse consequence. The conflict often results when one policy encourages employee behavior that violates a different policy, and management deals with it by taking corrective or disciplinary action. Policies may also cause an employee to engage in a dispute with another employee in a misguided effort to comply or get more favorable treatment.

- An absenteeism policy intended to encourage good attendance by penalizing absences for specified reasons leads employees to lie about reasons for absences, violating a truthfulness policy.

- A zero-sum bonus policy, according to which employees divide a previously established bonus amount, or merit pay systems based on rigid, zero-sum rating processes lead to unhealthy competition and conflict between those vying for a larger share of a fixed amount.

Good management of an organization's policies can minimize both direct and secondary conflict. But to manage policies effectively—at both the implementation and administration stages—managers must understand how policy issues either directly or indirectly cause conflict. The most important policy issues are discussed in the paragraphs that follow.

Loss of Control

Control has to do with who directs our actions and whether our personal expectations are met. Most of us like to control the events that affect us personally so that our needs and wants are fulfilled. That's why many people become entrepreneurs and work for themselves. Although most employees understand that hiring on with an organization and working for someone else carries some loss of control, they nevertheless like to maintain as much freedom of action as possible. They like, and need, to feel a level of personal empowerment that maintains their self-esteem and allows enough control over their work life for them to attain their expectations.

Workplace policies by their very nature limit the control employees have over their daily life. Policies are, in effect, contracts between an organization and its employees, but they are usually adopted unilaterally by management and imposed as a condition of employment. They govern employees' work life, telling them how to behave and what they will receive for such behavior. Regardless of how appropriate or fair such policies are, they reduce the control employees have over their life; and the more comprehensive and rigid they are, the greater the reduction. This situation does not necessarily cause identifiable conflict, but it forms the fertile soil from which conflict can grow from small and seemingly meaningless events to major issues, because employees are looking for a fight.

> A policy prohibiting use of a cell phone while driving the organization's vehicles may help prevent accidents, but it takes an element of control from employees and is difficult to enforce. If it is combined with dress restrictions, rigid work times, and other such controlling policies, employees may come to feel their lives are not their own.

Unfair or Unreasonable Requirements

Employees want and expect fair treatment and a fair reward from management in exchange for an honest day's work. What is fair and reasonable is usually an individual perception, however, and treatment that is unfair or unreasonable from an employee perspective is likely to cause conflict. Employees make their judgments about fairness both in an absolute sense and relative to how they see other workers being treated. Any policy that doesn't meet their basic needs or provides less benefit than what they perceive other workers in comparable situations are receiving is likely to foster conflict. From an employee's perspective, a policy is likely to fit into one of these problematic categories if it

- Imposes requirements that do not conform with generally accepted norms in comparable work environments

> • A policy prohibits all personal use of the organization's e-mail.
>
> • A policy requires significant, continuing long hours without additional compensation or other consideration.

■ Imposes inconvenience or requires extra effort that goes beyond normal expectations of the job without an appropriate reward or compensation

> A policy requires frequent short-term call-outs to work or expects use of an employee's personal car for business purposes without compensation.

■ Treats groups or classifications of employees differently for no defensible reason

> Different sick leave or absenteeism policies apply to operating and administrative employees who are otherwise similarly situated.

■ Doesn't meet the perceived needs of employees

> A pregnancy policy fails to recognize the potential impact of workaday stress on fetal growth and development.

Business needs may at times require management to implement policies that work against employee interests, at least in the short term. With effective collaboration and communication, however, enlightened management actions should rarely, if ever, be seen as unfair or unreasonable.

"Cliff" Standards

Standards are often necessary to establish triggers or limits in the allocation of resources. They specify when a policy applies or how benefit amounts are determined. Standards establishing triggers or limits rarely cause conflict when the consequences of failure to qualify are balanced with the circumstances and when they are supported by external norms, defensible from an economic or management point of view and under-standable to employees. Policies often award benefits based on objective milestones on an employee's career journey—milestones that employees understand they will attain over time. In such cases, employees may not be too concerned about failure to qualify at one point in time because they know they will qualify later. Or benefits are based on incremental sched-ules, so an employee may not be too concerned about a benefit amount that is possibly too small because the next higher increment is only slightly more favorable.

> A vacation policy that increases paid time off by one day for each year of service is not likely to be contested by junior employees.

The point is that similarly situated employees are treated similarly, employ-ees only slightly differently situated are treated slightly differently, and the standards applicable to an individual employee can become more favorable based on objective criteria such as time. Conflict is not likely in situations such as these.

But policies that make major distinctions based on minor differences or have all-or-nothing applications often lead to predictable conflict. When employees almost qualify but do not, the loss is seen as too great and they challenge the policy rather than "fall off the cliff." They usually feel either that the policy is arbitrary and unfair or that it unfairly, if not illegally, dis-criminates against them. Whichever the case, conflict is the result.

> A loss on a home sale policy that compensates only employees who lose more than $25,000 on the sale of a home in a transfer situation is likely to be contested by an employee who loses $24,900.

Punitive Provisions

Behavior policies are often enforced through punishments such as written warnings placed in an employee's file, demotion, time off without pay, discharge, or other penalties for failing to behave as required. Compli-ance with behavior policy requirements is necessary and appropriate for an effective workplace, but punishment nearly always leads to problems, including the following:

- Supervisors are reluctant to intervene in the early stages of a problem because they generally don't like to punish employees or to be seen as building a case against them.

- Supervisors may show favoritism.

- Communication declines because employees are afraid management will shoot the messenger.

- Punishment loses its effectiveness over time as employees become insensitive to sanctions.

- Employees emphasize avoidance rather than cooperation as they seek ways to get around the rules and punishment rather than contribute to the organization.

- Employees develop attitudes of apathy, anger, resentment, and frustration over the long term.

- Punishment often escalates rather than resolves conflict and leads to more disruptive and costly resolution processes up to and including lawsuits.

Granted, employees must conform to appropriate rules, and discharge—the ultimate workplace punishment—is necessary from time to time when employees refuse to be coached or take certain actions that standing alone may warrant termination (such as stealing or starting a fight). In most policy situations, however, punishment has only negative consequences. It almost always leads to conflict between the punished employee and management, as the employee is likely to contest the fairness of the policy itself, the appropriateness of application in the particular case, the extent or level of punishment, or any other concern that seems ripe for contest. And because penalties are likely to cost the employee both money and self-esteem, the challenge is likely to be aggressive.

Unhealthy Competition

Policies such as pay for performance or bonus programs that allow employee actions to determine the allocation of rewards are often used to provide incentives for desired behavior. They may be healthy and encourage improved organizational performance when they

- Communicate what management believes is important

- Communicate the need for excellent performance

- Provide incentives for excellent performance

- Communicate the need for poor performers to improve

Such policies do, however, have a darker side, which can lead to counterproductive conflict. The potential darker side includes the following:

- The wrong behavior may be rewarded because performance is often difficult to assess, or supervisors may be reluctant to make required distinctions.

- Supervisors may be charged with favoritism, which may be perceived or real.

- If potential rewards are too great, employees may try to manipulate the system, with damaging consequences.

- Zero-sum policies are likely to cause unhealthy competition and personal conflict among employees, impairing organizational effectiveness.

- A salary program based on forced ranking of employee performance can lead to charges of favoritism against the supervisors doing the ranking.

- Competition for a larger portion of an established bonus pot can cause employees to manipulate targets or results, withhold information, refuse to cooperate, or even sabotage the efforts of another in an effort to gain advantage in the allocation of the reward.

Direct competition for rewards can be very counterproductive from the organization's viewpoint. Just as important, however, it can also build distrust and dislike, creating an atmosphere in which even worse conflict on different issues becomes a way of life.

Poor Communication

Employees must understand what is required if policies are to be effective and cause a minimum level of conflict. Unfortunately, management communication of policy requirements is often inadequate for the following reasons:

- Management doesn't get the word out.

Management's only communication of major policy changes is bulletin board postings, which employees rarely read.

- The policy obfuscates with doublespeak; its language is so complex, unclear, or vague that employees do not understand it.
- Communication is conflicting.

> Different supervisors communicate different understandings of a policy, each of which may or may not reflect the appropriate information.

- Management talks to employees and fails to listen to their questions and respond appropriately.
- There is noise in the system and employees are not able to really hear the new policy.

> - Management makes an oral announcement on the work floor while distracting work continues.
> - Management announces a change in compensation policy at the same time as a layoff announcement, which distracts employee attention.

Without real awareness and understanding, employees do not know what they can rely on from management or what management expects and relies on from them. This lack of mutually understood expectations leads to uncertainty, disappointment, distrust, and ultimately conflict when employee behavior does not meet management expectations or management actions disappoint employees. Only effective communication—broadly defined—can create the awareness and understanding required to minimize such conflict.

Inflexible Application

Policies typically cover future, generally recurring actions, and few can anticipate all issues or cover all eventualities. Circumstances arise that the designers didn't anticipate, unforeseen changes make policies less appropriate than initially envisioned, or perceptions of fairness evolve over time. Under these circumstances, rigid application of a policy by unthinking, inflexible administrators may not meet employee or organizational needs or may be perceived as unfair or unreasonable. In such situations, employees may expect management to change its interpretation or make special exceptions for them. Management may refuse to do so because of concerns about charges of discrimination or about setting troublesome precedent for the future. Regardless of the reason, when management relies on the literal language of a policy and doesn't exhibit the flexibility to respond to changing employee needs or desires, conflict is likely to occur, whether or not the "right" decision was made to appropriately balance conflicting interests.

Discriminatory Application

While appropriate flexibility is needed, too much flexibility in policy administration can raise the specter of discriminatory application, either real or as perceived by employees. When policy administrators change interpretations or make exceptions for an individual employee, other employees expect comparable treatment in the same or similar circumstances. If the original exception is properly considered and applied on a uniform basis in all future comparable cases, it probably represents the type of policy evolution that may be needed in a living, vibrant workplace. But if an initial exception based on poor judgment, favoritism, convenience, or management's fear of an employee's reaction is not applied in future similar cases, conflict is likely. Oiling the squeaky wheel nearly always causes problems. Employees in comparable situations will observe the differences of treatment, conclude that certain employees were given favored treatment, and feel they are being discriminated against.

Concerns about discrimination are particularly relevant with policies that depend on an interpretation of the facts or require significant management judgment in their application. In such cases, personal decisions of an individual manager are the primary factor in determining the consequence of employee actions. Direct conflict and allegations of discrimination often result when employees disagree with the manager's understanding of the facts, interpretation of the policy, or decision as to consequences.

- A policy prohibiting transmission of offensive e-mails is subject to interpretation as to what is offensive.

- A policy prohibiting horseplay turns on management's interpretation of what constitutes horseplay.

REDUCING POLICY-BASED CONFLICT

Management cannot prevent all policy-based conflict. If it all was the result of challenges by troublemakers or the ignorant, prevention might be possible; management could get rid of the troublemakers and educate the ignorant. But preventing conflict is not so simple. Some conflict is inevitable because policies address individuals and groups with divergent interests that often clash. Managers and affected employees often have different objectives; work time impinges on social life, cost consciousness competes with higher employee pay, and so on. And employees themselves often have competing needs or desires, as when several are striving for one promotion allowed by a policy, or when seniority rules that favor one individual necessarily hurt another.

Thus, some conflict seems inevitable, and management cannot eliminate all of it. Instead, management must implement policies that respond to differing interests, avoid exacerbating differences or creating additional ones, and facilitate effective resolution of those conflicts that do arise. Ideas for accomplishing these objectives are outlined below.

Don't Implement Unneeded Policies

We are aware of the problems created in society when legislatures pass laws that unreasonably impinge on personal liberties, violate commonly accepted mores, or are unenforceable. Prohibition and attempts to regulate private, consensual sexual conduct are among the most visible examples. The same concept applies in the workplace.

Most employees understand what behavior is acceptable in the society of which the workplace is a part. If they don't understand at the start, they respond well to education, training, effective supervision, and a climate of mutual trust. For these employees, an unnecessary policy is more than redundant—it can be a demeaning exercise in the ills of micromanagement. And the small minority of employees who refuse or are unable to comply with normal social norms are typically no more likely to respond to formal policies. Dealing with such employees requires individual, one-on-one actions regardless of whether a policy exists on a particular issue. Therefore, formal policies intended to mold behavior to commonly accepted norms may have a negative effect, except perhaps in more egregious situations, where spelling out penalties for failing to comply may be important.

> A policy prohibiting theft may be necessary, not to advise employees it is unacceptable, but to advise that they will be discharged for a first offense.

Difficult issues also arise when management implements policies that prevent employees from exercising their own judgment in areas where that judgment is normally sufficient. Such policies are often by their very nature difficult to fairly enforce because they require substituting management's judgment on a case-by-case basis for employee judgment. Further, they detract from employee feelings of self-worth and personal control and are likely to lead to resistance, reduced trust, unintended consequences, and increased conflict.

Management must make its own determination about whether a policy is appropriate by balancing the business need for it against the adverse consequences that could flow from it. Concerns often may be better addressed by other means, such as education, training, and good management practices. In such cases, management should avoid implementing policies or consider getting rid of those that already exist.

> - Has employee dress deteriorated to the point that it is a legitimate problem, and must it be addressed with a dress code policy rather than education and supervision?
>
> - Must employee breaks be formalized and monitored, or can employees be motivated and trusted to manage their own time? Will employees find a way to compensate for a restrictive break policy by resting on the job?

Derive Policies from Core Values

An organization's core values are the necessary and enduring set of guiding principles that should drive everyone's behavior and decisions. Values tell managers and employees how they should act as they try to attain the goals of the organization. They guide the choices people make, suggest which matters should be given most attention, and provide predictability in the workplace. Like the policies that flow from them, values may be evidenced by a written, formal core ideology, or they may be informal, part of the stories and myths that describe the organization. Whichever the case, to be effective they must be well understood by all.

Policies can provide guidance for handling most transactions involving employees. But they cannot always be written with absolutely clear language that means the same thing to everyone, nor can they always anticipate all issues or concerns. Gray areas nearly always remain. Without core values, when the meaning of a policy is not clear or gaps appear, the parties have no guidance for resolving difficult issues. Absent a foundation in core values, the only guidance employees have in such situations is their own judgment and self-interest and the fear of suffering the consequences of management's after-the-fact condemnation of their actions. Management's only alternative may be to stand over employees as an enforcer on a case-by-case basis. Thus, without well-understood workplace values, policies often lead to conflict because on many issues each party marches to the beat of its own drummer rather than in lockstep with the other.

When policies are based on and reflect core values, conflict is minimized for the following reasons:

- Management and all the parties have a common reference for what the language means and how it is intended to be interpreted and applied.

- Senior managers, administrators, and other decision makers have a basis for exercise of consistent judgment.

- Employees who are comfortable with the organization's values are likely to be comfortable with the substance of aligned policies.

- The organization's culture is more likely to support its policies.

A warning is in order. While all policies should be driven by values, not all values should be enforced with detailed policies. Doing so raises the possibility of values clashing with reality, or of their being implemented in ways that are implicitly contradictory or in conflict with how employees should be treated. When this happens, employees become frustrated, don't know what to do, and may create conflict. Thus, policies should be based not only on values, but also on good judgment as to how they square with reality and with each other.

- Emphasizing a customer service value drives management to establish a detailed policy for what should be said to customers, but the instructions don't fit all situations and the policy angers certain customers instead.

- A public service value drives management to pressure individual employees to support a particular charity, but its insistence violates its value of respecting employees' personal decisions.

Consider the Systems Implications of Policy

The need for systems thinking in conflict management was discussed earlier and will not be repeated here. It is important to emphasize, however, that policies are part of an existing system and function as a whole through the interaction of its parts. This means that each policy should fit with other policies and processes. Change in one affects others and often requires that they be changed also.

> - A retirement policy that is end-loaded and encourages long service doesn't fit with physically demanding work where turnover is desired.
>
> - Implementation of a new bonus policy is likely to motivate different employee behavior and therefore require different supervisor practices.
>
> - Implementation of a zero-tolerance harassment policy may necessitate changes in employment orientation procedures and education programs.

To address systems concerns, management should consider the following:

- Involve a broad cross section of individuals who are familiar with most or all parts of the system in the formulation and implementation of policy.

- Do an impact analysis on prospective policy that identifies places and people likely to be affected, either directly or indirectly. Consider additional actions to minimize any adverse effects that are predicted.

- Consider the relative leverage opportunities of various policy options, and use the option by which the least change will get the greatest result with the least likely conflict.

> An organization is experiencing excessive turnover from employee job bidding. It could impose policy rules that limit employee rights to bid from one job to another or provide a financial penalty for doing so. A higher-leverage, less conflictive approach might be to address the reasons employees are leaving jobs and make small changes in the seniority system that remove employee incentives to bid for other jobs or improve the overtime work procedures employees object to in departments they are bidding out of.

- Synchronize policies. In an effective organization, all individual policies work together, supporting each other and fostering the same behavior.

- A compensation system that rewards individual initiative is inconsistent with a rigid break policy that limits employees' freedom to manage their own time.

- A rigid absence control policy limiting personal time off may need to be supported by a policy that allows employees to exchange work shifts.

Involve Employees in Policy Implementation

Workplace policies almost always involve balancing competing interests. These can be best balanced by recognizing that although an organization and its employees have many different interests, they also have many in common, and collaboration presents the best opportunity to meld them in ways that are mutually beneficial. Collaboration requires both management and employees to contribute their information, expertise, and energy and work together to complement each other in a synergy that allows the combination to be greater than the sum of its parts. More specifically, it allows employee participants to

- Bring to the process a better understanding of employee needs, wants, concerns, and other such considerations

- Challenge conventional wisdom and management's mental models by participating in dialogue

- Convey an employee view of what really goes on in the workplace and what issues are real and not real

- Assist management in effectively communicating the result to all employees

- Assist in implementing policies by serving as supportive ambassadors

It is usually not appropriate or practical to have all employees involved in all the nit-picking of policy formulation. Although they often have much to contribute, they also have other work to do and usually have limited expertise in specific issues, so their direct involvement often would not be cost-effective. Several more limited forms of involvement, however, are feasible in most situations. They include the following:

- Management by walking around, whereby managers and supervisors discuss the issues involved, reveal that a policy is being considered, solicit employee feedback, and convey the information to those working on the policy

- Formal communications that announce a policy is being considered and solicit informal employee feedback through supervisory channels

- Employee surveys that request written input on the issues being considered

- Employee focus groups that facilitate discussion of the issues being considered and invite oral feedback

- Employee participation on teams that are charged with obtaining information, designing a policy, or overseeing its implementation

- Announcement of tentative decisions and requests for feedback before final implementation

Practices such as these do more than obtain information for constructing a better policy. They also reduce resistance to policies employees don't like by eliminating the surprise, helping employees understand both sides of the issue, and giving them the feeling (which must be based on reality) that their ideas were considered in the final decision.

Employee participation through these and other practices offers great value, but one proviso is in order. Some involvement of nonunion employees, particularly their participation on teams, can raise concerns that management is in fact forming and dominating a labor organization in violation of the National Labor Relations Act. The act does not prevent nonunion employee involvement in policy formulation, but managers would be well advised to seek legal counsel to ensure it is done appropriately.

Effectively Communicate Policies

Effective communication of policies can realize some of the value of employee involvement and significantly reduce conflict. It works for two reasons.

First, knowing the rules is necessary for employees to abide by them. Most employees will willingly comply with reasonable behavior policies they know about and understand, but they are more likely to violate those they aren't aware of or don't understand. And violation brings potential conflict. This means that policies must be communicated to all employees before they become effective and to new employees when they join the organization, and policies must remain an open book while they are in force.

Second, early advance communication minimizes the likelihood of conflict arising even from unpopular policies. Announcing and explaining policies well before their implementation date allows employees who may be negatively impacted to think about them, rationalize their appropriateness, prepare for compliance if necessary, or protest in a nonthreatening setting where no impact has yet been felt. When such policies are actually implemented, employees are less likely to protest because they have known about the planned change for a substantial time, have had an opportunity to adjust, and didn't object earlier.

> Announcing a no-smoking policy months in advance of its effective date gives smokers time to adjust to the change, both physically and psychologically, and seek smoking cessation help if needed, thereby minimizing the likelihood of conflict.

Initial communication should not be cursory, but should include whatever information is necessary to ensure that employees have a thorough understanding of relevant provisions and the rationale behind them. A simple announcement may be appropriate in some cases, but more extensive communication, such as a detailed explanation of the background behind the policy or a significant training program, is more likely to be needed.

> A change in work hours can be easily communicated so employees understand when to report to work. However, while easily understood from a mechanical perspective, the change potentially affects car pools, child-care arrangements, and other personal concerns. Therefore, complete communication of the business need and rationale is important.

Policy communication should fit with the organization's usual procedures and be handled similarly to communication on other issues of comparable importance. The process should not imply more or less importance than actually exists. Following are examples of approaches that may be considered:

- Oral communication, either in small groups or one-on-one
- Recorded messages via the organization's telephone system
- Written announcements, either hard copy or electronic
- Training programs in which managers, supervisors, policy experts, or employees involved in policy formulation are the trainers
- Continuing feedback, interaction, and communication throughout the development period
- Maintaining policies on the organization's web site or using other processes for continuing availability

Provide Fair Administration

What is a fair policy, from a substantive perspective, will vary from case to case. In each case, management must balance the interests of all parties involved and reach its conclusions by considering the need for a policy, the organization's core values, employee input, and other issues discussed in the preceding pages. But substantive fairness is only half the issue. Unfair administration of fair policies can also cause major conflict.

Employees are likely to see policy administration they perceive as unfair to be punishment—which often impairs their self-esteem, reduces their trust in management, incites discrimination charges, and causes other conflictive behavior. Therefore, developing policies that are substantively fair is of little value unless employees believe the policies are fairly administered.

Several principles are important to ensure fair administration. They amount to a due process of policy administration: those principles and rules that protect the individual rights of employees from the disproportionate power of the employer. (Due process issues are especially important when employee discipline and discharge are involved. Disciplinary due process is discussed in more detail in Chapter 6.) Suggested principles are as follows:

- Provide early initial communication sufficient to put employees on notice as to what is required of them.
- Offer relevant information. In addition to communication of the policy itself, management should provide employees with relevant, non-

confidential information relating to its administration. This information should be sufficient to allow a concerned employee to make his or her own judgment about the need for the policy, its fundamental substantive fairness, and how it is being administered. It might include background data relating to the policy itself, the company's assessment of the facts in a particular case, how similar cases have been handled, impact of a different handling on the organization or other employees, or other similar information.

- Provide access to experts. Organizations often require questions or complaints to be processed through the chain of command, with employees having access only to their immediate supervisor, perhaps with an appeal farther up the line. Such requirements are seen to maintain the authority of the supervisory force. But supervisors and line managers may not be familiar with policy details and even with reasonable advance preparation may not be able to adequately deal with the minutiae of complex policies. Therefore, confining employee discussions to the organizational pecking order may deny an employee the right to a meaningful discussion. On the other hand, allowing employees to discuss concerns directly with policy experts, perhaps in the presence of their supervisor, often provides them the best opportunity to get their questions addressed in ways that minimize conflict.

- Allow an employee to bring a support person when discussing a concern or protesting a policy. In most cases (absent some unlawful act or violation of a union contract), management has the right to make the final decision regarding policy questions, and this right is not affected by who participates in discussions leading to that decision. However, allowing a concerned employee to be accompanied by a support person can be evidence of management's openness and willingness to do what is right and can provide an employee with the confidence to be more forthcoming with information and to accept a final decision. Therefore, management has little to lose and much to gain by allowing a support person to be involved.

- Balance flexibility with nondiscriminatory application. Management must treat each employee as an individual and fully consider every aspect of his or her particular case while at the same time avoiding even the perception of discrimination among employees. This presents a difficult task—often raising a Hobson's choice between responsiveness and needed consistency—and there is no easy or certain way to accomplish it! To do so, management must not allow policy statements to stand alone. Instead management should develop a "common law" of precedent in policy administration. Management should always do what is right in the case at hand, as the right decision will not cause precedent that cannot be dealt with. To ensure that the right issues are considered, all decisions should be documented in the organization files so that each decision can be compared with prior similar cases. Thoughtful awareness of precedent and comparison with the case at hand can lead to flexible but nondiscriminatory administration that best meets the needs of management and employees alike.

- Be responsive. Employees often can live with any answer, as long as they have an answer; they are looking for certainty and predictability as much as a favorable response. Nonresponsiveness in the form of stonewalling, obfuscation, or delay introduces uncertainty that may be a bigger problem for the concerned employee than a negative response. It builds resentment and antagonism, which are likely to make any answer unacceptable when it is finally received, and ensures that conflict results.

Build Dispute Resolution Processes into Policies

On the surface, management may appear to have little incentive to build formal dispute resolution processes into its policies. Most complaints or potential conflicts arise when employees challenge an employer's policy or its administration. An employee typically is the charging party, and management simply wishes to maintain the status quo—and usually has the capacity to do so. Thus, an argument can be made that management is in control, and relinquishing some aspects of that control through a dispute resolution system only gives complaining employees another bite at the apple and makes their challenge of management easier.

But the cost of employees' not having an easy, fair way to resolve policy complaints is significant as well. Continuing conflict over the appropriateness or application of a policy is counterproductive and can be costly. The level of conflict, and consequent cost, can range from an unhappy, unproductive worker to active resistance in the form of subtle sabotage or fomenting of discontent among other employees to the filing of lawsuits in cases where there is appearance of violation of a legally protected right. All of these potential consequences are negative and costly.

Thus, management needs to provide mechanisms that smoothly and expeditiously resolve as many disputes as possible as early as possible while at the same time maintaining the level of control felt necessary to manage the business. The best chance for attaining this balance is to provide an internal dispute resolution system that ensures the use of due process in the application of policy. Options for such a system are discussed in Part 3.

Internal dispute resolution processes reduce conflict in two ways. First, they provide the discipline that causes management to make more balanced and better-reasoned policy decisions, which are less likely to foster conflict. A supervisor or administrator who understands that all the facts will come out and that a senior manager or other third party may review his or her decision is likely to make a more reasoned decision than a person making one in a vacuum. And, second, employees who have a chance to protest with the protection of due process are more likely to have confidence that management intends to make the right decision because it has been willing to expose its vulnerability. Accordingly, they are less likely to complain than those who feel they have been treated arbitrarily.

Update Policies to Keep Up with the Changing Times

The workforce and the nature of work have changed dramatically in most organizations over the years, and they continue to change with increasing speed. In the past, employment was typically seen as a long-term relationship between a large firm competing in expanding markets and hourly wage workers or salaried managers with spouses at home. But today's employment relationship is very different. Increased participation of women, the prevalence of part-time or temporary workers, increased risk of permanent job loss, and other similar factors have changed the basic employment contract and introduced continuing uncertainty into the employment relationship. Thus, many policies adopted in earlier times are not now matched with who works, how they do it, and how the relationship fits with institutions such as the family, education processes, the social welfare system, and the global economy. Policies adopted today may not fit tomorrow's changing workplace.

Policies that don't fit the world of which they are a part, or don't address the changing needs of the employees to whom they apply, cause conflict. This means that managers and policy administrators must continually implement, administer, reexamine, and change all of an organization's policies. In this way, policies become living, evolving systems that are able to keep up with the changing world.

KEY POINTS

1. Policies intended to ensure workplace effectiveness, justice, fairness, and peace often instead cause significant counterproductive conflict.

2. Conflict resulting from policies can be direct, as between employees and the organization represented by the policy; or secondary, where they provide an incentive for unacceptable employee behavior or conflict among employees.

3. Counterproductive conflict can be caused by either the substance of a policy or its administration.

4. Management cannot prevent all policy-based conflict. It can, however, do a number of things to reduce its amount and severity. These include the following:

    *   Not promulgate unneeded policies

    *   Derive its policies from core values

    *   Consider the systems implications of policy

    *   Involve employees in policy implementation

    *   Effectively communicate policies

    *   Provide fair administration

    *   Build dispute resolution processes into policies

    *   Update policies to keep up with changing times

Managing Change Effectively

"When it comes to change, people like only those they make themselves."

—French proverb

P eople often see change as a confusing jungle, fraught with fear, threats, and potential conflict. Business as usual, with less uncertainty and fewer confrontations, is more comfortable. But no organization can remain viable over time without change. Change will be foisted upon it by external forces, and, more importantly, management must continually make innovative changes within the organization to hopefully stay ahead of those forces. Also, employees across the organization need to be allowed and encouraged to introduce change because they often are closer to the action and in a better position to know what needs to be done and how to do it than are their managers and supervisors.

This chapter will address management-initiated change because it so often has a major effect on employees and is the change that most often causes conflict. And where its value exceeds its expected cost, including the cost of potential conflict, management generally must proceed with change even when conflict is predictable. It must plow ahead and take actions to minimize the resulting conflict.

Fortunately, options do exist for minimizing the conflict caused by change. Conflict may occur either because people don't like the substance of what is being done or because they object to the process used to do it. Objection to the process is often the biggest issue, and it usually is the one that can be dealt with more easily. Therefore, even when management may not realistically avoid making difficult changes, it usually can minimize conflict by handling them appropriately. Accordingly, the purpose of this chapter is to discuss ways to manage the change process to minimize conflict.

CHANGE THEORY

A great deal of research and writing has been done on the subject of organizational change. While the results may differ in detail, a basic theory emerges that is helpful in understanding how to manage it with minimum conflict. This theory is reflected in the notion that change happens when people in various roles engage in a process that converts the current status to something different.

Roles

Several different, though related, participant roles exist in any effective change effort. They may be characterized as follows:

- The change driver is the person or group who identifies the need for change, develops a vision of what can be, and exercises their initiative to cause change to happen. The driver may be managers or employees from any level within the organization.

- The sponsor is the person or group with the authority to sanction a contemplated change and commit resources to make it happen. The sponsor is responsible for understanding the need for change, deciding what actions are feasible, and designating those who will make it happen. Sponsors may or may not be the change driver, but they typically are at the top levels of the affected organizational unit.

- Implementors are the individuals or groups who are responsible for making a change happen. They develop and enact the steps required to make it a reality and manage the day-to-day process. Implementors typically work for the change driver.

- Targets are the employees or groups who are expected to change. Their behavior determines whether the new policy will stick and become institutionalized or be just another passing fancy. Targets may elect to accept change or to resist it through conflict with its drivers and implementors.

Obviously, the same people can perform more than one role, or each role may be handled by a different person.

- A senior manager may be the driver, sponsor, and implementor; or a supervisor may help implement a change that applies to him as a target.

- Employees surface a concern and drive change. Senior management is the sponsor, supervisors are the implementors, and all employees are targets.

Process

An organization is not static but rather is an entity in which the interaction of driving forces that tend to cause change and restraining forces that tend to resist it create an equilibrium, or status quo. An organization in equilibrium can change only when the drive to change exceeds the target's resistance and creates a disequilibrium that unfreezes the status quo. This is a process that moves individuals or groups from their current, often flawed state of established equilibrium that makes up the status quo, through a transition that involves disengaging and developing new attitudes, to the desired state, which becomes the new status quo.[8] Management typically initiates change when it is dissatisfied with the status quo and has a vision of a better state and the resources to carry out the change.

Most conflict occurs during the second stage—the disengagement and transition from the past—which frequently is filled with uncertainty, instability, and stress. This uncomfortable stage occurs when the equilibrium and relative comfort of the present state have been disrupted but the stability and predictability of the new state have not yet been attained. The targets resist the implementors through some form of conflict.

Resistance is the action of the targets to maintain the status quo. The level of resistance will be largely determined by how desirable or undesirable the targets perceive both the substance of a change and how the implementors are proceeding with the change process, as indicated by their first steps. Resistance can take many forms. Targets often can use traditions, laws, or policies to overtly prevent implementation. They can also simply fail to act, drag their feet, or engage in disputes with the drivers and implementors to make change more difficult, slow it down, or stop it.

Implementors have two fundamental options for dealing with resistance imposed by the targets. They can force change by using power and authority to overcome resistance, or they can control the quality of the change—its substance, the implementation process, and how both are perceived by employees—to reduce the targets' resistance and get their acceptance and support by making the matter less objectionable. This involves making the best decision about what specific changes to implement and how best to go about them and is the essence of minimizing change-driven conflict.

Ideally, the quality of changes implemented by management will foster acceptance by employees, but gaining acceptance is often a difficult process at best, especially when employees perceive a change as negative. Daryl Conner, building on earlier work by Dr. Elisabeth Kübler-Ross, has identified eight phases people go through in reaching acceptance.[9] They are:

1. *Stability*—the status quo that exists prior to a change.
2. *Immobilization*—the initial reaction of shock or disorientation, during which the target doesn't know how to react.
3. *Denial*—during which the target rejects change-related information and believes that if he ignores it, the change will go away.
4. *Anger*—the period of frustration and hurt, during which targets lash out, blame others, take hostile actions, and otherwise try to stop the change.
5. *Bargaining*—when the targets begin to accept reality and look for ways to avoid or minimize the negative impact.
6. *Depression*—the frequent reaction when the full weight of a negative change is acknowledged.
7. *Testing*—the period during which the targets learn to work with the new change.
8. *Acceptance*—when the new reality becomes the new status quo.

Conflict management issues arise during the denial, anger, and bargaining stages, when employees are not willing to go along and their resistance takes the form of overt challenges to management. These situations suggest a slightly expanded model that specifically addresses conflict management issues. Drawing heavily on Conner's eight phases, we have constructed such a model with the following phases:

1. *Stability*—the status quo before a change.

2. *Immobilization*—the initial reaction of shock or disorientation, during which the target doesn't know how to react.

3. *Disagreement*—the initial negative reaction to a planned change. A disagreement may be initially private, as the target knows the announced change is problematic but hasn't yet decided how to react.

4. *Surfacing*—when the disagreement becomes public, perhaps when the target advises the implementors or sponsor that a difference of opinion exists.

5. *Dispute*—the status when either of the parties escalates the disagreement with action intended to do something about it. The target makes the disagreement clear and emphatic and may make threats or take job actions such as strikes, lawsuits, or other activities to resist the change. The sponsors and implementors may take actions, perhaps in response to the target's resistance, to force the change.

6. *Resolution*—whatever activities are necessary to resolve the dispute, manage the resistance, and get on with life. Hopefully, resolution is attained through collaboration, problem solving, mediation, or other positive practices that lead to agreement among the parties. Unfortunately, however, resolution may be through more negative means, such as settling a strike or getting a court decision whereby one party forces its will on the other.

7. *Depression*—the frequent reaction when the full weight of a negative change is acknowledged.

8. *Testing*—the period during which the targets learn to work with the new change.

9. *Acceptance*—learning to live with the dispute resolution. This is usually easy if the substance of the dispute was resolved to the parties' mutual satisfaction. But when the resolution was imposed by coercion, acceptance is likely to be more problematic if it happens at all.

10. *Stability*—when the change becomes the new status quo.

In summary, change happens when management effectively deals with employee resistance and any disagreements or disputes that follow. If management overcomes the resistance with force, acceptance and a productive new stability are a difficult proposition. But if management minimizes resistance through collaboration that produces an agreeable resolution, then acceptance, support, and a positive new stability are more likely. To effectively deal with resistance and the impact of consequent conflict, management must understand why employees are likely to resist change and take actions to minimize it rather than to overcome it by force.

CAUSES OF RESISTANCE

Resistance to management-initiated change exists in all workplaces. It may be passive, as when employees disagree with the actions being taken but do not talk about their disagreement or escalate it to a dispute. This type of resistance may be expressed in foot-dragging, reduced productivity, low morale, anticompany verbal campaigns, or other negative employee actions that management may or may not be aware of. The fact that employees have not surfaced or escalated the resistance does not detract from its negative impact, however, and if continued it can become an insidious cancer that sucks the vitality from the organization.

Resistance may also be active, with employee targets engaging in a dispute with management. Employees may overtly refuse to comply, confront individual supervisors, file grievances, engage in sabotage, file lawsuits, seek a union if they do not already have one, strike if they do, or take other explicit actions intended to prevent management from proceeding. Their resistance can escalate to major organizational occurrences with costly consequences. Active resistance, however, does have the advantage of being out in the open and available for resolution.

Management's best bet for dealing with resistance, whether passive or active, is to minimize its occurrence in the first place. To do so, managers must understand its causes. Causes of resistance are in reality an extension of the causes of conflict introduced in Chapter 1. They have their basis in the same fundamental human issues and play out as a complex combination of concerns working together to thwart change. Following are some of the primary reasons that employees resist management-initiated change.

Substantive Disagreement

Substantive disagreement occurs when employees believe their work life—broadly speaking—will be negatively affected by a planned change. The belief could relate to specific concerns about wages, hours, and working conditions or to less tangible issues such as psychological needs, feelings of job security, and expectations for the future.

Employees' substantive concerns are often based in reality. Management, as the entity responsible to many stakeholders, must from time to time make those hard decisions that are necessary from the organization's viewpoint but that inevitably will hurt some individual employees. It hopefully will minimize the need for such changes by planning ahead to avoid them, balancing employee needs with the needs of the organization, and making decisions with empathy for those affected. But when they are required, it is management's duty to make them, and some level of substantive resistance is generally unavoidable.

> • Management combines two jobs into one to improve efficiency, and affected employees are fearful of a staff reduction.
>
> • Management changes the medical insurance policy to make it affordable, and employees fear they are losing a benefit.

Misunderstanding the Facts

Resistance often arises when employees have incorrect perceptions and misunderstandings about whether a change is good or bad for them. A key reason for such misunderstandings is that employees have different information than management has. Perhaps because of a closed style, poor communication processes, negligence, or legitimate issues of confidentiality, managers often do not involve employees in the decision process or share with them all the information behind a planned change. In other cases, management shares information but employees do not believe what they hear because of a lack of trust. Whatever the reason, employees who do not have all the information they need are likely to assume the worst and resist.

Different Perspectives

Targets may also resist because their perspective is different from that of those who are sponsoring or implementing change. Employees' perceptions are often determined more by their beliefs than by what they see or hear. They look to their work and the employment relationship for much of their personal identity and self-esteem, and they see management's changes through the lens of their own needs and interests. This perspective colors what they see and causes their expectations of the impact to be different from management's. Unless the different perceptions are corrected, conflict is likely.

> A management plan to move an employee to another job may be seen by the employee as punishment for unsatisfactory job performance, while management sees it as a good-faith effort to place the employee in a role better suited to his talents.

Inertia

Values, beliefs, biases, and other deep-rooted influences on our lives create the culture we live in, and needs and expectations arising from this culture cause us to value the status quo. Our culture provides us with a psychological equilibrium, or human inertia, that unconsciously causes us to develop habits, cling to certainty, and oppose change to our current situation. Most of us are more comfortable with what we know or can reasonably predict than with what we don't know or cannot predict. Therefore, since change nearly always involves some level of uncertainty and upsets this built-in inertia, employees resist it.

Loss of Control

Employees like to feel they control their own lives, and management-sponsored change represents a loss of that control. Change not only takes control away in the particular case, but also reminds employees of the extent to which someone else governs their lives over the longer term. Further, the uncertainty that almost always accompanies new situations reminds employees that they don't know what to expect next and exacerbates the real or perceived loss of control.

> - When management initiates a dress code, employees may resist because they object to someone else controlling something as personal as how they dress.
>
> - An employee who was about to retire anyway may object to a company-initiated retirement because he wants to control his own exit.

Indictment of the Past

People also resist change because they believe it is an indictment of what they have believed or done in the past. Change can occur for many reasons. It may be needed because the status quo is wrong and needs to be made right, because there is room for improvement in the status quo, or because circumstances are changing and the status quo must be changed to keep up. Unfortunately, it is easy for employees to forget that circumstances change over time, the information base grows, and better ways of doing things are discovered. When they do forget, they view all change as correcting something that was wrong, and therefore as a condemnation of what they have been believing or doing. When this happens, they often resist and cause conflict.

> An incumbent sees introduction of technology into a job as implying he has not been performing adequately.

MINIMIZING RESISTANCE

The collision of management's drive to change with employee resistance causes workplace conflict. If resistance is strongly felt and emotional, and management mounts powerful initiatives to overcome it, major confrontations are inevitable. Disagreements involving one or a few employees can escalate in severity and become disputes in the form of personal warfare or functional strife that includes many employees, has major organizational impact, and is costly to resolve. Management may win the battle by crushing the obvious resistance yet lose the war when hidden resistance and conflict continue unabated and make effective implementation impossible.

Thus, management's best option is to minimize—rather than try to overcome—resistance by addressing its causes and paying attention to the quality of the change. This ensures that its substance is appropriate and the process for handling it is effective. Since management's role often includes taking difficult, unpopular actions, it cannot expect to avoid all resistance. This is particularly true when the cause is a substantive disagreement, where the facts are what they are and management must proceed in the face of sure employee resistance. But management can always address resistance to the change process by planning how it goes forward and avoiding as many of the causes of resistance as possible. Doing this will minimize the likelihood and intensity of consequent conflict. Some suggestions for minimizing resistance are discussed below.

Don't Surprise Employees

Surprises may be great for birthdays, anniversaries, and celebrations of other happy occasions, but they usually don't work for workplace changes. Unless management is offering free trips to Hawaii, paid days off, or other extra benefits, it should prepare employees in advance. Even with positive surprises, the party getting the biggest shock may be management; there always appears to be room for giving more or doing things differently, and employees may prefer a different course. Management may be shocked to learn that even its best intentions turn sour because employees strongly prefer a different way of handling a change and are willing to engage in conflict to get it.

A lesson from effective negotiators helps make the point, particularly if the change will be seen as negative. Negotiators have observed that people often need time to adjust to the idea of accepting a proposal that is less than they wanted. When such a proposal is first presented, the recipient can see only his interests and his preconceived notion of how those interests should be met. Immediate acceptance is unlikely. If the receiving party is given time, however, he can think about the proposal, explore possible advantages or easy accommodations, and rationalize reasons for accepting less than he originally wanted. Even if few or no advantages are discovered, psychological accommodation during this "acceptance time" can make a previously untenable proposal seem more acceptable and reduce the likelihood of conflict.

Providing acceptance time also facilitates management-initiated change. The immobilization, denial, and anger stages discussed earlier take some time to work through, and in the bargaining stage, which includes many elements of negotiation (certainly when a union is involved, but also when efforts are made to involve nonrepresented employees), extra time helps employees accept something they initially believe is of more value to the organization than to employees. Given time, they can often find reasons to accept change or make a psychological adjustment that allows them to live with it. This is particularly true if during the acceptance time employees have an opportunity to affect the final decision, as discussed more fully below.

The old saw of "tell them what you are going to tell them, tell them, and then tell them what you told them" provides a model for avoiding surprise. When time and circumstances permit, management can tell employees what it plans to do, involve them in working out the details, and at a later time announce its decision, to be effective at a future date. Employees are not likely to object to the study and planning process, and failure to object to a plan after significant acceptance time reduces the likelihood they will object to actual implementation. This process not only provides time for psychological adjustment but also allows employees to make whatever personal or physical arrangements are needed to minimize possible negative effects.

> • Management needs to change to a more restrictive policy on personal use of the organization's e-mail system—a change that is not likely to be viewed with favor by employees. On February 1, management publicly announces that it is concerned about existing abuses, is studying the problem, will be seeking input from employees, and currently anticipates that it will announce its findings around April 1. After appropriate study, on April 5 management announces a new policy, to be effective on May 1. On May 1 management then communicates a brief reminder that the new policy is now effective.
>
> • An employee is not performing well and needs to be moved to a job that better fits his talents. On July 1 his supervisor mentions her concerns and what she is considering to the subordinate and asks for a reaction. She considers the reaction, and on July 5 (if the employee input has not changed the plan) advises the subordinate that the change will be made effective August 1.

Give Employees a Voice

In situations where employees cannot be intimately involved in the process, due to the size of the organization or the substance of the change, avoiding surprises and providing acceptance time through advance notice may be the best that can be done. But more significant employee involvement can provide even greater benefits in reducing resistance and conflict, and it should be used where feasible.

Employees are less likely to resist a change if they have been involved in its formulation. As discussed above, involvement provides employees with acceptance time and a better understanding of the need for a change. More important, it also gives management an opportunity to elicit ideas and information to make decisions that are more likely to work. Involving employees brings their knowledge of, ideas for, and concerns about business matters to the decision process and tables them for effective dialogue and problem solving. It ensures that their needs and interests are considered and, to the extent feasible, reflected in an ultimate decision that provides gain for all those involved. Employees whose needs are being met (or, where this is not possible, who understand that management has made a good-faith effort to meet them) are less likely to cause conflict and more likely to be committed to the success of the change than those employees who did not receive similar consideration. Further, employees are more likely to accept decisions they were involved in because their perspectives were considered and they were allowed some element of control over the process.

Many processes are available for involving employees in planned change. They include the following:

- Informal supervisor-subordinate discussions with feedback to the decision process

- Formal surveys through hard copy or electronic means

- Information-gathering focus groups

- Progress updates during the development process that provide employees an opportunity to react and voice their opinions

- Teams or committees that work with management throughout the entire process

Practices such as these engage employees in the change process in ways that provide input to improve the final decision, increase acceptance time, and, equally important, surface potential conflict in advance so it can be managed—hopefully to the benefit of all concerned.

A final proviso: as discussed in the previous chapter, labor law prevents direct dealing with union-represented employees and imposes constraints on dealing with nonrepresented ones in ways that are construed as creating and dominating a labor organization. Therefore, managers contemplating employee involvement, particularly formal approaches such as use of employee teams or committees, should probably seek legal counsel to ensure that what they do is appropriate. For more details on implementing change where a union is present, see *Managing Change in a Unionized Workplace*[10] by Kirk Blackard.

Communicate Changes Effectively

Change can cause conflict when employees don't understand it and therefore don't know how to comply, and also when they understand it and choose to resist. Management must address both causes using effective communication.

First, management's communication should allow employees to understand what is expected of them. Even when employees do not want to resist a change, they cannot comply if they do not understand what is being done or management's expectations. And if they don't comply, conflict is likely to result. Therefore, management should spell out any new requirements in detail so employees understand them and know how to comply. And the communication must fit the circumstances, which includes providing extensive training when needed to support broad, complex change.

Second, management's communication should sell the change. To the extent possible, it should address issues such as the background circumstances, the organization's need for change, why the particular plan is the best option for meeting that need, and the process for making the decision. As previously discussed, such information should be provided as early as possible to allow appropriate acceptance time. With such communication, employee resistance to a well-conceived change is likely to be minimal.

- New work hours may be communicated with a simple announcement of the new times and an explanation of the reason for the change.

- A new bonus or pay-for-performance program may require extensive training so employees understand its complexity, how it works, and what type of behavior is being encouraged.

Communication of a planned change should be integrated with an employee involvement process to the extent feasible. In small organizations where most or all employees can be directly involved, need for additional formal communication may be minimal. In larger organizations where all employees cannot be involved in the complete process, however, formal communication will be necessary. It may take many forms, from short oral or written announcements in the case of simple, straightforward changes, to detailed training programs for larger, more complex ones. Whichever the case, management should involve as many employees as feasible, explain why change is necessary, and make new expectations clear.

Ensure Effective Supervisor-Subordinate Relationships

The interface between supervisors and their subordinates is where the rubber meets the road in change management. Regardless of what the "organization" does, change is likely to cause conflict if first-line supervisors do not handle their roles effectively. Supervisors' actions can create mistrust in management, garble communication, cause misunderstanding, and make employees feel they are losing even a modicum of control. The positive effects of extensive employee involvement or communication programs at the corporate level can be negated by poor handling at the supervisor level.

To be effective, supervisors must understand, accept, and be honest about their role in each change and take full personal responsibility for all changes they initiate. Trying to dishonestly shift the responsibility or blame to "they" will nearly always be transparent, destroy trust, and cause conflict. Unless legal, ethical, or moral considerations suggest otherwise, if a change is a corporate one over which a supervisor has little or no control, she should nevertheless support management and avoid second-guessing the organization's decisions, even when from a business perspective she believes they are bad ones. Disagreement with more senior management on business issues can be handled privately as appropriate within the organization's culture. Supporting senior management's decisions may be particularly difficult when supervisors, as is often the case, are also a target of a negative change. But that is the burden they must shoulder to be effective.

To effectively explain and support a change, supervisors need to have a detailed understanding of its substance and implementation details well before the employees they supervise need this information. Thus, it often is appropriate to cascade information through various organizational levels, in effect making all supervisors implementors. When this happens, individuals at each supervisory level are deeply involved in communicating to their subordinates and training them when appropriate. Such involvement makes supervisors part of the process, which usually improves their understanding and commitment to change. This commitment can then be transferred to employees under their supervision.

Finally, the style with which supervisors communicate is a major factor in determining whether conflict will result. Being overly assertive and dogmatic, simply passing on an order in unequivocal terms, is likely to threaten employees and generate an equally dogmatic and negative reciprocal response from them. On the other hand, downplaying a change while saying as little as possible and avoiding difficult issues destroys trust and allows potential conflict to go underground, where it may erupt into a full-fledged dispute at a later date.

Collaboration is the supervisor's best shot at minimizing conflict. Collaboration balances the assertiveness necessary to ensure employee understanding with the necessary cooperation to work together to minimize potential negative impacts and exploit opportunities for mutual gain. To attain this balance, a supervisor must not only communicate the substance of the changes to be made, but also engage employees in dialogue. The goal of dialogue is to engender employees' trust, understand their needs and interests, determine how the change will affect them, develop opportunities to limit the negative effects, and to the extent feasible ensure that change is a gain for all.

A supervisor facilitates a team discussion in which the advantages of a change are directly tied to the needs and interests of her unit and its employees. She points out how a change will increase the gain for everyone who embraces the new system.

Provide an Outlet for Conflict That Does Develop

No matter how much advance notice and voice in the process employees have, and no matter how effective communication and the supervisor-subordinate relationships are, all conflict cannot be eliminated. Some change has negative effects that cannot be removed or minimized to a level that employees feel good about or are willing to accept. In these situations, management's objective becomes one of containing the damage, preventing its escalation, and dealing with it over time. Managers must prevent conflict from going underground and becoming a silent, insidious killer of morale and commitment, or erupting into full-blown disputes that torpedo organizational performance and cost dearly to resolve.

Supervisors are the first line of defense in this management action. When a controversial change is implemented, they must become a sponge for employee feedback and venting. They must be readily available to employees, engage them in dialogue, listen to and hear what they say, show sincere empathy with them, and act on those concerns that are within their authority or ability to address. Lower-level supervisors should also ensure that more senior managers are made aware of employee concerns.

Managers who are driving an unpopular change should listen to feedback from the supervisory force but also should obtain direct information through "management by walking around." Being visible and willing to take the heat, honestly listening to concerns and complaints, and responding candidly and thoughtfully can help build trust and minimize conflict even when it is not possible to do what employees want. In addition, information that is obtained may warrant a change in plans or provide opportunities for previously unforeseen responses to employee concerns.

Management's listening to feedback and its response acknowledges an employee's right to have concerns and valid complaints. This acknowledgment encourages the venting process, shows respect for the individual, and transforms the negative energy to a right of positive self-assertion. Regardless of the future outcome, it prevents the employee from feeling put down by the process.

In certain difficult cases or in larger organizations, such informal feedback channels may not be adequate. While they should not be displaced, they may be supplemented with more formal channels for employee reaction and venting, such as paper or electronic surveys, focus groups, or electronic chat rooms. If such processes are used, however, management must take great care to be honest about their purpose and not create unrealistic expectations. The purpose for which management is eliciting information should be made clear, and management should not imply that it is reevaluating a decision unless it is. In addition, if management asks for such information, it should be prepared to share the results with the employees who contributed it and address the issues raised in a forthright manner. Not doing so fosters distrust and can further escalate conflict. Other ideas for surfacing conflict are discussed in Part 3.

Deal Effectively with Conflict That Is Surfaced

When management becomes aware of conflict, it must deal with it—either informally or formally. Failure to address it head-on and in ways that employees know about and understand will only lead to further escalation. Part 3 discusses systems that are particularly helpful for addressing conflict resulting from management change.

KEY POINTS

1. Resistance to management-initiated change is a frequent cause of organizational conflict.

2. Change is the process of moving from the status quo, through a transition, to another status quo. Targets of change go through predictable phases in adjusting to change they perceive as negative.

3. Resistance to change—and consequent conflict—may be passive and unseen or active and confrontational. It may occur for many reasons.

4. All resistance to change cannot and should not be avoided. Instead, management should minimize—rather than try to overcome—resistance through actions such as the following:

- Don't surprise employees.

- Give employees a voice.

- Communicate changes effectively.

- Ensure effective supervisor-subordinate relationships.

- Provide an outlet for the conflict that does develop.

- Deal effectively with conflict that is surfaced.

CHAPTER 6

Hiring and Maintaining the Right Workforce

"The employer generally gets the employees he deserves."

—**SIR WALTER BELBEY**

I n poker, we play with the cards we are dealt. But in the workplace, effective management can deal itself the proper complement of employees to accomplish the organization's purpose. When the appropriate complement exists, employees are right for the organization, the organization is right for them, and conflict is minimized. But when employees and organization aren't right for each other, conflict is likely to take root and grow.

Employees are wrong for the organization when they are unable or unwilling to perform as expected in spite of management's best efforts to help or provide them an incentive to do so. Some people simply are not able, for a variety of reasons, to do the required work. Others march to the beat of a different drummer, refuse to follow the rules, and create controversy regardless of what management does.

Those who are unable or unwilling to comply with appropriate standards of performance or behavior are clearly wrong for the organization. Management must minimize the number of such individuals it employs, deal with whatever conflict they cause, and help them change when feasible. In many cases, however, it ultimately must remove them from the organization.

But not all conflict is caused by deficient or difficult people. Instead, it often is caused by good and competent people who react in rational and predictable ways to the incentives, needs, and pressures in their organization. As discussed earlier, much conflict is caused or can be prevented by management itself: by the way it staffs the organization, manages the people, and deals with problems. When this is the case, management can change itself or the work environment to fit with employees and minimize conflict.

But there are limits to what can be done. Some unpleasant work is a fact of life. Some needs cannot be met. Some pressures cannot be reduced. Given the economic and practical realities of the business world, management often cannot create a workplace that meets the needs of all employees. When this is the case, the organization may not be right for certain individuals.

- Management cannot create work to keep too many people busy when the market and customers do not require it.

- Management cannot create or maintain jobs all employees view as meaningful and challenging when the work itself is boring or unpleasant.

- Management cannot train employees to do work requiring knowledge or expertise that exceeds their capabilities, educational foundation, or inherent interest.

Thus, to ensure that the organization and employees fit, management must carefully manage how employees are brought into the organization and how they leave. It must have an effective employment process and be willing to correct its inevitable mistakes by dismissing employees when doing so is appropriate and necessary. The purpose of this chapter is to address both issues by suggesting some important principles that will serve as a guide to minimizing organizational conflict.

EMPLOYMENT PROCESSES

Management needs to hire the right number of the right type of employees in order to get an employee complement that minimizes conflict. This requires a strategy that accurately describes the number and type of employees needed by the business and identifies tactics that enable managers to find and attract individual employees who meet those needs. Ideas for effective strategies and tactics are discussed below.

Employment Strategy

Having the wrong number of employees in an organization often causes conflict. If an organization is overstaffed, those employees who are not meaningfully occupied are likely to develop poor morale and bad work habits. They also may engage in unhealthy competition for the work that does exist or have feelings of insecurity about the continuing viability of their jobs. Situations such as these often lead to conflict among employees or with management, and the conflict may be exacerbated if management addresses the situation with even the best-managed reorganizations, layoffs, or other changes.

At the other extreme, if an organization is understaffed, the pressure and excessive work hours needed to get the job done often cause supervisors to become dogmatic and overly demanding, and employees to become tired and stressed out. When this combination occurs, the die is cast for conflict.

Similarly, the seeds of conflict are planted when employees do not fit the work to be done. Overqualified employees feel they are underappreciated and undervalued and often become frustrated, cynical, and counterproductive. Incapable or underqualified employees become equally frustrated with their inability to meet the demands of the workplace in spite of their best efforts and may rebel against those requirements of management they perceive as unreasonable. Even the best management, which offers appropriate education, training, counseling, and patience, becomes frustrated when employees do not respond as needed because they do not have the capacity to do so. Some level of conflict is an inevitable result in either case.

Notwithstanding the potential for conflict, employers often approach hiring in an ad hoc manner and hire too many, too few, or the wrong type of people to do the work that needs to be done. This causes staffing to be out of sync with the needs of the business, leading to conflict and other organizational difficulties.

- An organization has an increase in business but decides to do the additional work with the people available rather than hire those who are needed, and the employees suffer burnout.
- A job on the organization chart is vacated and the employer hires to fill it without considering that the business no longer needs that role.
- An employer gets a short-term contract and hires "permanent" employees to meet the needs it creates, resulting in overstaffing when the contract expires.

Instead of an ad hoc process, management should use a strategic employment plan based on the work that needs to be done and what is actually going on in the organization. In such a plan, management doesn't worry about just filling jobs but instead thinks broadly about how to obtain the talent to do the work required to make the organization successful. It considers factors such as the current workload, predictable business cycles, business plans, anticipated attrition, and other current issues, as well as the organization's longer-term strategic vision and mission.

With a strategic plan as a foundation, management is more likely to hire the number and type of people who will minimize conflict. A strategic employment plan that will accomplish these objectives should, at a minimum, address the three considerations discussed below.

Maintaining Staffing Flexibility

Staffing needs of most organizations change continually in ways that are difficult or impossible to predict. Dealing with such change and uncertainty requires carefully managing both the employee complement and the work to be done by the organization's employees. The first can be accomplished with judicial use of temporary employees, and the latter by outsourcing appropriate work.

Hiring some employees on a temporary basis allows an organization to fit the size of its workforce to its changing needs. Temporary employees can be used to supplement the workforce during especially busy cycles or to fill in during illnesses, vacations, or other extended absences. They can also be used more strategically to deal with unexpected increases or decreases in workload resulting from unforeseen changes in the nature or size of the business itself without retaining unneeded employees, engaging in layoffs, reducing workweeks, or making other difficult adjustments.

Strategic use of temporary employees involves maintaining a core group of "permanent" employees to accomplish the most predictable and stable work and using temporary workers to handle work that is less certain. This hiring strategy, when implemented with care, honesty, and sensitivity, can enable the organization to offer all employees, both "permanent" and temporary, the type of work and stability that meets their expectations. And when expectations are met, conflict is less likely.

Outsourcing, or contracting work out to other employers, can be used to stabilize the workload handled by the organization's employees. Organizations have typically outsourced work that others can do better or at less expense or work that is not central to the business. Having such work done elsewhere enables the organization to concentrate on its core competencies. Outsourcing some of an organization's core work can be used to attain employment stability in the face of a workload that is unexpected or of uncertain duration. When outsourcing for this purpose, however, care must be taken to maintain permanent employees' basic expertise and capability to do the work so that it can be done internally when the need stabilizes.

Maintaining the Right Number of Employees

Organizations often hire too few or too many employees. Hiring too few may result in stressed-out employees, excessive overtime rates, high absenteeism, rapid turnover, quality breakdowns, and other problems and conflicts. Paradoxically, hiring too many employees causes most of the same problems. Employees become stressed because they are concerned that their jobs will evaporate. Absenteeism soars because employees aren't challenged, turnover increases because workers see no future in their jobs, and quality suffers because employees are not busy enough to keep their attention from wandering. In addition, unit costs spiral because production per employee is too low.

No magic formula exists that tells management when to hire or how many new employees to add in a particular situation. When considering hiring, however, management should ask itself questions such as the following:

- Do problems such as those discussed in the preceding paragraph exist, and, if so, do they suggest understaffing or overstaffing?

- What does the business plan suggest future needs will be?
- Are apparent needs in response to a real business demand or an operational problem that might be solved in another way?
- Do the needs justify hiring full-time, permanent employees?
- Can some or all the duties be handled elsewhere in the organization?
- Can the system be streamlined for better productivity? What attrition levels can be reasonably predicted?
- Can and should needs be filled internally?
- What other considerations are appropriate?

Rational consideration of such questions and actions based on a balanced view of the answers should lead to staffing levels that meet, but do not exceed, organizational needs and minimize the associated causes of conflict.

Establishing the Right Hiring Criteria

An effective hiring process must start with a thoughtful description of the work to be done. This description can be used to establish hiring criteria that guide recruitment and employment decisions, provide candidates a clear idea of what to expect, and help establish pay ranges for individuals who are hired. Unfortunately, descriptions of the work often take the form of narrow "job descriptions" that do nothing more than list specific tasks of a currently existing job. But circumstances often change, and employees who have been hired to fill specific, narrowly defined jobs are usually narrowly qualified and unable to adapt.

Using hiring criteria that attract well-rounded candidates is often the approach most likely to minimize workplace conflict. When hiring criteria are broad, the work to be done is described in a more fluid, matrixlike manner. Descriptions focus on the general tasks to be performed within broad qualification categories on a departmental or organizational basis and include the qualifications and competencies necessary to perform all those tasks. Individuals are then hired to meet these broad needs rather than to meet specific tasks associated with a particular job.

Hiring for breadth rather than depth may require more initial training and orientation than hiring for a specific job. However, the combination of more broadly qualified employees and additional training builds a staff complement that is flexible and adaptable to continuing changes in work requirements and in the needs and desires of individual workers. This flexibility, and the ability to cope with continuing change, will in turn reduce the level of conflict that would likely result if employees were less able to adapt.

Employment Tactics

Correctly deciding on the right number and qualifications of employees is only half the task. The other half is actually finding, recruiting, and hiring individuals who meet the criteria. This tactical part of hiring includes all the detailed tasks required to fill a job opening: recruiting, screening, interviewing, testing, making the hiring decision, contracting, and whatever else is necessary. Strategic employment planning is of no value if these tactical processes do not deliver and the wrong individuals are hired.

A discussion of managing organization conflict is incomplete without some guiding principles for a hiring process that minimizes conflict. These are briefly discussed in the paragraphs that follow.

Consider the Whole Person

Establishing broad and flexible hiring criteria accomplishes nothing if the individuals actually hired do not have equally broad qualifications. Hiring such individuals requires consideration of three different types of qualifications.

- *Credentials*—any licenses, certificates, permits, or educational accomplishments required for the individual to perform the work or fill the job.

- *Skills*—those competencies the candidate must bring to the job in order to handle the work, with the assistance of whatever training the employer is willing to offer.

- *Traits*—the distinguishing personal characteristics of the candidate that will allow him or her to fit within the organization's culture and operating methods and adapt to future change.

Employment processes often concentrate on credentials and skills because they are relatively easy to assess and more immediately relevant. Determining whether a candidate has appropriate credentials usually involves an easy, yes-no investigation. Assessing skills is somewhat more complex but still usually involves a relatively concrete assessment of whether an individual does or does not have the ability to do specified tasks. Both are relatively objective and easily defended against protest.

Assessing traits, on the other hand, is much more difficult, time-consuming, and risky. It involves often personal, subjective assessment of style and personality and raises the specter of prejudice and discrimination. Assessing traits may require expensive and unpopular testing, and subsequent decisions are easy to contest and difficult to defend. Thus, employers often avoid fully exploring this aspect in their consideration of candidates.

Employers who skimp when assessing traits and fail to consider the whole person are likely to hire employees who don't fit the organization's culture and changing needs. When this happens, employees are not able or willing to deliver on management's expectations, and conflict develops. Such conflict has costs in reduced productivity as well as in the cost of resolving the conflicts. These costs are likely to exceed those necessary to hire the right person in the first place.

Go Slow

The employment process is often driven by high overtime rates, needed work going undone, delayed expansions, or other circumstances creating dire need for new employees. Pressure builds to simply find a body to fill a job quickly and stop the bleeding. Two mistakes that can cause conflict are likely to occur under these circumstances. First, in its haste to fill jobs, management often accepts individuals who are available but who really don't meet its hiring criteria. Managers rationalize that almost having the required skills, or having most of the needed traits, is enough and hire unqualified employees who are unable to deliver on expectations. At the other extreme, management may find an "overqualified" candidate with credentials or skills that exceed requirements. For personal reasons this candidate is willing to accept a job that will prove neither challenging nor interesting. When an overqualified person is hired, the organization is usually unable to deliver the work satisfaction or rewards the overqualified worker expects. She or he becomes frustrated, and bad behavior follows from one or both parties.

A research center staffed primarily by Ph.D. scientists is in dire need of a lab technician, a position that typically requires a high school or, at most, a junior college education. In its haste, management hires a person with a four-year science degree. After a short time, the person becomes frustrated because he feels overqualified for the technician job and cannot compete for jobs filled by the Ph.D. scientists.

The conflict that results from failure to fit employee qualifications to job requirements is usually difficult to resolve because it involves fundamental, systemic issues that the parties are unable or unwilling to change. Often the only way to resolve them is to start over—by the organization and the employee parting company. When this happens, everyone loses. Management is much better off to take the time and incur the additional cost, if necessary, to hire the right person or persons in the beginning.

Inform Potential Employees

A good employment process should facilitate a marriage in which both parties are satisfied and have their basic expectations met. This requires each party to know as much as possible about the other before the vows are taken. Most hiring processes aim to have management learn as much as feasible about the applicants so that only the best qualified can be hired. Applicants are interviewed, tested, and investigated, and management leaves no stone unturned in its effort to ensure that employees are right for the organization. But employment processes often fail to inform applicants of what they should expect, and applicants fail to ask because of ignorance, complacency, or fear. Without such knowledge, new employees may be in for the type of disappointments and frustrations that lead to counterproductive conflict.

To minimize employee disappointments and frustration, managers must inform job applicants of what to expect. Information should be provided in the following areas:

- *Job requirements*—information about the tasks the individual is expected to perform on an ongoing basis, possible temporary assignments and other flexibility arrangements, normal hours of work, likely overtime or extra work requirements, available training, and any other information that helps applicants understand what will be expected of them if they accept an offer of employment.

- *Pay and benefits*—beginning pay rates and monetary benefits, and enough information about the system of pay adjustments to allow applicants to reasonably predict future income; information on nonmonetary benefits such as time off, breaks, or food service; and any other information that helps potential employees understand what they can expect of management if they accept an offer of employment.

- *Organizational culture*—information on the values, environment, and unwritten rules of business life that provide guidance in areas such as how early people generally come to work and how late they stay, how much autonomy they have, how they typically communicate, how they ordinarily relate to supervisors and managers, and the extent to which there is a sense of family among employees. Since organizational culture is unwritten and usually unstated, it is difficult to communicate. It can often best be conveyed by giving applicants a tour of the workplace, having potential peers participate in the employment process, or engaging applicants in other such activities that get them closer to the workplace.

> Having job applicants interviewed by peers, who are the persons most knowledgeable about the work to be done and with whom new employees will directly relate, has two advantages. It improves the quality of the hiring decision and provides the applicants with the best understanding of what the workplace is really like.

In summary, during the employment process management should learn about potential candidates but also ensure that they learn about the organization so both can make an informed decision about whether to enter into a relationship.

Follow the Law

The employment process is fraught with legal requirements and pitfalls, which are primarily an outgrowth of various laws proscribing discrimination based on race, sex, national origin, ethnicity, religious beliefs, pregnancy or related medical conditions, age, disability, and uniformed service. Since these requirements are often difficult to interpret and apply, they can lead to conflict regardless of management's behavior, as applicants who believe they have been discriminated against can pursue a remedy regardless of the merits of their claim. Management can, however, take actions to reduce the likelihood of such conflict.

Hopefully employers comply with the law because it is the right thing to do, but they should also comply because doing so reduces costly conflict. Disputes are likely for two reasons when management fails to follow the law:

- Applicants who are not hired for inappropriate reasons are likely to file administrative or legal action against the potential employer.

■ Illegal, discriminatory hiring builds employee complements where future conflict is more likely than in a legally constituted, diverse workforce.

Following the law during the employment process usually results in a more diverse workforce—one comprising employees who represent the diversity in the surrounding community's population. Properly managed, such diversity leads to cognitive disagreement on issues of importance and the resulting synergy of thought that is necessary for a high-performing organization. Balanced diversity also reduces counterproductive conflict. It creates a workplace in which those who are in the minority feel more comfortable because they are part of a similarly situated group. In addition, where minorities represent a critical mass, on-the-job discrimination is less likely because management and majority employees are more aware of their presence and of the appropriateness of treating them in a fair and nondiscriminatory way. And if discrimination does occur, it is likely to be addressed in a more timely fashion because those discriminated against have the support systems that reduce the fear of coming forward.

DISMISSAL

Sometimes the employment process fails in spite of management's best efforts. Even with strategic employment practices, unforeseen circumstances or mistakes in judgment can result in too few or too many employees. And even with the most effective tactics, sometimes the wrong person is hired and, notwithstanding the help of management and fellow employees, does not perform acceptably. In some cases his job performance will not measure up, and in other cases he can do the work but will persist in causing problems and continuing unacceptable conflicts. Thus, sometimes management's only option is to dismiss an employee or employees.

Termination of employment has been called workplace capital punishment for good reason. Whether an employee is dismissed for lack of work or discharged for unacceptable performance, the impact of losing a job is a major one. Job loss almost inevitably causes financial difficulty, embarrassment, and loss of self-esteem. It is a life change that can destroy marriages, upset family stability, and precipitate a downward cycle among all those who are affected. It is, therefore, an action over which employees are likely to throw down the gauntlet.

Terminating employees is also costly to the organization involved. The time and effort required to "make the case" are usually not insignificant. When the case is made, the fear, rumors, and gossip that often accompany dismissal frequently detract from the morale and productivity of the remaining employees. In layoffs workers may empathize with the laid-off employees and see themselves as the next to go, and in discharges they may not know the whole story and develop sympathy for popular terminated employees. Even when management has made the right decision, organizations are vulnerable to wrongful-dismissal suits, particularly when the dismissed employee is within a legally protected category. And finally, when replacements are necessary, recruiting and employing them is a costly proposition, and in times of low unemployment an unacceptably long time may pass before an acceptable replacement can be found.

Thus, dismissing employees to eliminate conflicts and problems often gives rise to even bigger conflicts and problems, at least in the short term. They can be minimized, however, if management is guided by the principles outlined below.

Avoid Dismissals When Possible

Layoffs due to lack of work are likely to be blamed on external economic realities—which may in some cases be a legitimate cause. It is equally likely, however, that management has failed to pursue strategies that make layoffs unnecessary. And while the need for layoffs cannot always be avoided, it can be minimized with the right strategic planning and actions.

- Developing diverse, countercyclical business units can contribute to employment stability.

- Maintaining a controlled-growth strategy and strategic employment processes avoids massive buildups followed by layoffs in the event of a business downturn.

- Effective training and development programs make employees more flexible and better able to adjust to change.

When the best-laid plans go awry, or the proper strategy was not pursued, management may be faced with too many employees for the work to be done. Even in these cases, however, management can consider other alternatives. Layoffs for lack of work should be the last option after other alternatives for handling overstaffing have been considered.

- Opportunities to bring back work that has been subcontracted or to terminate temporary employees may exist.
- Product might be stockpiled for future sales.
- Needed maintenance, fix-up, or clean-up activities might be rescheduled to provide work during a short-term situation.
- Reduced work hours may be considered.

Most such options carry some downsides, but they should be considered to avoid layoffs and the pain they cause to both individuals and organizations. Even when they are not feasible, conflict resulting from layoffs is likely to be reduced when employees are aware that such options have been considered and rejected for valid reasons. This can be particularly true when employees are involved in exploring the potential options and reach their own conclusion that they will not work.

The need to dismiss an employee for poor performance or bad behavior (for cause) can often be eliminated with proper management attention. A common method of dealing with employee problems has been the use of progressive discipline, which involves attempts to correct behavior through a series of progressively more severe penalties for bad behavior or poor performance. The process typically includes sequential steps, such as an oral warning, a written warning placed in the personnel file, a disciplinary suspension without pay, and ultimately termination of employment if behavior or performance does not improve. Certain steps are often repeated if performance improves temporarily and then deteriorates.

While this process may warn employees involved and help in defending a discharge, it rarely corrects fundamental problems and has a number of downsides. As discussed in Chapter 4, supervisors often are uncomfortable with the punitive aspects of progressive discipline, so they delay appropriate actions until the problems are out of hand or treat their favorite employees less harshly that others. Over time the threat of punishment simply becomes part of the work environment and loses its power to have much effect at all. Fear of punishment causes employees to avoid confrontation rather than address their problems. And finally, while punishment may induce short-term compliance, it also produces anger, apathy, resentment, and frustration that in the long term only exacerbate problems and conflict among those involved.

A different approach, which emphasizes personal responsibility and decision making, has been adopted by a number of leading companies. This positive discipline approach, discussed in detail by Dick Grote in *Discipline Without Punishment,*[11] includes the following elements:

- Be clear about the organization's expectations and the employee's responsibilities

- Offer the training and education necessary to make appropriate performance feasible

- Recognize and reinforce good behavior and performance and provide feedback when performance is inadequate

- Provide coaching by supervisors and counseling by professionals when appropriate

- Conduct oral discussions of the extent to which employees are, or are not, meeting expectations and carrying out responsibilities

- Issue written reminders if needed

- Require decision-making leaves with pay, followed by an employee commitment to improve or to leave the organization's workforce

Positive discipline is much more likely to correct performance problems than punitive progressive discipline. But it also fails in some cases. When it does, and employee behavior or performance does not improve, discharge for cause may be necessary.

Make a Disciplined, Balanced Discharge Decision

A decision to dismiss an employee should not be taken lightly. Unfortunately, some managers are too quick to act, while others are wimps, unable to face up to making and implementing difficult decisions.

For those who are too quick to act, dismissing an employee often seems to be the easiest way to fix a problem or resolve an ongoing conflict. Supervisors and managers often forget about the hurt it can cause and the problems it can create, thinking only about the time and effort required for other alternatives. They jump to quick conclusions that everything that can be done to avoid discharge has been done. Other managers fail to take needed action because of the likelihood of hurting the individuals involved and because of the potential cost and disruption to the organization. In addition, firing someone is a difficult confrontation and a traumatic personal event for most managers and supervisors, so they often tend to rationalize poor performance, make excuses for bad behavior, or pursue fixes that have little chance of success in their effort to avoid their own discomfort (perhaps fueled by sincere empathy for affected employees); so they don't make the difficult termination decisions that need to be made.

Management's failure to face up to its responsibility in a timely fashion usually causes more conflict and problems down the road. With the passage of time, employees become more invested in the organization and lose alternative options, so the impact is greater when they are terminated and the action itself is more likely to cause conflict. Delaying appropriate discharge also allows bad behavior to spread to others, impacting the broader organization's performance. Other employees often know a person needs to be fired and lose confidence in management when it fails to act.

> At the time of a discharge for poor performance or bad behavior, management often observes that the action should have been taken long ago. Both the individual and the organization would be better off if management had been willing to bite the bullet when the need first became obvious.

Unreasonably delaying inevitable layoffs for lack of work causes many of the same problems. More important, failure to take decisive action in times of economic distress can increase the risk of having to take more severe actions later on.

Thus, management must thoughtfully balance the potential pros and cons of dismissing employees. The right balance will, of course, depend on the facts of the individual case. The chances of reaching that balance are substantially increased, however, if management follows a disciplined decision process that includes considerations such as the following in both discharges for cause and layoffs for lack of work:

- Avoid spontaneous dismissals. In egregious for-cause cases, suspend the employee subject to a future decision.

- Ensure that affected employees have an opportunity to present their case, with help from an employee or union representative if requested.

- Clearly articulate a defensible reason for all dismissals.

- Consider the history of how other employees similarly situated have been treated. Be sure there is a valid reason for any differences.

- Review relevant legal considerations. A legal dismissal is not always fair, but an illegal one rarely is.

- Discuss the impact on the individual and the organization if an employee in question is not dismissed.

- Provide for a predecision review. This review could be by higher levels of management, a peer committee, external lawyers, or other knowledgeable individuals.

- Consider giving employees dismissed for cause the option of binding arbitration by an external neutral. The presence of this review will bring a high level of discipline and credibility to the entire process.

Handle Dismissals to Minimize Conflict

Some dismissed employees understand the reason, gracefully accept management's decision, and do not generate conflict. In clear cases, employees often agree with the organization's need to reduce staffing levels or to discharge those involved in egregious behavior, even when they are the ones affected. And in more questionable cases, dismissed employees often prefer, all things considered, to avoid the conflict and the emotional and financial cost of protesting. When management's decision is reasonable and the affected employees' response is balanced and logical, conflict usually does not escalate, as discharged employees are likely to cut their potential losses and get on with their lives. But this type of ending is unlikely when the discharged employees' decisions are based on emotion or personal animosity. When logic loses out and feelings take over, conflict is not likely to go away. And often, feelings are affected less by the substance of what is done and more by the process of how it is done.

Because employees often react less to what is done and more to how it is done, management can substantially minimize the emotion, hard feelings, and personal animosities involved in most dismissals by ensuring that the implementation is handled appropriately. The type of handling that is appropriate will vary from case to case, depending on individual circumstances. In all cases, however, dismissing an employee is a significant and difficult event that requires advance planning of what should be done before, during, and after the actual discharge discussion. The following paragraphs outline several principles that should guide that planning.

Avoid Surprises

If employees understand before the termination discussion that dismissal is likely, they have time to rationalize their situation, consider any possible benefits that a job change might present, get their finances and lives in order, and prepare a reasoned response. Therefore, when feasible, the dismissal discussion should do little more than confirm what the individual already knows or suspects, perhaps communicated in an investigatory interview during which he was able to review the facts from his perspective and make his case. Employees who are discharged for cause should be given adequate warning through the positive discipline process if the problem is continuing poor behavior or performance, or through clear rules where a one-time incident justifies discharge (e.g., stealing or initiating a fight). When employees are to be laid off for lack of work, the entire workforce should understand in advance the realities of the organization's economics and staffing situation, the likelihood of staff reductions, the basis of layoff decisions, and at least in general terms how each person fits those criteria. Supervisor communication, daily newsletters, in-house television networks, the organization's intranet service, and other similar communication processes are all options for ensuring this understanding exists. At a minimum, covered employers must comply with the federal Workers Adjustment and Retraining Notification (WARN) Act, which essentially requires companies with at least 100 workers to give affected employees 60 days' notice if a substantial portion of the workforce is going. Employers should also comply with applicable state and local laws.

Plan the Timing

Opinions vary as to the best timing of a dismissal. In all cases, however, two timing issues should be thoughtfully considered: when the termination will take effect, and when the termination discussion will be held with the employee or employees involved.

When the date is within the control of management, a bad effective date can add insult to injury from an employee's perspective and increase the likelihood of a protest. Management's flexibility may be limited in for-cause cases involving severe misbehavior, where there may be a need to have the offending employee off the property immediately. However, such situations usually can be addressed with suspensions, with or without pay as deemed appropriate.

To the extent that management does have the ability to set the effective date, it should consider issues such as the following:

- Don't schedule an effective dismissal date that coincidentally takes unfair advantage of the employee or unfairly advantages the organization.

> Don't schedule a dismissal just prior to the time an employee's pension vests unless taking away pension rights is a justified action for the offense.

- Avoid dismissals, particularly layoffs for lack of work, during holidays and special times.

- Avoid scheduling layoffs for economic reasons in proximity with other actions that appear contradictory.

> Laying off employees at the same time an expensive upgrading of office facilities occurs is likely to appear inconsistent even if both actions are logical parts of a major corporate transformation.

- When possible, don't dismiss employees when they have other major personal issues to deal with. Management can consider deferring a dismissal or, if this is not feasible, offering certain benefits, such as temporary continuation of paid medical insurance, to minimize the personal impact on those involved.

The date and time of the dismissal discussion should also be carefully considered. Management should balance the personal situation of the individual involved against the likely impact on the business when deciding day and time.

> - Advising an employee early in the week may allow him to get immediately to work looking for a job and prevent a weekend of moping, but it also may be more disruptive to the workplace than a Friday afternoon discharge.
>
> - Demanding that a dismissed employee leave the workplace immediately after the dismissal discussion implies a lack of trust (which may or may not be justified) and may encourage a protest.

Respect the Employee's Privacy

Being dismissed, for whatever reason, can be embarrassing for the individual involved. Management should, therefore, to the extent feasible, help the employee manage that embarrassment by respecting the employee's privacy and maintaining the confidentiality of the process in two principal areas. First, management should ensure that the dismissal discussion itself is private—not only conducted behind closed doors but also handled so that employees in general do not know it is taking place.

> A discharged employee should not have to exit an unusual private meeting with the big boss directly into a bullpen of curious co-workers.

Second, management should carefully consider what information is to be shared with remaining employees, who have a legitimate interest in what has happened. As a general rule, management should avoid sharing any details other than that a discharged employee will be leaving and that the circumstances surrounding the departure are confidential. Sharing more information may be appropriate, however, when necessary to quell rumors, clarify rules, or deal with other special circumstances.

Conduct an Appropriate Discharge Discussion

The discussion in which the employee is advised of his discharge is the single event most likely to escalate or minimize consequent conflict. Therefore, the person holding the discussion should be fully trained, and the meeting should be carefully planned and often scripted and rehearsed. Following are some items to be considered:

- Include the appropriate people, consistent with the privacy issues discussed above. A direct, person-to-person discussion—and not a phone call, e-mail, or other impersonal communication—should always be used when advising individuals of a dismissal for any reason. As a general rule, management should include the immediate supervisor and a more senior manager or that manager's representative (such as a human resource staff member) in the discussion. The employee to be discharged should be allowed to have a fellow employee or union representative accompany him.

- Get to the point and present the bad news. State the reason for the termination in a few short sentences and tell the person that he has been terminated.

- Be honest. Don't cop out and make the discharge seem unjustified in an effort to avoid hard feelings.

- Listen to what the employee has to say and answer his questions honestly and concisely.

- Do not negotiate. A thoughtful, informed decision considering both sides of the case and the employee's likely response should have been made in advance—based on an earlier investigation that provided the employee an opportunity to make his case.

- Avoid use of words that could trigger legal issues and possible liability.

> Suggesting the need for a "new approach" or "new blood" could raise concerns about age discrimination.

- Explain all severance details, such as how long the employee will be paid, how insurance will be handled, references, outplacement services, and other information of importance to the employee being discharged.

- Explain exit procedures, such as when and how the employee should vacate the workplace.

Let the Employee Leave with Dignity

Some circumstances require immediate departure, security measures, or other actions to protect the organization and its employees and assets. In such cases, little dignity may be deserved, and management should take those actions required to protect the organization's interests, up to filing criminal charges in appropriate cases.

> An employee fired for stealing the company's trade secrets from its computer systems may need to be escorted immediately from the workplace and not allowed to return to his office.

In most, less egregious, circumstances, however, a discharged individual is not a threat and should be treated accordingly. To the extent feasible, dismissed employees should be allowed some control over the situation, including input into when and how they leave, what is communicated to remaining employees about the departure, and other factors that will protect their dignity without jeopardizing organizational interests.

Soften the Landing

Nothing can be done to remove all the negative effects from most dismissals or to absolutely prevent the continuation or escalation of associated conflict. Dismissals are inevitably difficult for all parties involved. But the fairer and more generous an organization is with the people it must let go, the less likely it is that problems will continue or worsen. And management can consider a number of things to soften the landing.

When deciding whether and how to make dismissal easier for employees, management must consider available possibilities from various perspectives. First, it must not do anything that is inconsistent with an honest characterization of the reason for discharge. Doing so would be unethical and could provide the discharged employee with a basis for legally contesting the discharge.

> Management should not write an unblemished letter of reference for an employee who has been fired for dishonesty or stealing.

Further, treatment of employees who are being discharged is a legally complex area, where certain actions are required and others are prohibited, so any action considered should be carefully reviewed for legal compliance. Within this context, management must balance what is right and fair for the employees involved against the cost or benefit to the organization and consider options such as the following to soften the blow of dismissal:

- Provide as much notice as possible in advance of the last day at work. Significant notice is probably more feasible in a layoff for lack of work than a firing for cause.

- Continue to provide affected employees with as much information as possible.

- Offer a severance payment. Such payments may be part of a normal policy for layoffs. In dismissals for cause, they might be considered where the issue is poor performance but are less likely to be appropriate where the dismissal is for bad behavior.

- Allow employees to resign in lieu of being fired when doing so is justifiable.

- Offer favorable recommendations, either at the time of discharge or upon request, assuming such recommendations are justifiable under the facts of the case.

- Make prompt payment of any wages and pay due for accrued benefits, such as unused vacation or sick leave.
- Consider continuation of certain benefits for a period of time after the date of discharge.
- Do not protest unemployment compensation claims.
- Provide outplacement counseling and services.

There is a tendency for employers to try to soften the landing for employees who are laid off for lack of work, but to do little or nothing for discharged employees, especially those discharged for bad behavior. Assisting discharged employees is often in the employer's best interest, however, because it reduces the likelihood that they will continue to protest and is likely to be seen as fair in the eyes of remaining employees. In either case, softening the blow is likely to achieve benefits that exceed the cost.

Meet the Needs of Remaining Employees

Dismissed employees are not the only ones who can cause conflict, and the organization must continue to function after firings and layoffs. Without great care on the part of management, dismissing employees may negatively affect those remaining to such an extent that any organizational advantage sought by the dismissal is offset by declines in morale and productivity.

To minimize ongoing conflict, maintain organizational effectiveness, and preserve the ability to recruit and hire in the future, management must, to the extent feasible, retain the loyalty of those employees who remain. This may be especially difficult in layoff situations, where many employees are likely to feel they will be the next to go. The following should be considered:

- Be open and honest about everything that is going on. Especially during layoffs, management cannot communicate too much.
- Handle the dismissal correctly, as discussed above. Remaining employees usually can understand why dismissal is necessary, but they cannot understand if people are treated badly.
- When possible, remove continuing evidence of a larger workforce decimated by layoff.

> • Avoid having employees work on a half-empty office floor.
> • Quickly remove names of dismissed employees from rosters.

■ Make additional changes to reinforce the idea of a broader transformation and a fresh start.

> Coincide layoffs with an organizational restructuring.

■ Avoid serial layoffs. If necessary, do it and get it over with, but don't dribble out dismissals over an extended period of time.

KEY POINTS

1. Conflict is likely when employees and the organization aren't right for each other. To ensure a fit, management must maintain the right employee complement.

2. Management's first obligation in maintaining the right employee complement is to hire the right number of the right type of employees. Doing so requires an effective employment strategy and appropriate tactics.

3. An effective employment strategy establishes hiring criteria based on the work that needs to be done and what is actually going on in the organization.

4. Appropriate hiring tactics are necessary for finding, recruiting, and hiring individuals who meet the established criteria.

5. An effective employment process doesn't always prevent problems, and sometimes employees must be dismissed. When this happens, management should

   • Avoid dismissals to the extent feasible

   • Make disciplined, balanced discharge decisions

   • Handle dismissals to minimize conflict

   • Meet the needs of the remaining employees

Fostering Appropriate Supervisor Behavior

"Integrity is the one absolute requirement of managers."

—PETER DRUCKER, *Management, Tasks, Responsibilities, Practices*

I nstitutions and systems are major, underappreciated sources of workplace conflict, but they are not the only causes of conflict that are under management control. The personal behavior of individual supervisors can also lead to conflict between supervisors and subordinates, among employees, and between employees and management. Thus, a discussion of managing workplace conflict is not complete unless it addresses the personal behavior of supervisors—defined for this purpose as all those representatives of management who have supervisory responsibility over other employees. This chapter provides a perspective on supervisors as a potential cause of conflict and discusses how they can personally behave to minimize counterproductive conflict.

THE SUPERVISOR'S ROLE

Supervisors operate in a messy, systemic world in which their personal behavior affects employees and both affects and is affected by management systems. They operate where the rubber meets the road. They have more exposure, influence, power, and responsibility than any other members of the organization. Their behavior has a greater effect on the level and severity of workplace conflict than that of any other group of individuals. They can cause conflict both through their direct interface with subordinates and through how they administer the organization's processes.

Supervisors' jobs are not easy. As agents of the employer and representatives of more senior managers, supervisors must deal directly with subordinates they didn't personally hire, might prefer not to work with, and perhaps would fire if they had the authority to do so. They may hold the job the person they are supervising aspires to, and they must look out for their own self-interests as well as the interests of subordinates. They continually interact with employees, and their behavior can easily become a direct cause of counterproductive conflict.

> - A supervisor's overbearing attitude causes immediate, conflictive reaction from subordinates.
> - Employees resign from an organization because of their supervisor's yelling, screaming, intentional humiliation, and other egregious activities.

Supervisors also are responsible for administering the organization's policies and systems and often are the primary implementors of change or other initiatives. Because of this close identification, in some instances their personal mistakes are blamed on the systems they administer. Conversely, and probably more frequently, since their judgments and actions are there for all to see and challenge, they often get the blame for problems actually created elsewhere. Even though they may be implementing or defending unpopular decisions they disagree with, they get the blame because they are the most readily available scapegoat. People often frame disputes with a system as personal and want to shoot the messenger, the closest person, or the person with the highest profile when disagreements and problems occur. Thus, supervisors often are directly in the line of fire even when a dispute is actually with a broader management policy or a more senior representative of management.

- A performance-based pay system is intended to allocate pay on the basis of goal accomplishment. A biased supervisor disregards objective criteria and ensures that his favorite gets the best jobs and unearned favorable assessments, causing conflict with other employees. What appears to be a systems problem is really a personal supervisory issue.

- A performance-based pay system is intended to allocate pay on the basis of employee performance. The system has a forced rating component with no objective criteria. A competent, unbiased, fair supervisor does his best on the ratings, but one subordinate disagrees. The supervisor gets blamed, although the system is the problem.

The internal, personal forces that are attributable directly to the character, personality, and other attributes that the supervisor brings to the job from the beginning are only one driver of behavior. Influential forces resulting from the organization's processes or systems are a second, and perhaps more significant, driver of behavior. Supervisors, like employees generally, are affected by management systems, and deficient systems often contribute directly to counterproductive supervisor behavior.

A supervisor refuses to explain the reason for a decision to an employee or makes excessive demands that more work be accomplished. The supervisor appears to be insensitive and arrogant but in fact is badly overworked and under extreme pressure from his boss because the organization is badly understaffed.

Determining whether conflict is caused by internal, personal factors attributed directly to a supervisor or by the organization's systems is often difficult. When we look below the surface for the root cause of conflict, we often see both interwoven as parts of a larger system. Conflict that appears to result from bad supervisor behavior may be driven by organizational systems, and conflict that appears to result from a flawed system may not be caused by a systems problem but by a supervisor not administering it properly. Figure 7 illustrates this idea that systems performance and supervisor behavior are related causes and effects.

Bad supervisor behavior may be anomalous, the actions of a very few supervisors who are inherently counterproductive or don't get the message. Or it may be widespread across the organization and largely a function of organizational systems. In both cases, supervisors are at the interface

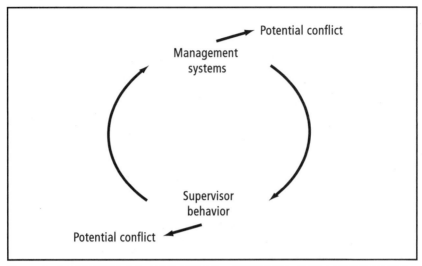

Figure 7 SUPERVISOR BEHAVIOR–SYSTEMS RELATIONSHIPS

between the organization and its employees, and their behavior can be a primary cause of counterproductive conflict but also the organization's first line of defense against it. To effectively minimize conflict, organizations must see that supervisors

- Ensure that their own personal style and behavior do not cause friction, frustration, personality clashes, or other conflict

- Represent the organization and its decisions, policies, and processes in ways that minimize the likelihood that they will cause conflict

MINIMIZING CONFLICT
THROUGH SUPERVISOR BEHAVIOR

When a supervisor's behavior is a direct or proximate cause of conflict, the effects are typically limited to the employees involved. But when it is an indirect or root cause, supervisor behavior affects systems, which in turn causes conflict among many employees.

Fortunately, supervisors can control their own behavior: how they directly interact with subordinates, as well as how they affect the organization's policies and systems. Attending to both of these areas provides their best opportunity to leverage their behavior to reduce conflict. The following sections outline ideas for attaining this leverage.

Foster a Mutual-Gains Climate

One usually thinks of climate in a broad organizational context: the prevailing attitudes, temperament, and outlook that provide a common, enduring experience for all employees. From this perspective, no single person is responsible for creating an organization's climate. Instead, it is determined by the aggregate of the actions of all managers, supervisors, and employees. Individual supervisors play only a small part in fashioning it.

But a special microclimate exists between a supervisor and subordinates in their small part of the larger organization. This climate contributes to the aggregate that is the larger organization but, more important, can provide the continuity, coherence, and predictability that allow a supervisor and subordinates to work together effectively with minimum conflict. Whether the microclimate has this positive effect depends on how the participants perceive it. If supervisor or subordinates see their workplace as a zero-sum game where everyone is out to get all they can without regard to the impact on others, excessive conflict is the likely result. If, on the other hand, the climate suggests that working together can expand the available resources and create opportunities for mutual gain that will be fairly allocated, productive synergy develops, and counterproductive conflict is less likely. Supervisor behavior is the major determinant of whether the climate is seen as a zero-sum game or an opportunity for mutual gain.

Supervisors nearly always have more power than their subordinates and can easily cause a zero-sum climate by discounting employee contributions and needs or not treating them as legitimate. When this happens, employees often lose in contests of wills that unfairly resolve issues to their detriment. Equally important, they may be offended by their supervisor's perceived arrogance but fail to raise the issue. This leads to stealth conflict with all its associated costs. Even if a conflict is belatedly surfaced, an offended employee rarely gets to play the game because the supervisor controls the agenda, determines what needs are relevant, and defines what the public disagreement will be about.

> Employees often need to leave work to do personal business, but their supervisor does not allow such time off except in extreme emergencies. They complain, but their supervisor quickly dismisses their concerns. The subordinates don't have their needs met, but they suppress their disagreement and don't take the case further. Morale and productivity decline, and both parties lose.

> The subordinates later decide to surface the issue again and press for relief. But the supervisor sets the discussion agenda and states that he will allow more time off, but with pay being docked. The employees' desire for flexible starting and ending times, which would allow them to take time off without losing pay and would meet all their needs with no detriment to the organization, is never considered.

To foster a mutual-gains environment, supervisors must acknowledge and respect employee potential and encourage a productive synergy that increases the size of the resource pie. They also must consider the interests and needs of subordinates in order to ensure they get a fair shake when those resources are allocated. In this context, supervisors must accept that some disputes will occur but avoid treating them as win-lose contests of wills between fundamentally incompatible personalities or interests. Believing that the outcome must necessarily favor one over the other when parties have different positions discourages the exploration of options and prevents the synergistic use of differences to solve problems. Only a supervisor who believes the options can be expanded and all parties can benefit is likely to lead subordinates in a successful search for mutual gain.

Empathy

A mutual-gains climate requires mutual empathy among the individuals involved. They must walk in each other's shoes, at least intellectually, until each can vicariously experience the other's thoughts, fears, and needs. To truly empathize, individual supervisors must be aware of their subordinates' work and nonwork environments. They must know enough about their subordinates' work to understand the pressures it causes, accurately and fairly assess whether it is being done properly, make reasoned judgments as to whether help is needed, and, if so, provide the help. They also must know enough about their subordinates as individuals—their personal lives, families, likes, and dislikes—to appreciate the external motivations and pressures being brought to the workplace.

> A supervisor complains that an employee is making too many personal phone calls on work time. He doesn't understand that she is a single parent of an adolescent who ran away from home and attempted suicide. Her calls are to school officials and counselors, and she works longer hours to make up for time lost.

When supervisors really care, demonstrate their appreciation of subordinates as individual persons, and respond appropriately to employee needs, their subordinates' natural tendency is to react with reciprocal empathy, caring, and actions that support individual supervisors and the organization. With mutual empathy, conflict is less likely because supervisors are perceived as individual persons rather than just an employer. When conflict does occur, the parties are not likely to stereotype it as resulting from the other party's ignorance, incompetence, or meanness. Instead, they are likely to see it as an honest conflict of interests that two individuals working together can resolve in ways that benefit both.

Colleagueship

Mutual empathy and the personal credibility that goes with it should lead to supervisor and subordinate seeing themselves as colleagues. Colleagues are not necessarily close personal friends. They are co-workers and associates who balance friendship and objectivity in a way that allows them to focus on substantive issues rather than personal concerns. Colleagues often do not agree or share the same views, but the fact of their seeing things differently adds to their power and effectiveness because they have increased information and the ability to work together in search of new insights and answers. Just as important, they also are willing to expose their personal vulnerability and assume the risks that are necessary when exploring the unknown. A mutual-gains climate is likely to follow when all these characteristics come together in a supervisor-subordinate relationship.

Safety

Employees must feel safe for a mutual-gains climate to exist. They must reasonably believe they are physically secure and that their jobs will not be arbitrarily or unreasonably abolished or diminished. In particular, they must understand that by contributing more and working with their supervisor, they will not work themselves out of their jobs. But a mutual-gains climate requires more. Employees must also feel psychologically safe and not perceive or anticipate threats against their egos, their self-respect, or their reputations. Employees who feel safe in these areas have no need to protect themselves or defeat others, so they can listen, interpret what they hear in a nonthreatening environment, and respond with honest, supportive behavior.

Personal safety and job security are usually best accomplished through organizationwide systems, but supervisors have the key role in creating a feeling of psychological safety among subordinates. Supervisors must avoid threats, intimidation, coercion, and other actions that obviously create psychological insecurity. They should also avoid actions such as causing subordinates to lose face, which works more subtly to create unsafe feelings.

People usually lose face when their identity claims are challenged or ignored or when their claim to be seen as a certain kind of person is diminished. Supervisor actions that publicly challenge their subordinates' motives, intent, competence, or other personal attributes are likely to cause a loss of face and lead to win-lose conflict. Even private feedback can be a threat to employees when communication is strongly evaluative or judgmental rather than descriptive. Thus, the supervisor's challenge is to maintain an honest, open, nonthreatening relationship with employees that allows expectations to be stated and results measured and communicated without causing subordinates to lose face and feel threatened.

Maintain a Collaborative Management Style

A mutual-gains climate is of little value unless the parties work together to further their own and the organization's best interests. Working together requires each party to balance the assertiveness of her views and concerns with cooperation with the other's views and concerns. This balance, the essence of collaboration, is a major determinant of whether conflict will exist and what form it will take if it does.

Collaboration is often discussed as a preferred dispute resolution style. But collaboration is much more than a way of resolving conflicts. It can be used to attain goals, solve problems, create new opportunities, and accomplish other things that best meet the needs of all concerned. When such needs are met, the likelihood of conflict is diminished. Therefore, collaboration is an important tool for minimizing counterproductive conflict.

A single mother is experiencing difficulty balancing family and work responsibilities without excessive absenteeism. She and her supervisor collaborate to develop a new work schedule that accommodates both interests. With the new schedule, it is not necessary for her to be absent, and conflict is prevented rather than resolved after the fact.

Collaboration that minimizes conflict suggests a management style that is not always natural for supervisors. If it isn't natural, developing such a style often requires special perspectives and actions, as suggested in the paragraphs that follow.

See Complexity

A supervisor must see complexity in the environment in order to foster collaboration with and among subordinates. Collaboration implies working together to create or discover something new and innovative by melding different views and perspectives with a synergy that creates value. Those involved must recognize that simple, one-dimensional views and understandings are rarely accurate and are not enough to make the best of a situation. Rather, new insights require the complexity of several views, perspectives, and talents. Therefore, all the parties, relationships, systems, interests, points of leverage, and other factors that provide opportunities for working together must be considered to reach improved solutions.

An employee asks for a raise to a specified higher pay rate. The supervisor views the world only in the context of pay rates, so only three responses are possible: yes, no, or a compromise raise that is smaller than requested. There are no opportunities to work together to find a better answer. But if the supervisor sees the broader relationships and systems, other opportunities arise. The parties might discuss a performance improvement plan aimed to qualify the subordinate for a raise, a transfer to a job with a higher pay grade, or a myriad of opportunities for addressing the issue and avoiding the potential conflict.

See Abundance

A collaborative supervisor must also have an abundance mentality. People who don't see abundance view the world as a zero-sum game. They don't believe things of value, such as ideas, recognition, credit, power, or profit, can be used to expand options and increase value. These people, therefore, are reluctant to share value because they believe they or the organization lose when they do. People who see abundance, however, believe that breakthrough solutions are possible and that there is plenty out there for everyone. They recognize the unlimited possibilities for expanding the size of the resource pie by working together to make mutually beneficial things happen. When the resource pie is expanded, sharing is easier, and the likelihood of conflict is reduced because all involved have an opportunity to gain.

An employee feels undervalued and underappreciated because her supervisor does not give her credit for her results. Although she suppresses these feelings, her morale and productivity are low, and conflict with her supervisor is just below the surface. The supervisor finally figures this out, takes her to lunch for a full and open discussion, and begins to credit what she does and praise her before her peers. The recognition and praise address the suppressed conflict, make the employee feel better and become more productive, and also improve the supervisor's standing with her boss, who has observed the entire process. Giving away credit has in fact multiplied its value.

Be Realistic About Self

A supervisor should, however, temper his abundance mentality with a realistic assessment of his own limitations. An unrealistic perception of his own expertise may lead to a know-it-all attitude that discourages cooperation; misunderstanding his authority may lead him to make decisions that cannot be implemented; and inappropriate use of power may build resistance to his initiatives. A collaborative supervisor, on the other hand, understands that creating something new often requires more than his own knowledge, understanding, and ability. He must know when his capacity is limited, and when it is better to rely on his subordinates. He must understand the limits of his ability to impose his will through authority or power. He must also know that most subordinates are willing to freely make up for his limitations by sharing their expertise, ideas, and feelings in ways that expand the size of the resource pie if they see a potential for mutual benefit.

Articulate Shared Goals

Collaboration requires supervisors and subordinates to share common goals. Significant shared goals provide the parties with a larger purpose to work on together and allow them to subordinate their own interests and contribute to others as well as themselves. Shared goals also provide the initiatives that are necessary to attain mutual benefit and offset the human tendency to pursue one's own agenda, be guided by arbitrary thinking, or continually defend one's own turf.

Supervisors should ensure that shared goals exist and are articulated. Supervisors typically are expected to explain, support, and obtain buy-in for broader organizational goals that cascade down from more senior management and perhaps manage development of subsidiary supporting goals. They may also need to lead a process to collaboratively develop mutual, stand-alone goals for their own work group. In both cases, they must take the initiative to ensure that goals are understood, accepted, and seen as a guide for action.

Lead Collaborative Efforts

Finally, supervisors must actively lead collaborative efforts. While collaboration often happens spontaneously, continuing and effective collaboration that is in the interest of the organization usually requires the active involvement of a strong leader. In leading collaborative efforts, supervisors must coordinate the time and effort of people who know what they are doing and are willing to work together. They usually must provide a vision of shared goals; form networks of communication, commitment, and support; furnish needed resources; train subordinates in how to collaborate; assist in dividing the resulting rewards; and otherwise provide the persistence and continuity necessary for success. This type of leadership motivates and empowers subordinates to contribute their best efforts in ways that minimize conflict and best serve the organization as well as its employees.

Handle Rewards Appropriately

Rewards are usually thought of as the organization's formal systems covering pay, bonuses, time off, and other explicit things of value that employees receive in return for their labor. Often governed by policies and administered by special departments or executive management, they frequently become a root cause of conflict, as discussed earlier. Supervisors must defend the organization's formal reward policies and play a role in implementing their details but in the end may have little direct influence over them.

Although individual supervisors may have a limited role in formal rewards, they have within their discretion a broad array of opportunities to informally reward employees—or themselves. Informal rewards include all the many things supervisors can do outside the formal organizational structure to meet employee needs and wants. Employees often view them as equal to or greater in value than formal rewards.

- Giving employees time and attention either on or off the job
- Sharing information with employees
- Seeking advice from employees and listening to responses
- Paying sincere compliments for a job well done and displaying other signs of appreciation and respect

Supervisors can also informally reward themselves, sometimes unfairly, through actions they believe will enhance their own standing, prestige, or power.

- Being secretive with information to increase one's relative power
- Insisting on being addressed with honorific titles
- Taking credit for work done by subordinates

If a supervisor inappropriately handles rewards to subordinates or unfairly rewards himself, conflict is the likely result. Three primary considerations should govern the use of informal rewards if conflict is to be minimized.

Use Informal Rewards

Supervisors should recognize their subordinates' needs and use informal rewards accordingly. Most people need to feel accepted and valued by others, and informal rewards meet this need. Being the source of attention, the recipient of information or praise, or being listened to makes us feel more valuable. Conversely, the absence of such rewards can be hurtful, disappointing, and demotivating when we expect them but they do not occur.

This feeling of being devalued when informal rewards are withheld is tied to the key difference between formal and informal rewards; formal rewards cost money, while informal ones do not. Because informal rewards are free, a supervisor's failure to use them is more likely to cause conflict than if they were costly. Most subordinates understand limits to costly formal rewards, as they can mentally balance the cost to the employer against their contribution to the enterprise. But cost-benefit balancing is not necessary with free, informal rewards. Since subordinates understand they are free, they resent supervisors who don't give them when they are earned.

Using informal rewards nearly always results in mutual gain. Giving them doesn't use them up but instead usually conveys value to both the giver and the recipient. Thus, supervisors should look for opportunities to reward both subordinates and themselves by sharing informal rewards.

> • Sincere thanks and a "job well done" make both subordinate and supervisor feel good.
>
> • Seeking advice rewards subordinates with a sense of empowerment and is likely to educate the supervisor and improve his decision process.

Be Sincere

Notwithstanding the value of informal rewards and the opportunity they present for mutual gain, their excessive or inappropriate use can cause conflict. If a supervisor bestows them insincerely or when they are not deserved, employees will see through the façade and understand that their purpose is manipulation. And since informal rewards are free, subordinates who see a supervisor granting them and expecting something in return can only assume manipulation is the objective.

Employees may see insincere praise or other informal rewards as threatening. Most rewards are based on some type of evaluation, and even sincere, positive evaluations from someone higher in the pecking order often make the recipient uncomfortable. Employees are likely to see those with even a hint of insincerity as attempting to demonstrate status. Further, when informal rewards are used insincerely, employees learn to take them for granted, and they no longer function as rewards even when well deserved and sincere. They become like the boy's yelling "wolf" too many times in the fable; when the cry was really needed, it did no good.

> A supervisor's paying compliments when they are not deserved is likely to be seen as "sucking up" in an attempt to curry favor rather than as sincere feedback. On the other hand, sincerely paying compliments when they are deserved rewards both subordinates and the supervisor.

Don't Discriminate

Just as with formal rewards, supervisors must not inappropriately discriminate in their use of informal ones. While discrimination in formal rewards may cause more overt disputes because more concrete evidence usually exists, discrimination on informal issues is just as likely to lead to conflict—often suppressed—with all its negative consequences.

Not discriminating means that those equally situated should be treated equally, but it does not mean that all subordinates and situations should be handled the same. Different situations and different people deserve different treatment, and treating them the same can be as bad as treating those similarly situated differently. Thus, supervisors must be objective in their assessment of people and use appropriate criteria to determine who should receive what informal rewards. Only such balanced objectivity can avoid discriminatory rewards and their consequent conflict.

Communicate Effectively

The importance of communication by managers and supervisors has been widely discussed and written about, and other sources are available for in-depth explorations of this important skill. Our purpose here is to discuss two key issues that largely determine whether supervisor communication minimizes or causes conflict. These issues are whether supervisors' words and actions reflect an appropriate attitude, and whether subordinates are engaged through an appropriate balance between telling and listening rather than being just talked to.

Attitude

Form is often more important than substance in communication; attitude usually conveys more than words, as music conveys more than the lyrics. Conflicts often result from adverse reactions to how something is communicated or from disconnects between what the communicator is saying and the impression he is conveying. One person may be offended by the communication style of another, or people perceive conflicting meanings because words say one thing and actions another.

- A red-faced supervisor, veins bulging on the side of his head, shouts that he isn't angry.
- A supervisor says she wants input but interrupts continually with her own views.

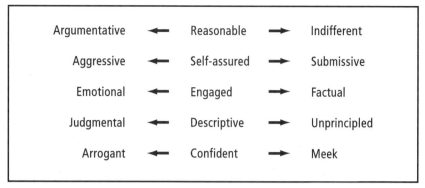

Figure 8 RANGE OF COMMUNICATION TRAITS

Attitudes that are offensive or inconsistent with supervisors' words usually arise from these individuals' predispositions, which reflect their personalities, demeanors, and expected behaviors. But personality traits often are neither good nor bad, and when they are inappropriate, their polar opposite may also be inappropriate. The point is that a supervisor's attitude, as reflected by his personality, must be reasonably acceptable to the listener, fit with the context in which the conversation is taking place, and support the words being used. This is called being congruent in our communication.

Figure 8 reflects a range of appropriate attitudes in several important areas that supervisors can develop and use. Traits at either end of the ranges are less likely to be helpful than those between the two, but it is imperative that supervisors manage their attitudes to reflect the points on the ranges that are consistent with their words.

Traits such as these often say more about a speaker than actual words and can lead to conflict if the supervisor doesn't demonstrate an attitude that supports, rather than detracts from, the words that are communicated. A supervisor whose communication embodies inappropriate traits obviously creates conflict. Just as obviously, a supervisor who exhibits appropriate attitudes consistent with the words spoken fosters positive perceptions by subordinates and minimizes conflict.

- A supervisor giving performance feedback must clearly describe the subordinate's performance and confidently state expectations without appearing overly judgmental.

- A supervisor showing no emotion in a discharge discussion conveys a noncaring attitude that increases the likelihood of conflict.

Engagement

Communication too often seems to involve supervisors telling subordinates certain information and perhaps listening to their responses in some detached way. While this may facilitate an exchange of information, it doesn't encourage an open, supportive relationship that minimizes conflict, which can only occur when supervisors engage their subordinates. And to engage subordinates, supervisors must attain an appropriate balance between telling and listening, between exploring and deciding. This requires the right balance of discussion and dialogue.

In a discussion, each party tries to persuade the other, presenting a point of view with the intent of having it accepted or winning a disagreement. One accepts the other party's position only if he becomes convinced the other is right, does not have the power to resist, or feels a need to give in to reach agreement.

Dialogue, on the other hand, is a conversation in which two or more people exchange ideas or opinions. The purpose of dialogue is not to win, but to explore complex issues and gain new insights and understandings. In dialogue, the parties suspend their assumptions, preconceived notions, and mental models in a free exploration of all their ideas, thoughts, and experiences.

A balance of discussion and dialogue is necessary for effective supervisor-subordinate engagement. Dialogue surfaces ideas and options, and discussion helps decide among them. Both are continuing parts of a communication process that allows supervisors and subordinates to be truly engaged. Figure 9 illustrates this process.

Engaging subordinates through a continuing balance of discussion and dialogue requires supervisors to take action on the following:

- Engagement requires both sending and receiving information. To foster effective discussion or dialogue, a supervisor must not only dispense information but also really listen to and hear what the subordinate is communicating. Really hearing on many levels allows supervisors to acknowledge their subordinates' feelings as well as the information they have to offer.

- Supervisors must be willing to explore their subordinates' ideas, thoughts, and experiences in an effort to develop better options. They must also encourage reciprocal arguments and exploration and argue their cases with subordinates when necessary.

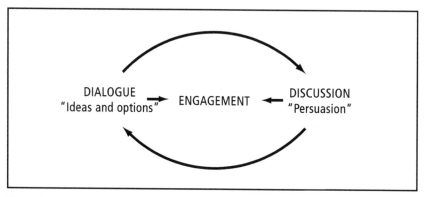

Figure 9 E N G A G E M E N T

- Engagement requires understanding as well as action. Actions arrived at through discussion often are less than effective because subordinates go along with supervisors when they really don't understand what is being said. Sometimes an understanding of the ideas and options developed through dialogue is all that is needed to make a particular action acceptable.

- Supervisors must recognize the extent to which what one says or hears is affected by beliefs, rather than vice-versa. They must be willing to suspend their beliefs, which are often based on their mental models, and participate in effective dialogue to get to the truth before engaging in discussion to arrive at a final decision.

Understand the Effect of Reciprocity

Conflict has its basis in reciprocity, or how the parties react to each other. Negative reciprocity can lead to a downward spiral in the relationaship between supervisor and subordinate, while positive reciprocity can lead to improved relationships and minimum conflict. Effective supervisors understand how reciprocity works and use it to minimize conflict.

Systems thinking helps explain reciprocity and how supervisors can use it to minimize conflict. In systems terms, conflict is driven by circles of relationships (called feedback loops) that in reality are reciprocal flows of influence that are both cause and effect. Both supervisors and subordinates are part of the process, and each of them influences and is influenced by what happens. Thus, each is at least partially responsible for the actions of

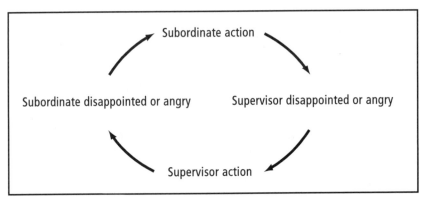

Figure 10 CONFLICT RECIPROCITY

the other. And each can cause conflict and can become a player in a circular, continuous cycle of escalation in conflict. The cycle can begin anywhere and works generally as indicated in Figure 10.

These situations can build over time, with conflictive actions by one party leading to conflictive behavior by the other in a continuing downward spiral.

> A subordinate uses e-mail inappropriately. The supervisor becomes angry, reacts arrogantly, and takes punitive action. The subordinate responds by starting rumors among peers and failing to communicate as necessary, which leads the supervisor to take further punitive actions, and the spiral continues downward.

How the parties reciprocate can also minimize conflict. Appropriate early actions will foster a positive cycle, and a conflictive spiral can be reversed when one party or the other acts counter to the negative influence being received. Either supervisors or subordinates can break the negative spiral, but supervisors have the most resources, are at lower risk, and are in the best position to break a downward cycle of conflict. While there may be fewer substantive opportunities to foster a positive cycle of reciprocity, supervisors nearly always have great flexibility in how actions are initiated (the process) and therefore can foster a positive cycle.

From a substantive perspective, supervisors may find it necessary to take actions that lead to disagreement, confrontation, and possible conflict.

They must establish expectations, provide appropriate policies and rules, and make the difficult decisions that from time to time negatively affect the short-term interests of employees. This is a necessary part of their role and cannot be avoided. Often the best supervisors can do is to sincerely consider the impact on employees and appropriately balance conflicting interests.

Regardless of the substance, however, managers and supervisors can implement and administer actions or policies in ways that minimize the potential cycle of conflict. Opportunities for doing this are discussed in detail in the Chapter 4. Exercise of such options allows supervisors to reduce the likelihood of a cycle of conflict by exhibiting personal actions that do not call for negative reciprocal reactions.

- A supervisor may develop a rule in collaboration with engaged subordinates and minimize conflict or unilaterally impose his own rule and cause conflict.
- Being open and explaining the need for a requirement limits conflict, while hiding the real intent causes it.

To reverse negative cycles begun by either themselves or a subordinate and to minimize further conflict, supervisors must act counter to the influence they are receiving and take actions that subordinates will respond to positively. Such reaction by supervisors may require an initial leap of faith, but any negative consequences are likely to be minimal if the actions are carefully considered and proportionate to the possible risks. Often, the only thing that is needed is for a supervisor to refuse to "take the bait" and react with restraint rather than with actions that are likely to escalate a conflict.

- Responding to belligerent actions with calm and reason rather than a belligerent response begins to reverse a cycle of conflict.
- Exceeding a subordinate's demand where doing so is otherwise justified suggests a supportive, trusting response that minimizes rather than escalates conflict.

KEY POINTS

1. The personal behavior of individual supervisors often causes conflict, but a supervisor's behavior can also be the best line of defense against conflict.

2. Supervisors both affect and are affected by the systems within which they work. To minimize conflict, they must pay attention to their own personal style and appropriately represent the organization's decisions, policies, and processes.

3. Supervisors must manage themselves to reduce both the direct and the indirect conflict their behavior causes. They can do this if they

   - Foster a mutual-gains, rather than a zero-sum, workplace

   - Maintain a collaborative management style

   - Handle rewards appropriately

   - Communicate effectively

   - Understand the effect of reciprocity

PART 3

Dealing with Conflict

CHAPTER 8

Surfacing Conflict

"Give every man thine ear, but few thy voice."

—SHAKESPEARE, *Hamlet*

arlier chapters discussed ways to minimize workplace conflict. The problem is that they don't always work. Although good supervisors, a trusting environment, effective policies, and positive management practices can substantially reduce conflict, some conflict will remain. Believing that an organization is always a peaceful cooperative of its members is wishful thinking—and a triumph of cover-up over reality rather than of management over conflict.

Management is often seduced into believing conflicts are not present because so many of them are not the big, public disputes that require attention—physical altercations, the policy violations that require discipline or discharge, the sexual harassment that leads to EEO investigations, the strikes, or other obvious situations. The attention given big or inherently public conflicts tends to mask the often smaller and largely private ones that commonly exist on a day-to-day basis. The problem often occurs when employees are unwilling to tell their supervisors what they know about conflict that does exist. When they are also unwilling to discuss their unwillingness to surface it, a conspiracy of silence evolves, which prevents management from seeing the stealth conflict that is embedded below the surface of the daily workplace routine.

A pattern of private conflicts can be costly to any organization. Management often counts only the cost of public conflict to which it is a party and which enters the organization's formal dispute resolution processes. Suppressed conflict, however, has many dark consequences and often is more insidious, counterproductive, and costly than the public conflict that gleans most of the attention. Its consequences and costs cannot be accurately quantified, as management cannot count what it cannot see and is usually oblivious to the conflict. But suppressed conflict clearly has many organizational costs. It

- Detracts from creativity and innovation because employees fail to communicate and work together

- Causes poor coordination and project integration when communication is bad and employees refuse to work as an effective team

- Leads to organizational paralysis, as people are unsure of their own power and authority and are therefore afraid to act

- Results in ineffective change initiatives when employees refuse to support changes or drag their feet to resist them

- Reduces initiative, as employees involved in unacknowledged and unresolved conflict develop poor morale and become demotivated.

Effective conflict management requires addressing that which is suppressed, and the first step is to surface conflict with those who are able to deal with it. Accordingly, the purpose of this chapter is to foster a better understanding of what suppressed conflict is, why employees suppress it, and what management can do to surface it.

SUPPRESSED CONFLICT

Suppressed conflict exists when two or more parties, one of which may be management, have a grievance between them but fail to express it or acknowledge the problem.

- Certain departments consider themselves fiefdoms, refuse to cooperate with other departments, and refuse to acknowledge discord exists.

- The boss's assistant acts like the proverbial "queen bee" and is very difficult to deal with, but no one is willing to confront her or her boss.

- Covert race, religious, or gender prejudice is present but not discussed.

Suppressed conflict also exists when employees acknowledge grievances between themselves but hold them in private, and responsible management representatives are not aware of them. It percolates below the surface and often plays out in the form of bitching, failing to communicate, ignoring requests, veiled insults, unfriendly glances, jokes at each other's expense, passive resistance, or other negative forms of behavior. It is often the germination stage for more active, visible conflict.

- A male employee makes sexual innuendos in conversation with a female employee. She confronts him, but the two are unable to resolve the problem and are unwilling to discuss it with others.

- Individuals are offended because their boss shuts them out of decision processes in which they believe they should be involved. They discuss the matter in a private meeting, but nothing changes and senior management never becomes aware of the problem.

The fact that conflict is suppressed and not acknowledged or obvious to management doesn't mean it isn't being dealt with in some fashion. The parties usually develop their own equally suppressed methods of dealing with it. Their actions, however, usually do nothing to resolve the basic issues and instead become part of a cycle of escalation. These methods, several of which may be seen in a single case, include the following:

- *Avoidance*—where parties pretend a conflict does not exist and to the extent possible forgo social interaction with others involved in it

- *Toleration*—where the parties acknowledge the conflict but take no action to make others aware of it or to resolve it

- *Self-help*—where a party takes private action to either resolve a conflict or escalate it to gain the upper hand

- *Surveillance*—where a party keeps tabs on an offender by gathering information for potential use in self-help or when involving a third party

- *Silent bargaining*—where the parties engage in informal, unstated, often undiscussed and implicit concessions that allow them to live together while not actually trying to resolve the real issues

- *Passive resistance*—where parties drag their feet or otherwise refuse to cooperate with the other parties

- *Exit*—where the parties seek a transfer to another subunit of the organization, resign from employment, or take other actions to get away from the conflict

Thus, suppressed conflict results when participants are unwilling to come forward or management turns a blind eye to what it should see. It is almost always costly, and employees often deal with it in ways that are counterproductive.

The first step to take in dealing with suppressed conflict is to surface it. Surfacing conflict means having those who will resolve it become aware of and acknowledge its presence. In cases where only the parties themselves are necessary for resolution, they may surface conflict by acknowledging it between themselves but keep it private from others, including management. Where third parties are required for resolution, conflict is surfaced when the appropriate parties are made aware of it. Surfaced conflict may or may not become public knowledge, depending on the circumstances. To decide how to cause conflict to surface, management must first understand why it exists.

WHY EMPLOYEES SUPPRESS CONFLICT

Most employees don't enjoy suppressed conflict. It creates uncertainty, anxiety, and fear, and it impairs both individual and organizational performance. So why do employees so often deep-six conflict and leave it to fester or escalate into more damaging disputes? Why don't they surface disagreements among themselves or with third parties who will help resolve them? Employees have many reasons (valid and invalid) for wanting to maintain the status quo and cover up disagreements. The actual reasons, which will vary from case to case, are likely to be one or more of the following.

Fear of Appearing Ignorant or Incompetent

Surfacing a conflict raises the possibility of exposing one's deficiencies or of being proven wrong, both of which can reduce an employee's credibility. Doing so can be especially troublesome to a subordinate when the supervisor is the one to see the deficiencies.

Fear of Escalating the Conflict

Sometimes it appears safer to let sleeping dogs lie than to run the risk of inciting reciprocal action by the other party that escalates a disagreement and makes matters worse.

Belief That Nothing Will Change

Surfacing conflict nearly always entails some risk. Therefore, the parties must balance that risk against the likelihood that matters will improve if they surface it. If they don't believe anything will change for the better, they are not likely to incur the risk of surfacing a conflict.

Desire to Protect the Other Party

Conflict often occurs between people who like and respect each other, and one party surfacing it may hurt the other. Just acknowledging conflict may cause anxiety, hurt feelings, or other emotions that detract from a person's self-esteem. And surfacing a disagreement with a third party (perhaps the other party's supervisor) raises the same concerns plus the possibility that the supervisor will take action that is not in either of the conflicting parties' self-interest.

Resentment of Supervisor Conduct

When supervisor reaction to conflict is aggressive and intimidating, employees feel humiliated, bullied, insulted, and threatened. This creates a wall of antagonism and resentment that destroys trust, halts communication, and drives conflict farther underground.

Fear of Punitive Management Reaction

Surfacing conflict subjects an employee not only to the risk that an issue will not be handled appropriately, but also to the concern that management will shoot the messenger and punish him for being involved in the first place. Such punishment could be either informal or through the organization's formal disciplinary process.

An employee is often late relieving another employee because of personal problems at home, and this is causing hard feelings and frequent arguments between them. They are reluctant to raise the issue with their supervisor, however, for fear that he will give them less consideration for future opportunities or issue a written reprimand to the employee who has been late.

Ignorance

Organizations often are large, bureaucratic institutions with their own culture and rules for managing conflict—rules that frequently are not well publicized or involve impossible-to-understand gobbledygook. When this is the case, employees are reluctant to come forward because they are not confident they can do it without embarrassing themselves or causing other problems they would rather avoid.

Fear of Indicting the Past

Conflict frequently evolves over a period of time and involves many separate but related activities. Admitting to the presence of a current conflict may suggest that the one making the admission made mistakes in the past.

A supervisor is reluctant to address an employee's poor work performance because he recommended her for employment and gave her several good performance reports.

The reasons employees don't surface conflict can be summarized in three simple concepts: fear of the consequences, ignorance of how to go about it, and doubt that it is worth the effort and risk. To address these issues, management must create an environment in which it receives the message and responds appropriately when employees come forward. Unfortunately, even when employees overcome their concerns and attempt to surface conflict, management often, because of ignorance, indifference, inattention, or other priorities, fails to listen to what is being said, to see what is being demonstrated, or to acknowledge what it really knows. Like the people in the story of the emperor's new clothes, it pretends to see peace when discord is obvious. When this happens, it thwarts employee intentions and effectively causes the conflict to remain suppressed.

Management can, however, go a long way toward seeing that conflict is appropriately surfaced. It can foster a culture and systems that encourage employees to come forward and supervisors to hear them and acknowledge their concerns and needs. The following section presents ideas for how management can accomplish this.

SURFACING CONFLICT

Not all conflicts should be surfaced. Sometimes a willingness to live with inconsequential differences of opinion, to let minor slights pass, to ignore aggressive behavior, or to otherwise avoid unneeded confrontation helps grease the wheels of social interaction. Avoidance, toleration, and other ways of dealing with conflict are often the best approach. This is particularly true when the differences are minor, ad hoc situations that will soon go away and be forgotten, or when the parties have a short-term relationship that will soon dissolve, making the disagreement irrelevant.

But not all conflict is so easily ignored, especially that which occurs in the workplace. While some workplace conflict is minor and inconsequential, much of it is significant because of the unique circumstances involved. It may affect the disputants' current or future financial well-being and the sense of self-esteem so often intertwined with people's work. The relationship among the participants and the impact of conflict is likely to be long-term rather than short-term, and if not addressed it can affect other employees and the performance of the organization as a whole. Thus, while not all workplace disagreements should be surfaced and dealt with, many should be.

Surfacing conflict means different things in different situations. When management is not a party, and the disputants themselves are able and willing to resolve a dispute, it is surfaced when they acknowledge the conflict to each other: when each communicates to the other that he is aware of a conflict and feels responsibility for participating in its resolution. The disputants may elect to keep it private between themselves and not involve management or third parties, but the conflict is on the table for resolution by the appropriate individuals.

When management is not a party and the disputants are unable or unwilling to resolve a conflict without management intervention, it is surfaced when the appropriate supervisor, an ombudsperson, or another management representative is informed and acknowledges that the conflict exists. Management could be informed by either party, both parties, or a third party who has become aware of the conflict.

A conflict to which management is a party is surfaced when both parties acknowledge it: when the employee involved and an appropriate management representative with the responsibility for dealing with it make each other aware of the conflict, and some level of confrontation takes place.

- An employee feels a supervisor is not treating him fairly compared to another employee but has failed to raise the issue. He surfaces it by discussing his concern with the supervisor and having him acknowledge, though not necessarily agree with, the concern.

- A supervisor believes a subordinate's performance has been declining but has not raised the issue with him. She surfaces the conflict by verbally discussing the issues with the employee and having him acknowledge her concern.

There is a limit to what management can do to cause conflicts to surface. It cannot force issues to surface unless it is a party and knows about a problem with an employee. An employee who has a problem with management can surface that problem in his own time. And employees involved in conflict among themselves will themselves decide whether, and when, to surface it. They will elect whether to confront each other, to escalate a matter to a public conflict that is obvious to all, or to seek help from a third party, usually a manager or supervisor, to attempt to resolve their problem. Management cannot require them to take such actions. It can, however, create an environment that removes most of the reasons employees suppress conflict and provides the safety and incentive that will encourage them to surface their issues. The following sections outline some key things management can do to create that environment.

Listen

Effective listening has been defined as "(a) taking in information from speakers, other people or ourselves, while remaining nonjudgmental and empathetic; (b) acknowledging the talker in a way that invites the communication to continue; and (c) providing limited, but encouraging, input to the talker's response, carrying the person's idea one step forward."[12] This is an excellent definition of listening in the conventional sense, where people freely express their views. But people often don't express their views freely when conflict is involved, so listening to conflict also requires providing employees the opportunity and encouragement to surface their feelings and communicate them. Doing this requires management to provide employees easy, safe opportunities to surface conflict, to continually encourage them to use those opportunities, and to actively listen to what they have to say. Management can do a number of things to foster this type of listening.

Encourage One-on-One Conversations

Direct, one-on-one conversation between management and employees is the best way to surface conflict. Listening to people acknowledges their worth, increases their self-esteem, and builds their confidence to share important information. This shared information is likely to be the best and most current available about what is really going on in the workplace. Personal conversations also allow for questions and follow-up to ensure the best possible understanding.

Provide Safe Opportunities to Talk

Employees who are involved in conflict or who feel aggrieved are often reluctant to talk about their concerns for the reasons discussed above. They are unlikely to do so with supervisors (except in the most egregious circumstances) unless safe, easy opportunities are available. The following are some ways management can provide such opportunities.

- *Maintain frequent supervisor-subordinate contact.* The close personal relationship developed by two people working together in good faith provides the best opportunity for easy, safe communication. Don't fail to take advantage of it when possible.

- *Maintain an open-door policy.* Employees should understand that they have permission to talk to any manager in the pecking order at any reasonable time, and that no repercussion will follow if they do. This privilege may also include talking freely to human resources staff or others available to assist with conflict and employee problems.

- *Manage by walking around.* Senior managers should spend time with and be visible in various parts of the organization as often as feasible. This can be done in connection with other business activities or just for the purpose of being available to listen. It provides an opportunity to get feedback from employees about the overall work environment, how they like working in the organization, and whether they feel included or excluded.

- *Appoint ombudspersons.* Employees are often reluctant to grieve within their chain of command but would be willing to talk confidentially to a neutral third party who is trained to deal appropriately with their concerns. An ombudsperson, discussed in more detail in Chapter 11, can accomplish this purpose.

Geographic diversity, low supervisor-subordinate ratios, self-managed teams, working at home, and other such factors often make supervisor-employee contact difficult. If frequent personal contact is not feasible in the normal course of events, other communication options, such as frequent telephone contact, Internet message boards, and other expanded use of electronic communication, should be considered. Although use of such processes has some potentially negative effects—they can generate rumors and compromise confidentiality—they nevertheless can often reveal workplace moods and fears that are the precursors of conflict.

Elicit Formal Input

Sometimes person-to-person listening, perhaps supplemented by informal electronic measures, doesn't work or is not enough. When the organization's size or work practices unduly limit management-employee contact or the level of trust is so low that employees are reluctant to speak out, more formal alternatives may be necessary. Their purpose generally is to elicit information from a large number of employees on a confidential basis. Formal information-gathering practices could include activities such as the following:

- *Employee surveys*—formal, professionally developed, written or electronic questionnaires that ask employees to provide information in areas designated by the survey developer.

- *Employee focus groups*—small groups of representative employees meeting with a facilitator to provide verbal input. Groups may have an "open focus" and encourage discussion of any topic, or may be more structured to concentrate on specific areas of management concern.

- *360-degree performance feedback*—assessment processes that require all employees to give their bosses feedback on how they are doing. Such feedback often surfaces broad organizational concerns as well as issues between an individual supervisor and subordinate.

- *Physical, web site, or e-mail suggestion boxes*—typically thought of as encouraging suggestions for improved operations, they are also mechanisms for soliciting confidential employee input on any issue of concern.

- *Formal organizational assessments*—systemic studies that reach conclusions based on all available information, such as organizational performance, grievance and dispute resolution activity, individual interviews, and information gained through processes such as those listed above.

While processes such as these can provide good listening opportunities for management and can help surface conflict, they do have potential drawbacks. Just asking questions can build unrealistic employee expectations that management will initiate changes, which it may not be able or willing to do. At a minimum, employees expect feedback from their input, and management may hear things it doesn't want to communicate to employees generally. Accordingly, such broad-based queries should be used only after careful thought and consideration.

Remove Barriers to Effective Hearing

The ideas presented above should go a long way toward encouraging employees to surface conflicts, but they do little to ensure that management really hears what is said. There is a real difference between listening to what is surfaced and hearing what is communicated. An organization can have supervisors available to employees, use both informal and formal information-gathering processes, receive a great deal of information, and still not really hear the organization or its people. Various barriers often affect what both individuals and organizations hear and prevent the real understanding and acknowledgment necessary to have conflict surface effectively. All levels of management must deal with such barriers by behaving differently—not always at polar opposites, but in ways that encourage rather than discourage hearing all that is communicated. Table 1 summarizes some typical barriers that management constructs for itself and suggests more appropriate management behavior.

Dealing with barriers such as these to attain the preferred behavior requires continuing management effort in areas such as supervisor selection, training, and assessment and all the other practices that develop effective supervisors. If these barriers are not removed, management may appear to listen but is unlikely to hear the real message.

Table 1	Hearing Barriers	
BARRIER	PREFERRED BEHAVIOR
Setting the agenda in ways that limit the issues to be discussed	Making all issues of employee concern open for discussion
Believing that listening connotes lack of authority or power	Believing that hearing is a win-win proposition
Believing that employee venting is enough and no action is required	Recognizing that employees expect to be heard and responded to
Having preconceived ideas about what you want to hear and hearing only that	Hearing with an open mind
Maintaining biases against the person speaking or the subject	Valuing input from all sources on all subjects
Letting emotions win out over hearing	Balancing emotions with objectivity
Reacting inappropriately to hot-button words or actions	Responding with measured actions

React Appropriately

Employees will continue to surface conflict only if they believe management really hears what they say—and they will decide whether they are really heard on the basis of how management reacts. Therefore, after removing the barriers to hearing, supervisors should pay particular attention to their responses. The following should improve the chance that management will understand what is communicated and react in ways employees feel good about:

- Listen to the underlying meaning as well as the words. Employees surfacing conflict are often reluctant and intimidated, so they are likely to play it close to the vest and say as little as possible to get their message across. Listeners must be aware of this and note what was not said as well as what was said.

- Avoid immediate reactions that are critical, judgmental, or threatening or that in any other way justify the fear an employee probably has about raising a concern. The time may come when judgments have to be made about what was said, but the conversation in which an issue is raised often isn't that time. Opportunities to gather more information, reflect, and think about the response will usually moderate a management representative's first tendencies and help convince employees that they have been heard.

- Take care when asking questions. Some questions are often necessary for understanding and clarity. They should not, however, be seen as an interrogation or as an attempt to unduly control the direction of the conversation.

- Be open with disagreement. Employees may surface conflict or issues that involve their supervisor, other supervisors, or management generally—and the receiving management representative may have a different view of the matter. If this is the case, he should be honest and open about his views and clearly explain the reasons for them. Avoiding an appropriate confrontation only provides time for the concern to fester and grow.

- Do not try to solve the problem alone. Many conflicts are best solved without supervisor intervention, and essentially none should be solved by a supervisor dictating an answer. Even when supervisor help is appropriate, full consideration, data gathering, and other investigation may be needed. Intervention normally should be in the form of collaboration rather than a dictated answer.

Empower Employees

Fear is a recurring theme in the list of reasons employees suppress conflict: fear of appearing ignorant or incompetent, of being vulnerable, of punitive management reaction, of escalating the conflict, of hurting the other party. There are many reasons for such fears, but no doubt the most significant arise from the power disparity between supervisors and subordinates, and between employees and management as an entity. As discussed in Chapter 3, workplace power may be coercive, utility based, or collaborative. Subordinates often hold collaborative power that is substantially equal to that of management, but management and individual supervisors hold nearly all the coercive and utility power.

Unfortunately, employees involved in conflict are often fearful of management's coercive power. Managers at all levels have a larger scope of responsibility, control over more resources and functions, and access to more information than their subordinates. And they have the authority, either directly or indirectly, to fire, demote, or promote their subordinates.

Some organizations treat employees as servants rather than colleagues, use their bodies rather than their minds, and aim to catch employees making mistakes rather than to reward positive behavior. Under these circumstances it is no wonder that conflict occurs and employees would rather stonewall it than have management know about it. They are afraid management will use its coercive power to take unfair advantage of them. To address this fear, management must take steps to level the playing field by empowering its employees.

Employee empowerment is a controversial concept in some quarters. Some represent it as a panacea for all organizational ills, while others see it as management losing control over its business, like turning the prison over to the inmates. In reality it is neither. In the conflict context, empowering employees will not ensure that all conflict is appropriately surfaced, nor will it lead to anarchy. Properly conceived and practiced, empowering employees gives them more confidence to address their conflicts privately when appropriate and to surface them with management when necessary.

In empowering employees, management minimizes its use of coercive power and allows employees to use the huge store of collaborative power they already have. Management maintains control through values, objectives, and systems rather than force. Although empowering employees is a comprehensive way of managing that goes well beyond conflict management, it clearly is an effective tool for reducing fear and encouraging employees to handle conflict appropriately.

Volumes have been and will be written on employee empowerment, and, as with other management areas, our purpose here is not to replicate them or to exhaustively explore the subject. Here we will examine four principles that are important in empowering employees to surface conflict: they must understand the organization's ideology and direction, have the know-how to act, have appropriate information, and be allowed the freedom to act.

Ideology

To effectively use their collaborative power, employees must understand where the organization wants to go, what it wants to accomplish, and how they can contribute to it. This means that the organization's ideology—its values, fundamental purpose, business strategy, and milestone goals—should be clear to all. A well-articulated ideology provides a central reason for being that people can feel good about, rally around, and work together toward. It also provides an element of control by setting broad boundaries within which all employees—subordinates and supervisors alike—must work. This allows management to feel comfortable with empowered employees and employees to feel comfortable with management.

Properly framed and articulated, an organization's ideology should implicitly provide a broad philosophy for handling many day-to-day occurrences, including the management of conflict. It provides employees guidance in assessing conflict situations and a reasonable level of predictability as to what management's reaction will be when conflict is surfaced.

> In organizations where customer service is a strong value, employees know to go to great lengths to avoid conflict with a customer. They also feel safer in challenging a supervisor's criticism of an action taken for the purpose of helping a customer.

Know-How

To really use their collaborative power, employees must be able to decide what to do and how to do it. Management must hire employees with the capacity to handle the roles to which they are assigned. It also must provide them with the education, training, and experience to do their jobs and deal effectively with conflict. This combination of capacity and development provides employees with the confidence to use their initiative and creativity. Training in areas such as communication, team processes, and negotiations can help employees resolve most of the conflict they encounter, and familiarization with the organization's communication and dispute resolution processes will encourage them to surface that which they cannot resolve without assistance.

Appropriate Information

Empowering employees requires management to share with employees not just information relating to their specific jobs, but broader information on issues such as goals, accomplishments, problems, concerns, organizational performance, and most other information available to management. From a conflict management perspective, relevant communication should include a clear statement of the behavior expected, the processes through which disputes are resolved within the organization, generic feedback as to the results when significant conflicts are resolved, and any other information that will help employees understand the risks and rewards of surfacing conflict. Old concepts of privileged information must be reassessed and employees trusted to handle sensitive information appropriately, and old tests of need-to-know as determined by management must be reconsidered in favor of need-to-know as determined by management or employees, or perhaps "want-to-know" by employees.

Sharing of appropriate information generally makes employees feel they are in the loop and that management trusts them and is willing to treat them as partners in a mutual enterprise. Sharing provides employees with the knowledge necessary to do their jobs with creativity and innovation and allows them to monitor their own contributions and behavior against external standards, which tends to motivate them to act responsibly. From a conflict management perspective, appropriate information helps employees make informed judgments about the risks and rewards of surfacing conflict and builds trust that management will react appropriately if they do.

Freedom

Employee freedom to act means autonomy within boundaries. It suggests supervisors who act as colleagues and coaches rather than dictators; decisions being made by those closest to the work rather than the organizational hierarchy; and employees who have the confidence and initiative to act first and explain later if necessary. Freedom to act also includes the freedom to engage in appropriate conflict, resolve one's own whenever possible, and seek help when necessary.

Boundaries are necessary to channel energy in the right direction and ensure that autonomy does not become anarchy. A clearly articulated ideology provides a broad set of boundaries that offer general direction for employees and management alike. But additional, more specific, boundaries are usually helpful. These may take the form of role descriptions, organizational policies, cultural norms, decision-making procedures, alternative dispute resolution processes, or other guidelines that provide a common set of assumptions to govern the actions of the entire organization. Such boundaries help define what kind of behavior is likely to lead to conflict and how it will be handled if it does. When employees understand the boundaries within which they must operate, they can assess the risks associated with surfacing conflict within them. When boundaries are properly established, therefore, they free employees to surface conflict. Any management that establishes boundaries that take away that freedom needs to take a good look at itself and ask whether it is contributing to negative conflict.

Motivation

Empowered employees tend to be self-motivated. They understand their organization's objectives, see an alignment with their personal needs, and get direct feedback of results. In a collaborative environment with mutual respect and strong, visible leadership, little else is needed to foster the type of behavior that leads to organizational excellence. Employees' best reward is the satisfaction of a job well done. In addition, however, an organization's formal systems should provide an incentive to surface conflict whenever feasible. Appraisal and pay systems should support openness and candor, and discipline systems should not shoot the messenger. Instead, they should positively reinforce individuals who are willing to take the risk of coming forward. Management should also informally reward messengers who surface conflict. They can personally thank them for bringing their concerns forward, tell them how much they and the information provided are valued, visibly respond to their information in an appropriate way, and take other actions to convince them the initiative was safe and worthwhile.

Avoid Punitive Discipline

Not all conflict involves unacceptable behavior, but some does. Disagreements between individuals can escalate from healthy sparring to heated arguments, unacceptable harassment, or physical altercations. Conflict between an individual and management can involve an honest, constructive disagreement, but it can also arise when an employee violates the organization's policies and rules. Not surprisingly, employees who have behaved unacceptably and anticipate being taken to the woodshed when management learns about it are not likely to surface the conflict if they have a choice.

This reluctance to surface conflict is exacerbated if the organization uses progressive discipline processes that all but require punishment for every infraction. As previously discussed, progressive discipline has many variations, but at its core is the concept of administering warnings and successively more punitive actions, up to and including discharge, until the behavior is corrected or the employee is terminated. While punishment may improve behavior in the short term, in the long term it rarely solves the real issue, almost always drives conflict underground, and reduces contact and communication between subordinates and supervisors.

Unacceptable behavior is unacceptable, however, and cannot be tolerated. Management's challenge is to prevent recurrences of offending behavior while doing as little as possible to cause employees to suppress conflict. To do this management must avoid punishing employees and instead help them take responsibility for their own behavior. Dick Grote has discussed such an approach in *Discipline Without Punishment*. He recommends shifting responsibility for employee behavior from management to employees by using the following when dealing with unacceptable behavior:[13]

- Positive contacts—recognize and affirm employees who are performing well.

- Coaching sessions—clarify performance expectations, provide appropriate training, remove obstacles to performance, and provide feedback.

- Oral reminders—at the first formal disciplinary action, where the supervisor formally advises an employee that a problem exists, the employee is asked to respond, and both try to resolve the issue.

- Written reminders—similar to oral reminders, but formally documented in a written memo to the employee.

- Decision-making leaves—an employee is given time off with pay to decide whether to return to work committed to acceptable behavior.

- Terminations—not a part of the disciplinary procedure, but occasionally necessary if an employee does not meet his responsibility.

Although a disciplinary process with these elements may still tend to drive some conflict underground, it achieves the best balance between dealing with unacceptable behavior and surfacing conflict. More importantly, it treats employees as adults responsible for their own actions. Over the long term it tends to reduce the incidence of conflict in the first place.

Maintain an Effective Dispute Resolution System

Employees often suppress conflict because they are afraid that if they surface it, they will suffer adverse personal consequences. They also suppress it when they believe it will never be resolved. Maintaining an effective, formal dispute resolution system helps address both issues.

Chapter 11 discusses the advantages of formal dispute resolution systems and some principles on which they are based. Such systems have evolved as efficient, cost-effective ways of addressing disputes that without early intervention are likely to escalate to increasingly negative behavior or to expensive, time-consuming lawsuits. They have real value in this regard. In addition, they also can encourage employees to surface suppressed conflict by making it less risky and more predictable, provided that

- Employees know a system exists and understand how to use it

- The system helps employees resolve conflict rather than punishing the people involved

- Confidential avenues for surfacing conflict are provided

- Employees believe the process will foster fair resolution of their conflicts

- The system provides timely feedback as appropriate for individual cases and broad organizational issues

Developing dispute resolution systems with characteristics such as these, in which employees have the level of confidence that causes them to surface conflict, is not a simple proposition. It requires management commitment, organizational resources, and the active participation of empowered employees. Chapter 11 presents ideas for integrating these factors and developing effective processes.

KEY POINTS

1. Some counterproductive conflict will exist even in the best-managed organizations, and much of it will be suppressed and not apparent to management.

2. Suppressed conflict needs to be surfaced so those who need to resolve it become aware of and acknowledge its presence.

3. Employees don't surface conflict because of the fear of the consequences of doing so, ignorance about how to go about it, or doubt that doing so is worth the effort and risk.

4. Not all conflict should be surfaced; some should be ignored or tolerated.

5. Most conflict needs to be surfaced so it can be dealt with. An environment where employees are likely to surface conflict can occur if management

   • Hears what employees say

   • Empowers all employees

   • Avoids punitive discipline

   • Maintains effective dispute resolution systems

Engaging Conflict

*"Don't never interfere with something that
ain't botherin' you none."*

—TEXAS BIX BENDER, *Don't Squat
with Yer Spurs On!
A Cowboy's Guide to Life*

O nce managers know conflict exists, they are faced with the often difficult question of whether to get involved and, if so, what to do. Should management intervene at all? If so, when and how? What is its role? And how can it best carry out that role? To answer these important questions, management must consider issues such as the conflict's potential effect; how much time, effort, and money will be required to intervene; and what the chances are of improving the situation.

This chapter will address such issues by discussing management's role in two very different situations: (1) where only employees are involved, and (2) where a conflict exists between employees and management. It will also suggest basic management objectives for two phases of conflict—disagreements and disputes. Chapters 10 and 11 will then present more details on dealing with disagreements and resolving disputes.

ENGAGING EMPLOYEE-EMPLOYEE CONFLICT

In employee-employee conflict, neither the organization nor management as an institution is a disputing party. Instead, such conflict is between (1) employees of equal rank, (2) employees of different rank with no supervisory relationship, or (3) a supervisor and a subordinate as individuals. Employee-employee conflicts often do not appear to be any of management's business when they are purely personal and involve issues that have no relationship to the workplace, except perhaps that the workplace is what brought the parties together.

> - Two employees who are neighbors argue while at work about the boundary between their properties.
>
> - At lunch one employee continually asks to borrow money for food. This irritates the second employee, and now they will barely speak to each other.
>
> - Two employees in the same work group dated for a period of time and subsequently broke off the relationship. Now they are continually at each other's throat.

Employee-employee conflict may also be work related. This occurs when the issues involved affect or are affected by the work to be done, the workplace environment, or the supervisory relationship of the individuals involved.

> - Two peers argue over the level of funding for their particular projects, and the arguments get out of hand.
>
> - A supervisor has a demanding and arrogant personal management style along with the sensitivity of an anaesthetized hyena. The subordinate has a short fuse, and continuing arguments ensue.

Management frequently has a role to play in addressing employee-employee conflicts, even though they usually are personal in nature and often do not directly involve business subjects. In most cases it has a right to become involved, and in some cases, it has an obligation to do so. However, intervening in the wrong situations, or doing the wrong things after intervening, can cause additional problems and make managers wish they had minded their own business.

When Managers Should Intervene

Management often seems to be schizophrenic about its involvement in employee conflict. Sometimes it fails to get involved when intervention is badly needed, while at other times it takes the view that all conflict in the workplace is its business and cannot be adequately dealt with unless a supervisor or manager intervenes. A better approach is to balance the costs and risks of intervention against the value management brings to resolving the problems.

The costs and risks of management intervention in employee conflict include the following:

- Employees often will arrive at a better resolution without management intervention. They know the facts, usually have the capacity to handle conflict on their own, and, most important, know what the best solution looks like.

- When management intervenes on its own initiative, it is often difficult for it to be neutral in the ultimate resolution. Without management neutrality, one party is likely to remain unhappy, and a conflict that appears to be resolved really won' bet.

- Management intervention detracts from employees' sense of empowerment. It suggests to the disputants that they do not have the capacity to manage their own lives.

- Intervention costs money. Management staff must devote their time to it, and time is money.

- There is a risk that management intervention will drive the employees together against management. Sometimes employees resent what they see as an unnecessary intrusion into their personal lives.

Because of such concerns, management should mind its own business and stay out of many purely personal conflicts between employees. Employees are adults and should be treated accordingly. This means that management generally should not intervene unless there are affirmative reasons to do so. But when affirmative reasons do exist, appropriate managers and supervisors are obligated to get involved, and their failure to do so is an abrogation of their responsibility. Outlined below are some situations in which management typically should intervene in employee conflict.

Management Has a Legitimate Interest
in the Substance of the Conflict

Individuals may argue about matters that directly affect the organization's performance, that bring into question its values or purpose, or that directly relate to the effectiveness and efficiency that determine whether the organization's purposes will be accomplished. What is decided in such cases may be quite important, and management has a right and responsibility to intervene to ensure the organization's best interests prevail even though it is not a disputant. It may have an interest not only in ensuring that a disagreement is resolved and its negative impact stopped but, more important, also in ensuring that the substantive decisions that resolve it support organizational performance.

> Two managers argue continually over the size of their respective departmental budgets. Senior management has a real interest in how the issue is resolved and should intervene to ensure that broader interests are considered.

The Conflict Itself Has Negative Effects
on the Organization

Some personal disputes about issues bearing no relationship to the workplace nevertheless negatively affect the organization. The feelings, emotions, and actions of the disputants spill over into the workplace, reducing the efficiency and effectiveness of the parties involved. Employees think about the dispute rather than their work, spend their time fighting rather than working, and often create an environment that prevents others from contributing as much as they should. In such cases, management may have no interest in the substance of the conflict or how the matter is resolved, but it needs the negative effects removed from the workplace. It has a right to insist that this be done, and an obligation to other employees and stakeholders to insist that it be done.

> One employee coaches another's son in little league baseball, and they have an ongoing argument about the son's lack of playing time. The argument persists on the job site, where the parties argue rather than work, and their colleagues are beginning to become involved and take sides.

The Conflict Presents a Potential Risk to the Organization

Personal conflicts of current interest only to the disputants often hold the seeds of larger, more significant disputes. They can easily escalate and damage both the financial and public relations standing of the organization. Resolution is likely to be much more tenable at the early percolation stage than after the conflict has escalated to a full-blown dispute with polarized positions. Therefore, it is often in management's interest to intervene on the basis of the potential impact and not wait until a conflict is actually damaging the organization. While management might have no interest in how such matters are resolved, it has a real interest in ensuring that they are resolved fairly and expeditiously before harm is done.

- A lovers' quarrel can easily become a sexual harassment event—and the organization may become liable for its failure to intervene.

- A dispute over a purely personal matter could distract employees from their work, cause inattention to safety, and lead to devastating accidents.

There Is a Power Disparity Among the Parties

Power disparities can arise when one individual has a higher place in the hierarchy; holds more relative seniority, expertise, or information; has a more demanding physical presence; or otherwise has an advantage over another. In such situations, the more powerful may take unfair advantage of the weaker.

Does management have an obligation to protect a weaker employee in a conflict it otherwise has no interest in? If an obligation to intervene doesn't exist, are there business reasons for doing so? Management must walk a fine line when power disparities are perceived. It must be concerned about allowing one employee to take advantage of another in the workplace. However, it also must be concerned that intervention will only reinforce the feeling of disparate power, or that the parties will resent the intrusion and gang up on management.

There are no easy answers. The decision must balance issues such as the size of the power disparity, the magnitude of the issues in dispute, and the extent to which the powerful party is actually hurting the other. As a general rule, management should intervene if the disparity is great enough that (1) either party loses the capacity to make free and informed decisions concerning resolution of the dispute, or (2) the power disparity raises the likelihood that management's normal workplace commitments to the weaker employee will be compromised.

Deciding whether to intervene when an employee does not appear able to make a free and informed decision often presents a difficult dilemma. Managers may see a need to provide the weaker party with the information, expertise, or help deemed necessary for a free choice in resolving a matter. However, unilaterally providing such help tends to dictate what information will be considered and can have a disempowering effect that scuttles an agreement the employees themselves were prepared to make. The dilemma has no easy answer, but management's best approach is to look to process and structure, not substance. Management should ask whether organizational processes and structure prevent an employee from obtaining the information, expertise, and confidence she needs to ensure that the conflict will be fairly addressed. If the answer is yes, management probably should intervene. If it is no, management probably should stay out of the conflict.

- An employee has a personal dispute with another employee (not in his chain of supervision) two levels up in the organizational pecking order. Management does not intervene because the dispute is not affecting the work environment and both are fully competent and free to resolve the dispute as they wish.

- An employee has a personal dispute with his supervisor. The supervisor's boss intervenes because the subordinate has access to less information and has reason to fear repercussions from making his case with his supervisor.

With regard to the second consideration, the employment relationship is founded on an implicit or explicit social contract covering the rights and obligations of the employer and employees. Management should do whatever is necessary to deliver on its obligations under this contract. If a power disparity in an employee conflict is jeopardizing its commitments, management must intervene and ensure they are maintained.

Management is obligated to ensure that the workplace is free from threats of physical violence or unlawful discrimination, and should intervene if it sees these being compromised.

Employees Request Management Intervention

Employees may, for various reasons, request that management intervene in their disputes. They are most likely to do so when one party is weaker than the other and needs help, when the parties believe they do not have the capacity to address the conflict themselves, or (ideally) when they understand the organization has a direct substantive interest in the outcome. Mutual requests from all disputants to their supervisor are usually rather straightforward. There is no implication of one party ratting on another, confidentiality of the request is not an issue, and some sort of intervention is nearly always appropriate.

Other requests, such as confidential requests by one of the disputants without the other's knowledge, requests that go over the supervisor's head to her boss or another management representative, or requests to omsbudpersons or HR staff, can be tricky because they may reflect on the competence or trustworthiness of the other disputant or the complaining party's supervisor. Accordingly, the employees requesting help often don't want others, particularly those most directly involved, such as their supervisor or the other disputant, to know they asked for it. This presents a real "catch 22" for management because inappropriate intervention can easily exacerbate the problem or create another one. Intervening may violate the trust of the one requesting help, but neglecting such a request is likely to reflect a careless attitude by management and cause problems as well. When employees ask for help, however, management has little choice but to respond. Its real choices lie in how it responds, which is discussed below.

How Management Should Intervene

When management intervenes in employee conflict, it must help the situation without making employees' problems its problems, trying to solve employees' problems for them, or forcing resolutions in which it has no interests. These pitfalls destroy employee confidence, tend to make employees dependent, prevent learning, and frequently just shift the locus of the conflict to management itself. Instead, management should pursue a broad goal of not only having the dispute resolved but also ensuring that the disputing employees become more effective and contribute as much as they can in the future. This objective requires managers to treat disputing employees as competent, empowered members of the organization and to allow them to learn and grow as a result of conflict and its resolution. To do this, management's role in addressing employee conflict should normally remain limited, along the lines discussed in the following paragraphs.

Protect Organizational Interests

Employee conflict may affect organizational interests either directly or indirectly. The effect is direct when an organization's policy, business plan, or other interest provides the substance about which a conflict arose and also provides standards for its resolution.

> Two team members are involved in a continuing dispute because one is often late to work and the other resents it. Left to their own devices, they could decide to resolve the dispute by agreeing to reduce their hours of work and to both arrive at a later time. Management, however, has a direct interest in maintaining its current work hours.

Management has an indirect interest when the substance of a conflict is not material to it, but how it is resolved could affect a policy or an element of the business plan.

> Two employees are involved in a purely personal dispute that started when their children had a fight. They agree to resolve it by one of them requesting a transfer to another department. Management may refuse to go along with the transfer because of negative organizational consequences.

In both situations, management must see that the matter is handled in a way that does not cause unacceptable repercussions in the organization. Key concerns typically are to prevent continuing conflict from interfering with the organization's morale and performance and to avoid resolutions that themselves conflict with organizational interests. While management cannot dictate how employees feel and whether or not they agree or disagree, it may need to be clear that employees are expected, one way or another, to correct their workplace behavior and do so in ways that do not hurt the organization.

Address Management's Contribution to the Conflict

Conflicts that appear to be between employees are in fact often caused by management systems or actions. Earlier chapters discussed system causes of conflict and how factors such as management policies, organizational changes, or poor hiring practices can cause conflict. System-caused conflict is more often between employees and management—when employees violate policies or resist changes. Sometimes, however, a management policy, action, or failure to act is also the root cause of conflict between employees.

> - Two managers refuse to work together and continually bad-mouth each other because they are both vying for larger bonuses in a zero-sum bonus system.
>
> - Two employees with adjacent desks can't get along. One resents the fact that the other views pornographic web sites on his computer in violation of the organization's policy, which management has not enforced.

Management should understand the facts of all conflict to the extent necessary to determine whether or not it is part of the cause. If it is not, management may wish to limit its own role in the resolution. If it is part of the cause, however, management may need to participate in the resolution as though it is one of the disputants. This does not necessarily mean changing its policies or systems, as they may be best on balance, even though they lead to some conflict. It does, however, mean assessing the situation, collaborating with the parties to resolve the conflict, taking appropriate actions, and making sure expectations are clear when change is not appropriate. Management is not the sole issue in most cases of this type, as the people themselves are usually also part of the problem. Therefore, it should proceed in ways that help them learn, grow, and become better able to deal with the systems and environment within which they work.

Foster Improvement in the Disputants

In *The Promise of Mediation,*[14] authors Bush and Folger present conflict and its resolution as opportunities for moral growth. The people involved can become transformed through empowerment and recognition. Empowerment means each party establishes or regains a sense of strength, self-control, and security through clarifying goals, understanding options, enhancing skills, developing additional resources, making decisions, and taking other actions used in resolving conflicts. Recognition means moving beyond a focus on self and recognizing the other party: his situation, ideas, viewpoints, words, actions, and other characteristics that make him who he is. The objective of empowerment and recognition is to help the parties improve themselves and move beyond where they were prior to the dispute.

Although Bush and Folger write about how mediators can foster empowerment and recognition in mediation, the same objective should exist when management intervenes in employee conflict. Fast, half-baked, or forced solutions may make the immediate symptoms go away, but they are not likely to have lasting effects on the real problem or the individuals involved. The parties can effectively correct the problem and experience the self-worth, confidence, and security that reduce the likelihood of future conflict only when they understand themselves, the other disputants, the real issues, and the various opportunities for resolution. And this understanding does not come from someone else resolving a problem for them, but instead comes from a process in which the parties are forced to look at themselves, examine options, deliberate, and decide on their own course of action.

Provide Coaching and Help

Employees are not always experts in knowing how to resolve conflict or in applying the options available for doing so. They may need help, and management is positioned to provide it in the form of coaching, an intervention that is intended to help employees resolve their own conflict in ways that truly foster empowerment and recognition.

The nuances of this intervention are best illustrated by comparing sports coaching with legal counseling. Legal counseling generally involves advice or opinion given for the purpose of directing the conduct of another, with the counselor having a continuing role in accomplishing the other's purpose or carrying out a mutually developed plan. The lawyer is usually an active player with a continuing direct influence over the client's actions until a matter of mutual interest is resolved. A sports coach also gives advice and opinions but is not an active participant in the game being played. He is on the sideline, and the players on the field determine the outcome of the game by their own skill. This best demonstrates management's role in resolving conflict among employees in ways that foster empowerment and recognition.

Management's coaching of employees in handling conflict might include actions such as the following:

- Training before the fact on matters such as communication, listening, problem solving, and other matters that help minimize conflict and give employees the tools to deal with it when it does arise

- Training on a case-by-case basis after conflict arises to provide help in areas such as legal or technical requirements, interest-based negotiations, or other specific issues

- Providing input on substantive matters, such as what resources and options are available both internally and externally, and helping employees assess the pros and cons of various possibilities

- Advising employees on the availability of formal dispute resolution processes

- Other appropriate input that helps employees address their own issues

In summary, management should act as a coach, rather than as an active player, unless its own substantive interests are at stake.

> Two employees who share the same workspace have been engaged in a continuing controversy over how clean they should keep their workplace and who should do the cleaning. Management may wish to coach them in required cleanliness standards and the resources available to get it done but normally should insist they decide for themselves how the standards are to be met.

Provide Last-Resort Alternatives

Even with the best of coaching, employees are not always able or willing to resolve conflicts themselves: a more senior employee may be unwilling to relinquish power, self-interests may prevail, or a problem may be too intractable. Yet continuation of conflictive behavior often is not a realistic option. Something must be done.

As a last resort, management should intervene in the substance of employee conflict when it becomes apparent that the employees involved cannot resolve it. When it does intervene, however, management should ensure that it brings things to the table that the employees do not possess. Generally speaking, such things fall into the following categories:

- *Resources.* Sometimes conflict resolution is facilitated by resources that are not readily available to the disputants. When this is the case, management may need to intervene, determine the need for resources, and provide those that will help. Such resources could include help with personal issues through interventions such as lifestyle counseling or anger management classes, or hard resources such as the money to purchase whatever is necessary to resolve a problem.

■ *Motivation.* Sometimes employees don't resolve conflicts because they don't want to make the necessary compromises or concessions. They believe it is to their advantage to continue the conflict. Management may need to use its authority to up the stakes and provide an additional incentive for employees to resolve their problems. Ultimately, it may be necessary for management to take a stand that the behavior must improve or the employees must take their dispute elsewhere.

- Two employees share a computer and argue continually over availability issues. Management may need to intervene and provide the money to obtain another computer.

- Two employees have had several very heated, public arguments over a personal issue. Management may need to tell them (following appropriate procedures) that they will be fired if their behavior isn't corrected.

ENGAGING EMPLOYEE-MANAGEMENT CONFLICT

Employee-management conflict is between an employee or employees and management as an institution. It is not personal between employees and managers as individuals; managers are also employees, and personal conflict between them and their subordinates is employee-employee conflict. But employee-management conflict typically does involve individual managers or supervisors acting as agents for the organization and its management. Employee-management conflict is substantive in nature. Its basis is in actions and positions taken by management against employees or by employees against management, and management is by definition a disputant.

- A supervisor disciplines a subordinate for violating the organization's e-mail policy, and the employee protests that discipline.

- An employee protests the size of his pay increase.

- A supervisor assigns a job that the subordinate believes is unsafe, and the employee refuses to do the work.

Management has a bifurcated role in employee-management conflict. It is a party with rights and obligations to protect its own self-interest. In addition, management is responsible for ensuring that conflicts are resolved fairly and with minimal negative effect on the organization and its employees. These aspects of management's role will be discussed in the sections below.

Management's Role as a Party

Management's role as a party in conflict is to represent the best interests of the organization and all its employees, regardless of whether its actions tend to minimize, perpetuate, or escalate conflict in the short term. While minimizing conflict is no doubt preferable in most cases, management must do what is in the long-term best interests of the organization. It must consider the costs, risks, and other negatives associated with not resolving or perhaps escalating a conflict, the cost of the resolution process, and the value of resolving a conflict when it decides what actions it should take in a matter. When all sides are considered, it may do more than the facts of the immediate case justify in order to resolve the conflict and avoid greater damage. Or management may refuse to agree as a matter of principle, even though that position will escalate the conflict and increase its cost. This doesn't mean the value of resolution wasn't considered. It means that principles or other matters outweighed the cost and risk of not resolving or even escalating the conflict.

- An employee charges management with allowing a hostile work environment and asks for monetary damages. Management's decision process includes not only an assessment of the work environment but also the cost and risks associated with a potential lawsuit if the matter is not resolved quickly.

- Management may elect to fire an employee for continually violating a company policy, even though its action will almost certainly escalate the conflict.

Management's role as a party to conflict is a fundamental part of its authority to run the enterprise. Employees are generally bound to comply with its instructions, although in many cases they have a legal right to protest after the fact. In this context, management's role as a party normally includes the following:

- *Investigator.* Defines the issues and the problem, gathers and analyzes data, understands the needs of the organization and the employees involved, and gathers other information necessary for an appropriate decision.

- *Decision maker.* Manages the business in the balanced best interests of all stakeholders. This does not mean that management makes all decisions unilaterally, or that many of its decisions are not subject to challenge. Rather, it means that management should ensure that appropriate decision processes are available (which may include high levels of collaboration and employee involvement) and that those processes are used to arrive at the best possible decisions, considering relevant matters such as the value, costs, and risks.

- *Implementor.* Contemplates management action resulting from the decision process. As a general rule (except in cases such as a safety compromise, violation of the law, or moral/ethical lapse), management may implement its decisions, and employees are obligated to comply. Such decisions may involve refusal to comply with employee requests or management action up to and including a decision to discharge an employee. Employees may, of course, contest management's implementation of its decision. That is the essence of employee-management conflict.

- *Advocate.* Defends management's actions with employees in an effort to avoid escalation of conflicts and represents management's position at various levels in the dispute resolution process if that becomes necessary.

> Management looks at its financial situation, makes a decision to lay off several employees, and appropriately communicates its rationale to the affected division. Employees still challenge management's action with an age discrimination charge. Management's role then is to ensure that there was no discrimination and defend its actions, by hiring attorneys and testifying in court if necessary.

Management's Conflict Resolution Role

Counterproductive conflict is a cost that detracts from the bottom-line success of an organization, and management is responsible for minimizing that cost. One option is to be essentially passive and allow employees to control the resolution process. When this happens, management may insist on its position as to the substance of a dispute but nevertheless allow employees to determine the process through which it is resolved. Management might aggressively defend a decision or policy at the heart of a controversy but nevertheless allow employee disputants to decide when to surface the dispute, whether to appeal a decision internally or externally, or whether to litigate. In such cases, management implicitly relegates decisions as to how conflicts will be resolved to the employees with whom it has a conflict.

While delegating decisions to employees is often a positive management practice, allowing employee disputants to control the process for resolving their conflicts with management has many pitfalls. Doing so allows decisions concerning the resolution process to be controlled by individuals who, with respect to the situation in question, are likely to have interests that are different from those of the organization or other individuals in it. In addition, employees may not have the appropriate information, expertise, or resources to pursue creative or nontraditional approaches. They are likely to use processes that lead to substantive decisions based on who is right from a legal or policy viewpoint, or who has the power to coerce the other party to give in. Absent early concessions by one party or the other, litigation is a strong possibility. And settlements arrived at with the use of threats, forced through coercion, or decided by a third party through litigation are frequently costly and rarely address the real interests of either party. Such rights-based decisions seldom truly resolve the underlying problems in a way that prevents reoccurrence or accomplishes a purpose that goes beyond settlement of the immediate, surface dispute.

A wiser option is for management to have a strategy for resolving conflict, a plan that forms an alternative to an employee-controlled process that so often leads to costly litigation and further conflict. This means that management must provide effective, cost-efficient conflict resolution processes that are available to address both employee-management and employee-employee disputes.

CONFLICT RESOLUTION APPROACHES

The preceding sections discuss in general terms management's role in resolving various types of workplace conflict. Each role requires different approaches in different situations, and which approach is appropriate will depend on who the conflict is between (employee and employee or employee and management) and whether it is a relatively minor "disagreement" or a more significant "dispute." The management implications of these distinctions, first introduced and discussed in Chapter 1, are addressed in the following sections.

Disagreements

Disagreement is a state of dissatisfaction: a difference of thought, attitude, or belief resulting in dissent or unmet expectations. It includes that stage when the parties acknowledge to each other that each has something the other needs, wants, or has the power to withhold. Disagreements typically are characterized by differences that are expressed between the parties but have not yet been supported by actions or demonstrated by an event.

Conflicts are typically easier to resolve during the disagreement phase than later, after positions harden and actions are taken. Usually during this phase neither party has hurt the other or caused the other loss, so it is easy for the parties to look forward rather than backward. There is no present demand to remedy anything. The parties need only figure out how to avoid creating problems or loss in the future. This presents opportunities for cooperative, informal discussions in which the parties do not try to win, but rather collaborate to find a resolution that increases the size of the pie and offers the possibility of mutual gain.

Disputes

Unfortunately, not all conflict can be addressed or resolved at the disagreement stage. Some conflict is so deep or intractable that even the best and most sincere efforts of both parties are insufficient to reach agreement. Other conflict escalates so quickly that there really is no opportunity to address it at the disagreement phase—one party takes actions against the other immediately, the other party is unaware that a conflict exists, or the other party has no opportunity to respond. A dispute exists in these situations. It contemplates the often aggressive actions that result from unresolved disagreements: the arguments, quarrels, and fights based on tangible and concrete issues, opposing positions, and expectations for relief.

When disagreement becomes a dispute, it is still best to first seek agreement and mutual gain through informal, collaborative processes that emphasize the needs and interests of both parties. This approach will continue to work in many disputes. But more is often required. Mutual gain may not be possible, so the best the parties can hope for may be to compromise, and they may get to a situation where one wins and the other loses. When this happens, the size of each party's win, or who wins and who loses, may be decided by legal rights or power, and more formal conflict resolution processes are usually needed.

Implications

The differences between disagreements and disputes, therefore, are reflected in the level of severity of the conflict, usually as it evolves in different stages over time.

- An employee is frequently late to work, and his supervisor notes the habit. The supervisor discusses the behavior with him, and the employee has a different view of the policy. This is a disagreement. When no resolution occurs, and the supervisor gives the subordinate time off without pay as discipline, a dispute exists because action adverse to the employee was taken.

- An employee believes a transfer policy has been inappropriately applied to her and raises that concern with her supervisor and her HR representative. This is a disagreement. When the employee is not satisfied, she appeals to the division manager with no result and then files legal action alleging discrimination. This is a dispute.

Conflict resolution at its various stages is likely to have different characteristics. Practices that succeed for minor disagreements caught early often differ from those that work for major disputes or disputes that have escalated over time. Thus, addressing conflict requires a continuum of practices suggested by the typical characteristics of conflict resolution at the two stages, indicated in Table 2. Although disagreement and dispute are

Table 2 | Conflict Resolution Practices

PRACTICE	CONFLICT LEVEL	
	DISAGREEMENT	DISPUTE
Objective	agreement	often only settlement is likely
Process	more informal	more formal
Power	emphasizes collaboration	may involve coercion
Focus	interests	positions and rights
Negotiation	mutual gain	compromise or win-lose
People Involved	the parties	often a third party neutral

Table 3	Management Conflict Resolution Roles		
	CONFLICT LEVEL	
PARTIES	**DISAGREEMENT**	**DISPUTE**
Employee-employee	coach	counselor
Employee-management	administrator	advocate

presented as discrete stages of conflict, they really are points on a continuum. The parties involved should select the most appropriate practice for their particular situation from the continuum of practices the chart represents.

The stages define a range of characteristics, which suggests that the level of severity of a conflict is a key determinant of management's role in its resolution. Another key determinant is who the disputing parties are. This combination of considerations is reflected in Table 3.

The various roles can be described as follows:

- *Coach.* Works with the employees involved in conflict by suggesting processes and information to help them resolve their own conflict.

> Two employees argue over workplace issues. Their supervisor coaches them as to what resources are available to help and makes a private office available to them to discuss the problem.

- *Counselor.* Becomes involved in resolving employee-employee conflict by suggesting solutions or processes, insisting that conflictive behavior must change, and helping employees develop a solution.

> Two employees are involved in a conflict over a nonwork issue. However, at work they refuse to communicate and become involved in heated arguments. Their supervisor meets with them, makes it clear that their behavior must improve, and suggests one bid to another department.

- *Administrator.* Handles employee-management issues through communication, discussion, and other problem-solving techniques that address both employee and organization interests.

> An employee has been refusing overtime assignments. His supervisor discusses his concerns with him, and they work out a way to get all the work covered.

- *Advocate.* Continues to address both employee and organization interests when feasible but emphasizes and takes actions to protect the organization's interests whenever necessary.

> An employee files a sexual discrimination complaint with the EEOC. Management tries to get to the bottom of what is happening and also defends its position with the agency investigator.

The coach and administrator roles are similar. Their objective is to cause disagreements to be resolved in a mutually satisfactory way before they become disputes. Suggestions for accomplishing this are discussed in Chapter 10.

The counselor and advocate roles are also similar. They aim to resolve disputes in ways that protect the organization's interest while also considering the employees' needs and wants. Suggestions for accomplishing this are given in Chapter 11.

KEY POINTS

1. Management should not become involved in all conflict between employees. When deciding whether to do so, it should weigh the possible disadvantages of its intervention against legitimate reasons why it should become involved.

2. Management is obligated to intervene in some employee-employee conflict. When it does so, it should empower employees and help the situation without making the employees' problem its problem, trying to solve employees' problems for them, or forcing a resolution in which it has no interests.

3. Management has two roles in employee-management conflict. It is a party, and it also must ensure that the conflict is appropriately resolved.

4. Conflict resolution approaches often must differ, depending on whether a conflict is a disagreement or a dispute, and resolution may require moving back and forth between approaches.

5. Management's role in conflict resolution varies, depending on who the parties are and the stage of the conflict. It may include any of the following:

   • Coach

   • Counselor

   • Administrator

   • Advocate

Resolving Disagreements

"If we must disagree, let's disagree without being disagreeable."

—LYNDON BAINES JOHNSON

C hapter 2 introduced the conflict management cycle (minimize, surface, resolve, and learn) and outlined five objectives of the resolve phase. In summary, these objectives suggest that conflict resolution should acknowledge and fairly address the interests of both parties as well as underlying causes of conflicts to minimize the likelihood that these conflicts or similar ones will occur in the future.

These objectives are appropriate regardless of the severity of a conflict or when it is addressed. They are more readily attained, however, at the early disagreement stage than at the later dispute stage. At the disagreement stage, issues typically are not polarized, personal antagonisms are not likely to be a major problem, and the door is open to informal, collaborative processes that can resolve conflict in ways that are agreeable to all parties and that minimize the likelihood of future similar occurrences. Therefore, the parties have more opportunities to attain their conflict resolution objectives than they do after the matter has escalated to a full-blown dispute, where positions are likely to be hardened and there often is great pressure to simply settle the conflict and get on with more urgent matters.

- A supervisor coaches two employees who are involved in a personal conflict, and they are able to resolve it before either behaves unacceptably and their behavior becomes part of the problem.

- A human resources representative addresses a policy conflict before the employee involved appeals to the CEO.

- An ombudsperson helps address a discrimination complaint before an EEOC charge is filed.

This chapter will discuss principles for resolving early-stage disagreements and address some unique problems associated with resolving those between employees and management.

PRINCIPLES FOR RESOLVING DISAGREEMENTS

To enhance the likelihood of resolving disagreements in ways that minimize future conflict, organizations must use a collaborative, holistic process that not only resolves the presenting problems but also looks beyond and considers the future. Management can use the principles outlined in the following sections to accomplish this objective, either as a coach in employee-employee conflict or as an administrator in those between employees and management.

Describe the Conflict Properly

Conflict is a dynamic process that can play out in many different ways, depending on the people involved, the circumstances, and the perceptions of those circumstances. Further, conflict usually is not objective; it exists only when the parties perceive it to exist and often is a function more of the personal values, beliefs, and needs of the individuals involved than of objective facts. Thus, each disagreement is different from all others.

Different actions are required to resolve different conflicts. One solution does not fit all. Therefore, how a disagreement is defined largely determines how it will be resolved. Looking at one cause suggests one answer, while looking at several causes raises the possibility of several answers. Narrowly defining a conflict and the associated issues leads to narrow solutions, while thinking in broader terms opens minds to broader, more comprehensive solutions. Using broader options allows more effective, long-term resolution. Properly defining a conflict requires management to consider several key issues.

Focus on the Cause or Causes

We often define conflicts on the basis of the facts we can see and place them in pigeonholes with predetermined solutions. We like this approach because it seems easy, avoids uncertainty, and allows us to believe we have solved a problem by simply replicating what has been done in similar situations in the past.

> • An employee was absent several times in the preceding quarter. We characterize this as an attendance problem and discipline him under the attendance policy.
>
> • Two employees argue frequently and can't get along. We frame this as a personality clash and send them to charm school.

Most people do not enjoy conflict and thus rarely engage in it without some reason. Instead, disagreeing people usually try to achieve something that is in their own self-interest or the interest of those they represent. To effectively resolve conflict, therefore, we must discover its cause and the underlying interests of the parties. Discovering the root causes of conflicts opens additional opportunities for resolving them. Doing so allows the parties to consider their basic needs and interests rather than just the facts of the presenting event and helps resolve conflict over the long term.

> • An employee was absent several times in the previous quarter. Learning that his reason for being absent was sickness caused by job stress opens more effective options for resolving the conflict.
>
> • Two employees frequently argue and can't get along. Seeing that the senior employee believes he is a work leader and the junior employee doesn't understand this status opens resolution options that are better than charm school.

Treat Each Conflict as Unique

One of the biggest mistakes managers make in addressing conflict is assuming it can be resolved by employing previously used solutions because the presenting event is similar to ones encountered in the past. This allows them to follow precedent and use an easy, seemingly safe solution. In reality, no two conflicts are exactly alike. No matter how alike two situations may appear to be, they will differ in concrete ways, such as different time, place, and conditions, or in more subtle but nonetheless important ways, such as different environment, impact on related stakeholders, or underlying cause.

Viewing each conflict as unique demands thoughtful consideration of what disagreements are really about and of all available options for resolving them. Seeing the issues as unique increases the likelihood that in thinking about them one will develop new options for new problems, arrive at solutions that meet the long-term needs of the parties, and foster learning.

Look to the Future

All the king's horses and all the king's men couldn't put Humpty Dumpty together again. Likewise, in most conflicts we cannot roll the clock back, make things like they were, or undo what was done. Instead, when resolving disagreements we must consider what happened as a context for what is and can be.

Looking to the future does not mean refusing to acknowledge the past. In some conflicts, talking about past actions may be a form of venting or learning necessary to allow one or both parties to move forward. The past may hold important history that can help guide our future, so acknowledging and understanding what happened and why it happened is important. Although the past cannot be changed, it may suggest what an arbitrator or judge might do if called upon to decide who was "right" and who was "wrong," thereby suggesting remedial action that fosters resolution.

Looking to the future means acknowledging the past, understanding the present, and describing a problem in a way that allows the parties to fashion a solution that works in the future. It requires the parties to consider their future needs and interests as well as the future consequences of their actions, and to arrive at a solution that goes beyond the obvious to a more ideal and permanent resolution. The past provides a context; the present provides a platform; but the focus is on the future.

- A female employee accuses a male employee of sexual harassment in the form of leering looks and suggestive comments. The male employee denies that it ever happened. A supervisor involved in helping resolve the conflict should acknowledge both parties' perceptions after a discussion of what actually happened but emphasize the type of behavior that will avoid such conflict in the future.

- Management promotes one employee to fill a vacancy, and a second employee complains that he was more qualified and should have received the promotion. The job is already filled, and removing the first employee and replacing her with the second is likely to create more conflict than it resolves. Unless unlawful discrimination was involved, the complaining party must accept the decision, and both management and the employee must emphasize a future that ensures the employee is given fair opportunities.

Integrate the Right People

Management often tries to minimize the effect of disagreements by limiting the number of people who are aware of them or who are involved in their resolution. When a disagreement is between employees, their supervisor often tries to keep it quiet and settle the matter by imposing his will. Disagreements between employees and the organization are frequently addressed only by subordinate and supervisor, regardless of whether the supervisor has the authority or knowledge to resolve them. Often the chain of command is strictly honored, and employees are not allowed to talk to an individual with expertise in the area causing concern. This process may solve a problem at a superficial level, but the issues are likely to resurface later in another form.

An employee's supervisor denies her time off, which she believes she is entitled to under the Family Medical Leave Act. She disagrees with the denial and protests. The supervisor is not familiar with the act or the organization's policy and has made his decision on the advice of a policy expert. But the policy expert is not present in the resolution process, and the supervisor simply carries messages between him and the employee. As a result of not including the right people, the employee only gets a superficial understanding of the organization's view, and management never understands the employee's complete story. Thus, the issue is likely to surface again.

Rugged individualism may feel good to supervisors and enhance their feelings of power, but it misses opportunities for effective conflict resolution. It decreases the likelihood that the optimum resolution will be discovered and that whatever resolution is adopted will be acceptable to all involved.

From a substantive viewpoint, involving more people brings more information, knowledge, and opinions to the table. Each individual can become a valuable contributor to a synergy that allows all parties to gain and leads to better solutions than those likely from only one or two individuals.

While including more people increases the chances of agreement and mutual gain, such happy endings are not always possible. Management may need to insist that conflicting employees change their behavior even though they do not agree, or it may need to stand by its decision in a conflict with an employee even though the employee continues to disagree. Agreeing to disagree may be the best resolution that can be attained at the time. Under these circumstances, it is important for the resolution process to foster acceptance, even though there is no true meeting of the minds.

Integrating all relevant people in the process increases the likelihood that the solution will be accepted. This works in two ways. First, it usually adds important information that reduces the area of disagreement even when agreement on all aspects of a conflict is not possible. When the needs and interests of all parties are placed on the table, there is an opportunity to acknowledge and understand them, plus respond to many, if not all, of the issues. The narrower the area of disagreement, the greater the likelihood that the conflict will go away rather than escalate to a dispute.

Second, involvement leads to the understanding and empathy that foster acceptance. People resist solutions they don't understand, that are imposed on them, or that contain uncertain risks. Conversely, they usually can accept decisions that they have had a meaningful opportunity to influence and understand. This can only happen when all the relevant people are directly involved in the resolution process and are in the room when the decision is made.

Some specific actions managers can take to integrate all the right people in resolving disagreements are as follows:

- Insist that employees resolve their own conflict, with coaching as needed, whenever feasible.

- When involved in an employee-management disagreement, act as an administrator seeking a fair, effective resolution rather than as an advocate protecting only the interests of the organization.

- Allow employees to include a representative or support person upon request when addressing conflicts with their supervisor or with management.

- If a conflict involves matters of specialized expertise, have the person holding that expertise participate in its resolution.

- When resolving conflicts between employees and management, provide employees reasonable access to the person with the authority to make management's decision.

- A discharged employee should have direct access to the manager in the chain of command who authorized his firing.

- An employee with a policy disagreement should, when feasible, have direct access to the person with final policy authority. When this is not feasible, as in a very large organization, the employee should have access to a person who administers the policy and is fully familiar with its terms.

Take a Systems View[15]

Chapter 1 introduced the idea that conflicts are parts of a larger system; they are a function of interdependent people and interactions, each of which affects and is affected by other people and interactions. This means that resolving disagreements requires a systems view that recognizes that apparent causes are often like the tip of an iceberg, with the most significant issues submerged. Effective resolution requires addressing matters that are beneath the surface as well as those that are apparent.

Systems have multiple levels, and what happens at the lower ones can have a major effect on those above. Four levels that have been identified for business organizations are "events, patterns of behavior, systemic structure, and mental models."[16] These levels, which also apply in matters of conflict, are defined as follows:

- *Events* are defined as who did what to whom. They are those actions that are the obvious manifestation of a conflict.

> - Failure to promote an individual and the individual's complaining
> - A case of alleged sexual harassment and the facts surrounding it

- *Patterns of behavior* focus on longer-term trends and their implications. They are the way key variables or people act over time and are seen in the habits and predictable actions of individuals and organizations that can cause disagreements and lead to disputes.

> Departmental supervisors have a continuing pattern of nit-picking micro-management, which is perceived as distrust and leads to poor morale and conflict.

- *Systemic structure* is the pattern of interrelationships among key parts of the system. Structure might include hierarchy, process flows, how decisions are made, and many other factors, as well as the relationships among them. Systemic structure also includes factors such as organizational processes or programs that should foster productive synergy but that if working improperly can lead to counterproductive conflict.

> The interrelationship of job duties, qualifications, and seniority is part of the job assignment structure in an organization.

- *Mental models* are deeply held internal images of how the world works that provide us with familiar ways of thinking and acting. They include assumptions, stories, simple generalizations, or complex theories that we carry in our heads and that affect how we perceive the world and react to our perceptions. Mental models frequently drive the systemic structure, as they provide the value systems for managers who design and manage them. They also are the foundation of much personal conflict, as they are the basis of biases, prejudices, and self-centered wants that so frequently are at the root of personal conflict.

> Beliefs that management has about unions and unions have about management are usually parts of the mental models of the respective parties.

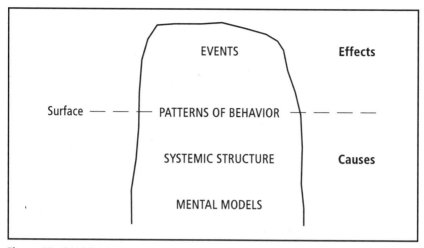

Figure 11 SYSTEMS VIEW OF CONFLICT

Thus, while disagreement events are usually clear for all to see, one must look to the patterns of behavior, systemic structures, and mental models that are below the surface to really understand them. Addressing the visible aspects of a conflict usually only addresses a small portion of the relevant and important issues and limits the opportunities for effective, long-term resolution. Addressing the parts below the surface often provides the real opportunities for resolution and learning. Successful conflict resolution hinges on consideration of all the interrelated parts of the larger system and requires asking why things happen, what the root causes are, and other queries into cause-and-effect relationships. Figure 11 uses an iceberg analogy to illustrate these concepts.

Disaggregate the Conflict

Considering the systemic roots of conflict opens it to a broader array of possible solutions. But usually the devil is in the details, and to understand its root causes and find all available resolution options, each conflict must be broken into manageable components, and each component must be addressed individually. More important, conflict is often the result of several contributing causes, and addressing only one of them will not resolve the conflict. Therefore, disaggregating the whole to isolate the various causes is the first step toward developing a range of options and finding the easiest and most feasible resolution. While it may be difficult, impossible, or perhaps unnecessary to find acceptable resolution for all components of a conflict, finding one may be enough to have the parties come to agreement.

Exactly how a conflict should be disaggregated will, of course, vary widely depending on the facts of each specific case. However, two particular opportunities—separating facts from their systemic roots and separating personal concerns from business or organizational issues—are appropriate in most workplace conflicts and will be discussed in the paragraphs that follow.

Separate the Facts from the Underlying Systemic Causes

Most conflict arises, not from the events of the particular incident, but from systemic causes that lie beneath them: the patterns of behavior, structure, and mental models affecting the disagreeing parties.

The facts are the obvious manifestation of a disagreement event: the who, what, when, and where that can be investigated and described. Facts do not, however, include the inferences that can be drawn from the events, such as fault, responsibility, or liability. In any conflict the parties may initially disagree about the facts, but in most cases they can be established through examination of relevant evidence.

The other levels of the system motivate action—often conflictive action—in different ways. Patterns of behavior cause people to act as they do out of habit. Systemic structure provides specific incentives or disincentives for particular actions. And mental models—our deeply ingrained images of how the world works—often color our view of reality. In most conflict, these factors are not only the cause of the conflicting actions but also the basis of the doubt, uncertainty, perplexity, aspirations, goals, or desires that escalate it.

Separating the facts from the underlying parts of a system, and each part from each other part, allows the parties and those who may be helping them develop resolution options for each aspect of a conflict. Addressing the facts usually requires specific actions or understandings relating directly to what happened. Considering patterns of behavior introduces a time component—the facts over time. And structure requires looking beyond the facts to what is causing the behavior. Addressing these hidden parts of a system requires going below the surface to understand what they are and then developing longer-term options for changing those that are causing problems. Once all aspects are identified and considered, the parties can then implement those actions that are most appropriate and most likely to create a long-lasting solution.

An employee has protested because he was not promoted to fill a recent job vacancy. The facts of the conflict are that a more qualified employee with less seniority was promoted. The employee's mental model contributed to the conflict because he grew up in an environment where seniority prevailed and therefore assumed that to be the case here. The structure also contributed because training programs are inadequate, and it was almost impossible for him to become qualified. Resolution options include addressing the facts by discussing the employee's qualifications compared to those of the one promoted, initiating some training as part of a performance improvement plan, and addressing the employee's mental models by providing evidence of the practice of promoting on the basis of qualification rather than seniority.

Separate the Personal from the Substantive Issues

Most workplace conflict can be separated into personal and substantive components. Personal conflict exists when individual relationships are characterized by friction, frustration, and personality clashes, while substantive conflict pertains to the conflict of ideas and differences about concrete business or organizational issues.

Conflict that appears to be caused by one component is often really caused by the other, and much conflict is caused by some of each. Substantive disagreement may actually contribute to conflict that appears to concern purely personal matters, and personal issues may contribute to conflict that appears to be a substantive matter. While addressing the apparent cause may provide a short-term cease-fire, it rarely accomplishes lasting peace. Instead, it may be necessary to resolve an apparent personal controversy by changing something that is actually substantive in nature, or to resolve an apparent substantive disagreement by addressing underlying personal issues.

- Two employees engage in continuing conflict, with the junior employee complaining that the senior one is nosey, meddles too much, and tries to give too much advice. This appears to be a straightforward personality conflict. But their mutual supervisor has asked the senior employee to provide some informal mentoring to the junior one on a confidential basis. When the three sit down and discuss the business need for mentoring and formalize the arrangement, the personality conflict goes away.

> • Two managers can't seem to agree on a budget issue, with each making strong substantive arguments for his position. But the real reason they disagree is that they are both arrogant, hardheaded, and unwilling to concede anything that would make the other appear to win. The immediate conflict can probably be resolved by mediating the budget dispute, but in the longer term it may be necessary to work on the personal styles of the participants.

SPECIAL ISSUES IN EMPLOYEE-MANAGEMENT DISAGREEMENTS

The principles discussed above apply to both employee-employee and employee-management disagreements. However, management has multiple roles and stakeholders that often give rise to special issues where disagreements between management and employees are concerned. Management's primary role is to make the organization perform. It is responsible to different stakeholders for many business decisions of a managerial nature that determine the scope, nature, and long-term viability of the organization. This includes responsibility to employees for fair and equitable treatment and to shareholders for accomplishing the overall purpose of the organization. In addition, it has both the authority and the obligation to direct the workforce in ways that foster organizational performance. These potentially conflicting roles cause certain pitfalls and dilemmas for managers dealing with disagreements between employees and management. These will be discussed in the following sections.

Pitfalls

Managers' administrative responsibilities and authority over employees often cause them to develop mental models that are not valid and that can easily get in the way of effective conflict resolution. Unfortunately, several are quite common.

Managers Assume That Employees See the World As They Do

Managers often have preconceived notions, based on their roles and perspectives, of how disagreements should be resolved. They expect employees under their supervision to see things the way they do, and when employees react differently than expected, managers see them as the problem rather than as a valuable resource.

In reality, however, each person experiences others and the world in a unique way, particularly when one individual is in a superior role and the other is subordinate within an organization. Managers are expected to see the big picture, while employees are often expected to focus more on the details. Managers are responsible for others, while subordinates are responsible for self. Managers have more power, and subordinates have less. These and other differences mean that managers and subordinates have different perspectives on any conflict and therefore are likely to have different views as to the resolution.

To get conflicts resolved effectively, managers must accept that their subordinates' thoughts, feelings, and needs are justified from their perspectives. This does not mean always agreeing with subordinates; cases will arise where decisions must be made and implemented over their objections. It does mean, however, that each employee's perspective is important and should be included in the decision process. It is included when the manager really listens, empathizes with the subordinate's perspective to know how she feels and to "walk in her shoes," and considers that perspective as an element of the decision. Such empathy fosters recognition and enables balanced and informed resolution. More important, its presence will be obvious to subordinates and will help make resolutions that seem to favor other stakeholders more acceptable.

Managers Assume Their Authority Will Prevail

Managers have the authority to direct the workforce. While legislation or the presence of a union may diminish it, their authority is nevertheless a substantial power over subordinates. In a nonunion workplace in an employment-at-will state, management has the legal right to take unilateral action of almost any type that does not violate the law. Even in a jurisdiction that does not support employment-at-will or where a union is present, an employer usually may take actions on its own initiative, and employees may protest and seek to reverse the actions only after the fact. Unfortunately, all this power seduces many managers into believing they can get their way by forcing their will on employees and dictating how conflicts will be resolved. These managers fail to acknowledge the many ways employees can resist when a decision is imposed on them.

When a decision imposed by management allegedly violates the law or a labor contract, employees have obvious, formal methods for resisting.

They may file actions with the many available agencies for enforcing employment law, file lawsuits, or proceed under the organization's ADR process (if it has one—to be discussed in the following chapter).

But the most pervasive ways of resisting are the informal ones, which are available to employees regardless of whether management is alleged to have violated a law or contract. These take many forms and can include simply refusing to support a resolution imposed by management, speaking out against it and creating morale problems, taking individual job actions that are just short of insubordination, and engaging in outright insubordination or sabotage. The impact of informal resistance can range from making the organization's performance less than it could be to bringing it to a standstill. When such resistance occurs, a manager who imposes a resolution may win the battle but lose the war.

Recognizing that management's authority may not prevail does not mean it should not be used. Instead, it means power should be used fairly, appropriately, and in collaboration with the employees involved. Chapter 3 discussed these concepts in the context of building trust to minimize conflict in the first place. The same concepts pertain when resolving existing conflict.

Managers Are Unwilling to Say No to Employees

Just as some managers try to use their authority to impose their will when resolving disagreements, others do almost anything to make employees happy, regardless of the impact on the organization. This most often happens when a supervisor has developed a close personal relationship with a subordinate or is afraid of conflict and concerned about continuing repercussions if it is not resolved to the complete satisfaction of a subordinate. In such situations, supervisors often give the relationship priority over the substance and in so doing make concessions to some employees they would not be willing to make to others or that are not in the balanced best interests of all concerned. They buy resolution without regard to the cost.

Ideally, conflict can be resolved in ways that meet the needs and wants of all parties. But this is not always the case. Sometimes when a subordinate is unhappy with a decision, management must draw the line. In deciding where to draw the line, managers should approach conflict with "detached responsibility." In *Listening to Conflict,*[17] Erik J. Van Slyke defines detached responsibility as "the ability to resolve conflict by separating the objective issues of a dispute from the personal issues. It is the process of managing the aspects of the conflict that are within your control . . . an acceptance of reality as opposed to a focus on the ideal." Detached responsibility helps balance the interests of the organization and the desire or need to make employees happy.

Supervisors and managers need to maintain detached responsibility in their relationship with subordinates—both in their normal day-to-day relationships and in dealing with conflict. This means managers must give appropriate consideration to all they do that is under their control and take action in the balanced best interests of all their stakeholders. They must treat employees fairly and with empathy but must balance this treatment with the need to avoid discriminating against other employees. And managers must also realize that while they can hope to positively influence subordinates' feelings, they cannot fix all employee problems or control how they react to a particular decision. Accordingly, they must maintain the boundaries between personal and substantive matters and be willing to stop short of completely satisfying certain employees when necessary to meet the needs of all stakeholders.

Thus, all disagreements cannot be resolved to the satisfaction of both parties, and employees may not be satisfied with a resolution management deems to be in the best interests of all concerned. When this is the case, the manager's role is to help the employee accept the decision. Causing an employee to accept a decision with which he disagrees is rarely easy, and often impossible. A manager's best hope for doing so is to balance the employee's continuing dissatisfaction with a clear, affirmative acceptance of him as a person. The manager must validate the subordinate.

Validation demonstrates that a person is valued without patronizing him. It acknowledges his right to feel the way he does, recognizes his right to perspectives and perceptions that may be different from management's, and demonstrates a willingness to consider all that he brings to the table. Effective validation allows an employee to win from the perspective of personal value and self-esteem, even if he loses on the substance of the matter in disagreement.

Validation requires appropriate management behavior throughout the entire conflict process: from the time a disagreement occurs, through resolution discussions, to the time a manager announces and implements her decision. This behavior requires managers to take understanding, empathetic actions such as the following:

- Listen carefully to everything the employee says
- Repeat the essence of the employee's communication back to her by using her key words
- Clarify by asking questions or restating points to ensure accuracy
- Use acknowledging gestures
- Paraphrase the employee's position
- Show respect for the employee's ideas and experiences
- Avoid trivializing the matter through jokes or sarcasm
- Provide contact with the most senior managers feasible
- Respect the employee's need for privacy and confidentiality
- Announce the decision firmly but with no hint of arrogance
- Acknowledge whatever right the employee has to appeal the decision

With validation, disagreements don't have to always be resolved with agreement. They also may be resolved when subordinates feel okay about accepting management's position because they feel good about themselves.

Dilemmas

A dilemma involves a choice between equally unsatisfactory alternatives. Unfortunately, employee-management disagreements often present situations where anything management does seems to be wrong. Some of the most frequently encountered dilemmas include the following:

- *Whether to hurt an employee and cause short-term conflict in order to benefit the organization in the long run.* Situations occasionally exist where interests cannot be reconciled, and it appears the only option that protects the interests of the organization also hurts an employee or employees. How should management balance the interests?

> After extensive training and coaching, a likable, committed, older employee still is only a marginal performer. Should management fire him, hurting him and his family, and risk escalating the disagreement to an age discrimination lawsuit or continue to tolerate his marginal performance?

- *Whether to be driven by precedent or creativity.* Consistently applying policy and maintaining consistent practices in similar situations help provide predictability and avoid allegations of discrimination among employees. But consistent administration often prevents viewing each conflict as unique and may drive management to insist on less-than-optimal resolution of certain conflicts. Often management must decide whether to stand by precedent and not resolve a disagreement to anyone's satisfaction or to make an exception to policy or the way things have been done in the past and accept the potential problems that creates.

Management has a policy against theft and a long history of firing anyone who steals. Should it follow precedent and fire an employee with long, commendable service who is observed taking a small tool home without authorization or find a creative option that preserves the employee's career?

- *Whether to negotiate with employees.* Negotiation in the sense of competitive bargaining—where one party asks for more than he expects and the other offers less than he is willing to provide, and through a series of concessions they meet somewhere in the middle—is not an appropriate strategy for management in dealing with employee-management disagreements. It destroys trust, favors employees who are the best negotiators, and makes management always susceptible to demands for more. But what should management do when, after it has done all it believes it should in a collaborative approach to resolving a disagreement with an employee, the conflict remains unresolved, and it is clear that a little negotiation will make the conflict go away? Should it stand by its position or make a concession to resolve the conflict and perhaps prevent a subsequent lawsuit?

In a same-sex sexual harassment allegation involving peer employees, the employer corrected a possible problem as soon as it occurred and believes it is without fault or liability. Should it offer some financial compensation to a complaining employee to make the problem go away?

There are no easy answers to these dilemmas. Management facing any one of them must consider the context and all the surrounding facts, balance the pros and cons, and make the decision it feels is best. The following principles should help in doing this:

- *Never compromise the organization's values.* Doing so may settle an immediate problem or avoid escalating one, but it will create more problems in the long run.

- *Minimize the harm.* Adhering to precedent or refusing to negotiate may be appropriate when deciding among two or more fair options for resolving a conflict. But they must not drive management to unfair or inappropriate decisions.

- *Be open and honest.* If management takes actions that hurt an employee, sticks to policy or precedent, or refuses to negotiate, be open and honest with the employee about what is happening and why.

- *Be willing to admit management error.* If a policy or practice was ill conceived, or circumstances have changed and it is now inappropriate, be open and honest about the situation and make a change.

- *Don't take the easy way out.* Making a decision that doesn't hurt an individual employee or rigidly adhering to policy or practice requires little thought, is easy, and usually is relatively safe in the short term, but it may be catastrophic in the longer term.

KEY POINTS

1. The best time for management to address conflict is at the disagreement stage. When possible, it should not allow disagreements to grow into disputes.

2. The best way to resolve disagreements is to use a collaborative, holistic process that

   • Describes the conflict accurately

   • Integrates the right people

   • Takes a systems view

   • Disaggregates the conflict

3. When dealing with conflict, managers must realize that employees don't always see the world as they do. They should avoid assuming their authority will prevail and be willing to say no when necessary and stick to it.

4. Management often faces difficult dilemmas when dealing with employee-management conflict. It must consider each one as unique and refuse to take the easy way out.

CHAPTER 11

Resolving Disputes

"The ultimate measure of a man is not where he stands in moments of comfort and convenience, but where he stands at times of challenge and controversy."

—MARTIN LUTHER KING JR.

est efforts to resolve them notwithstanding, some disagreements escalate into disputes. When this happens, management's role changes. In employee-employee conflict, it shifts from an informal coach (usually the employees' supervisor) aiming to help employees resolve their own disagreements to a counselor who insists disputes be resolved and provides more formal mechanisms for resolving them. In conflicts between employees and management, management's role shifts from an administrator seeking a fair and equitable resolution of a potential problem to an advocate who protects the organization's interest in more formal dispute resolution processes while also seeking a resolution that is fair and equitable for all.

Thoughtful managers must be aware of how much time, effort, and other resources they invest in dealing with conflicts and whether there are better approaches. If an organization does not already have a formal conflict resolution system, it should consider whether one would facilitate dispute resolution, improve organization effectiveness, and add economic value.

This chapter discusses factors management should consider in looking at available conflict resolution options and the needs of its organization to determine if a better approach is appropriate. It builds on Chapter 10's discussion of substantive ideas for resolving disagreements in an informal setting between the parties and envisions use of those same substantive ideas in the more formal and disciplined processes necessary for resolving disputes. Accordingly, it briefly reviews various process options for resolving disputes, outlines the potential benefits of formal dispute resolution systems, and presents an approach for management to use in deciding what practices it needs in its organization.[18]

DISPUTE RESOLUTION OPTIONS

As discussed in Chapter 9, one aspect of management's bifurcated conflict management role is to develop and implement a strategy for resolving disputes that provides an alternative to having employees control the process. Doing this requires a management concerned about counterproductive conflict to consider its particular circumstances and develop a strategy that uses one or more practices from a wide range of alternative dispute resolution (ADR) options. The first section below briefly discusses various options commonly used today. The second section discusses how specific practices can be used in three different ADR strategies that demonstrate increasing levels of planning, employee involvement, and cost: ad hoc practices, dispute resolution policies, and dispute resolution systems.

ADR Practices

Alternative dispute resolution is an umbrella term that covers a wide range of nonlitigious options that can be part of a dispute resolution strategy. These options include the following:

- *Open-door policy.* A formal open-door policy is often the first and least formal step in a dispute resolution system. Its goal is face-to-face, unstructured meetings, generally at the lowest feasible organizational level, that lead to agreed resolution of conflicts. It emphasizes the possibility that an early conversation among the parties, and perhaps their representatives or others, will resolve conflicts before they evolve to more significant disputes with their likely acrimony and costs. Most open-door policies not only open the chain of command to help resolve issues but also allow aggrieved parties to approach any person in the organization who is able to assist. This often includes human resources department staff, organizational thought leaders, or others who may by helpful in resolving disputes.

- *ADR policy.* A formal ADR policy statement establishes the rules for resolving disputes, provides due process, and fosters a full understanding of the dispute resolution options available to the organization's employees. Policies typically emphasize providing employees a simple, understandable procedure for resolving disputes in a fair, cost-effective manner, with guarantee of due process in disputes with management. Although due process has been variously defined and is often controversial in the workplace, it normally includes protections such as

  - Adequate notice of the employer's expectations regarding performance, behavior, and other matters relevant to the employment relationship

  - Informed and knowing acceptance of any policy that waives employee rights to judicial relief of statutory claims

  - Fair and impartial investigation of disputes

  - Access to appropriate information

  - The right to be heard and, if appropriate, to question one's accuser

  - The right to a representative of the employee's choosing, certainly in a formal decision hearing such as mediation or arbitration, and usually in the investigation. (This right is legally protected in many situations, and employers considering denying representation should probably consult with counsel.)

- *Facilitation.* Facilitation helps people resolve disputes in a relaxed, informal setting. Facilitators, who may be specially trained employees of the organization or external experts, listen to the details of a situation, ask appropriate questions, and perhaps engage in some level of fact finding. Their primary role is to work with the parties in a meeting or meetings, offer coaching, and encourage dialogue and discussion that enhance the likelihood of resolving a conflict.

- *Ombudspersons.* Ombudspersons are neutral members of the organization from outside the normal chain of command who provide confidential, informal assistance to employees in addressing workplace issues. They may serve many functions. Like an arbitrator or judge, an ombudsperson has an affirmative duty to actively encourage resolution of disputes and may take affirmative action to see that it happens. Like a mediator, he is strictly neutral and is not permitted to take sides, favor either party, or impose a resolution. And finally, like an attorney, an ombudsperson may investigate a dispute and seek information useful in resolving it. Since use of an ombudsperson is typically voluntary, she must have the complete trust of both employees and management.

- *Mediation.* Mediation may be voluntary or a requirement before escalating a dispute to other resolution processes such as arbitration or litigation. Mediation offers disputants a trained third-party neutral (who may be a trained employee or an external professional mediator) to aid them in resolving their conflict. Mediators are not empowered to impose resolutions—the parties must reach their own with the mediator's assistance—but philosophies differ as to the extent to which they should affect the result. Some more directive mediators concentrate on a current and readily identifiable dispute and, while not giving professional advice, become actively involved in the resolution process. Other "transformative" mediators concentrate more on helping the parties improve the overall workplace climate by empowering themselves and building self-esteem, with resolution of the specific disputes seen largely as a by-product of the process.

- *Arbitration.* Binding arbitration may be an alternative if the open-door policy, ombudsmanship, mediation, or other earlier resolution processes do not succeed. Arbitration is a more formal and structured process that in many ways resembles a courtroom trial. The parties typically select an arbitrator from an external panel of neutrals. The arbitrator examines evidence, hears testimony from the parties and other witnesses, and makes a final decision that all parties are bound to comply with. Appeal of the decision is limited to very special and egregious circumstances.

- *Med/arb.* Med/arb is an integration of mediation and arbitration that takes various forms, all of which aim to use the pressure imposed by a potential arbitration to motivate the parties to come to an agreement in mediation. A common variety has the parties first try to resolve a dispute with the help of a mediator, with the understanding that if they are not successful the mediator will change hats, become an arbitrator, and immediately render a decision that the parties must abide by.

- *Peer review.* Peer review panels may be used for various purposes but most often render final and binding decisions. Such panels generally comprise several specially trained peer employees and managers. Disputants typically select a predetermined number of employees from a larger panel to hear their case and render a decision, much as in arbitration.

- *Fact finding.* In neutral fact finding the parties select a third party to examine complaints, investigate the facts, and make a report. The parties may agree to be bound by the report or to use it only as advisory in their discussions. While neutral fact finding can be helpful in dispute resolution, it is not a widely used ADR practice.

- *Cost sharing.* Policies for compensating independent counsel or other cost sharing with employees who have complaints against an organization are often used as a way of easing access to an ADR process, encouraging its use, and building trust in it. Cost-sharing procedures vary but likely involve having the organization pay a substantial portion of the cost of an attorney of the employee's choice, up to an annual dollar limit.

- *Education.* Conflict management education in dispute resolution normally should be customized to fit the needs of the individuals involved, with somewhat different substance and levels of training for different groups.

  - Internal or external mediators, facilitators, and other employees who are intimately involved in dispute resolution activities may need to be trained in mediation or other appropriate conflict resolution skills or, at a minimum, in the policies and expectations of the particular organization.

  - Human resource professionals, EEO professionals, labor relations staff, and union leaders who are directly involved in the administration of programs should be trained in how they can be accessed, how they work, and how to encourage employees to use them, and perhaps also be provided an overview of dispute resolution techniques.

- Supervisors and union stewards should usually receive similar, if perhaps less detailed, training.

- The entire workforce covered by a policy should be trained in awareness of the policies and other appropriate conflict-avoiding practices such as communication and effective listening.

■ *Point person.* A conflict management point person, committee, or department is typically needed to manage the administration of a dispute resolution system that includes a significant number of the foregoing elements. The person's primary purpose is to make the system as effective and user-friendly as feasible. He typically does this through actions such as maintaining a relatively high profile, responding to employee questions, assisting with selection of third-party neutrals, maintaining a dispute resolution library and appropriate case files, and performing other duties of an administrative nature. In addition, in many cases it is appropriate for the dispute resolution point person or persons to conduct relevant training or to serve as the organization's ombudsperson.

■ *Feedback.* Feedback of appropriate, nonconfidential information from the ADR process to other management systems is essential for organizational learning. Appropriate feedback can minimize future conflict and improve the way it is resolved when it does occur. A conflict management point person is ideally situated to collect data, analyze it, and communicate it as appropriate.

ADR Strategies

Use of all these options is not likely to be appropriate in any single case; rather, management, in collaboration with employees, must decide on an ADR strategy and select those practices that support it. The following paragraphs outline three strategies that cover a range of needs. Processes appropriate for most organizations are likely to fall within this range.

Ad Hoc Alternative Dispute Resolution

In this minimal approach to ADR, management encourages employees to surface conflict, perhaps through an open-door policy or "management by walking around," and may provide training in open communications, active listening, or other such conflict-avoidance practices on an as-needed basis. Management maintains an awareness of ADR options that avoid litigation but proposes using them only on a voluntary basis after conflict surfaces.

> Management in the normal course of events becomes aware of a dispute. It encourages use of a third party to facilitate problem solving. At later stages it might encourage voluntary mediation or arbitration in lieu of employees' filing complaints with external agencies or resorting to litigation.

Ad hoc approaches provide alternatives that frequently are more effective and less risky for both parties than traditional approaches, and they can be used at a lower cost than more complex systems. However, they continue to allow disputants, rather than management, to decide what process will be used to resolve their complaints.

Dispute Resolution Policies

These policies are implemented before the fact and give management significant control over how disputes are resolved by spelling out procedures for surfacing and dealing with conflict. They must be fully communicated to all employees so that rules and expectations are clear.

> • A policy requires employees to work through the chain of command, formalizes an open-door policy, or offers assistance from the human resources department.
>
> • A policy provides for voluntary or condition-of-employment mediation and/or arbitration as a last step in resolving disputes.

While dispute resolution policies standing alone do little to minimize the occurrences or severity of conflict, they allow disputes to easily surface and make the process for resolving them more predictable, less risky, and usually less costly. Development and implementation of such policies requires both effort and cost, as they must be carefully crafted and properly administered, particularly if mediation or arbitration is to be required as a condition of employment. However, since they usually rely on employees to take the initiative and contemplate only a reactive role from management, the effort and cost associated with their ongoing administration is minimal.

Conflict Resolution Systems

Conflict resolution systems provide a clearly articulated policy with due process for all employees and a full understanding of appropriate ADR procedures. They also typically include a number of additional components, as described above, that provide a systemic process for minimizing conflict, surfacing and addressing that which occurs, and learning from the process to further minimize future conflict.

To reduce incidents of counterproductive conflict, minimize their severity, and provide effective ways to resolve disputes that do occur, conflict resolution systems must be systemic in nature. They must be a specific part of the organization's business and human resources strategy. To be viable and effective over the long term, they must be based on the idea that effective conflict management can transform a workplace, make it more efficient, and enhance the likelihood it will attain its purpose. They require significant allocation of resources—both money and people—and without a strong business driver, management is not likely to remain committed to them over the long term.

Conflict resolution systems can substantially reduce the cost of counterproductive conflict and pay real dividends to the organization, but developing, implementing, and maintaining them carries a price. To ensure optimal effectiveness, external assistance and a broad cross-section of employees should usually be involved in their development. Initial communication and training must be comprehensive and extended to all employees. In addition, ongoing administration of conflict resolution systems requires the attention of one or several employees, continuing training and education, frequent management attention, and out-of-pocket expense.

SELECTING AN ADR STRATEGY

A comprehensive dispute resolution system is the strategy most likely to minimize the effect of conflict in most workplaces. But is a comprehensive system cost-effective? Or is ad hoc alternative dispute resolution or a simple policy all that is needed or that can be economically justified in a particular situation? Each case must be evaluated on its own merits, considering all the potential benefits of ADR and the capacity and need of the organization.

ADR Benefits

ADR practices are used to resolve disputes among employees or between employees and the organization. But thinking only in terms of resolving disputes fails to recognize some of the potential benefits of ADR practices and may cause management to forgo their use or implement a narrowly focused program that misses opportunities. To avoid such pitfalls, management should take a broad perspective. It should think in terms of processes that will both minimize the cost of counterproductive conflict and contribute to organizational excellence. A broad-based system can accomplish these objectives in a number of ways. Some are concrete and easy to quantify, while others are more nebulous but nevertheless of real value. The following are the most important.

Reduces Litigation Costs

The most frequently discussed and easily quantifiable cost savings from effective conflict resolution is a reduction in litigation costs. ADR practices that surface and resolve disputes informally at an early stage and use mediation or arbitration when third-party intervention is needed avoid much of the costs normally associated with litigation. Legal costs are likely to be reduced or nonexistent, and management and employee time spent on each dispute is minimized. ADR processes such as mediation enhance the likelihood of mutually agreeable resolution, and arbitration is typically more predictable than a jury trial. More important, however, an effective ADR system addresses root causes such as systems problems, cultural differences, lack of trust, or poor communication and thereby reduces the number of disputes and the need for third-party intervention in the future.

Minimizes Wasted Time and Effort

Counterproductive conflict takes time and energy away from constructive business endeavors. Those involved in a dispute think about it, worry about it, and spend time trying to do something about it. Supervisors and managers become involved when the dispute includes them or employees need help in resolving theirs. This involvement diverts management time, energy, and attention from leadership activities that should leverage the efforts of all employees and tends to multiply the cost of disputes. An effective ADR system limits the occurrences of disputes and causes them to be handled in a more timely and efficient fashion, thereby reducing wasted time and effort by both the disputants and others.

Builds Trust in Management

Trust is an unwritten and usually unspoken contract that allows each party in a relationship to depend on the honesty, integrity, reliability, and justice of the others. Trust is necessary for an effective workforce, and its absence increases the cost of doing business by increasing adversarial activity and the costs associated with administering and enforcing policies, contracts, or laws to ensure that transactions among people are executed as expected. An effective conflict resolution system helps build trust. Allowing employees easily and inexpensively to include a third party in a contest with management demonstrates management's willingness and ability to deliver on its commitments. Shifting the focus from power-based settlement to effective problem resolution helps the parties deal with the power disparity between management and employees. More important, providing an accessible, fair, easy-to-use conflict resolution system exposes management's vulnerabilities within a setting that is reasonably predictable and controlled, thereby demonstrating to employees that management trusts them.

Enhances Bottom-Up Communication

Management frequently makes bad decisions because it fails to really listen to employees. It talks to them but does not have the inclination or systems to elicit their input or hear what they say. An effective conflict resolution system provides a process for listening and improves bottom-up communication. Consistent with confidentiality obligations, relevant data from cases handled by the system should be fed back to management. This feedback provides management valuable information to discern patterns of behavior, trends, employee concerns, or other issues existing in the workforce. More important, an ADR system should help give employees the confidence to become involved and provide direct input, because they know that any disputes that develop will be resolved fairly.

Supports Diversity

Diversity of thought in the workforce is necessary for the creativity and innovation required for optimum organizational performance. ADR systems encourage such diversity by valuing the differences that make people unique and providing a mechanism for employees to work out their differences and manage their conflicting interests in positive, respectful ways. They also help create a workplace where minorities and women prefer to work because they feel any discrimination or other inappropriate treatment will be dealt with quickly and fairly.

Fosters Cultural Change

Effective companies must change faster than the environment around them in order to stay ahead of a predictable business cycle of growth followed by decline. This means they must change their fundamental corporate culture from time to time, often at the peak of their success. Effective conflict management systems can surface problems, exhibit trends, and provide early warning of developing issues and the need for fundamental cultural change in the organization. If a system is not in place, implementing one can represent the first step toward increased openness, more employee involvement, or other fundamental changes that may be necessary for broad cultural transformation.

Fosters Confidentiality

The parties to a conflict would often prefer that its existence, related facts, and particularly its disposition remain confidential. This is not likely to happen if it is addressed through the court system or other public forum. Most ADR processes, however, are handled among the parties with very few additional individuals involved, thereby limiting the likelihood of broad public exposure. And some practices, such as mediation, have confidentiality as a cornerstone. Thus, if the parties want a dispute to be treated confidentially, it usually can be.

ADR Concerns

There are few downsides to a well-conceived and designed workplace ADR system that fits the organization's needs and is administered appropriately. Such systems are generally quite flexible and allow use of the dispute resolution method that is right for the parties and their specific disputes. They can, however, give rise to concerns in certain circumstances.

Failure to Provide External Precedent

ADR systems will not fulfill a need by either party to challenge or establish an external legal precedent. They are by their very nature internal—intended to avoid the court system where legal precedent is established—so their use precludes any effect on external precedent. If either party has a need for such precedent, ADR may thwart that need.

Inappropriate Issues

There is concern in some quarters that certain disputes, such as those raising constitutional civil rights issues, are inappropriate for private handling and should therefore be steered through the court system as a matter of public policy. It is argued that in such cases the public has an interest that can be protected only through public adjudication. The best approach seems to be in the eyes of the beholder. It can be said, however, that ethical obligations of attorneys to avoid illegal agreements and broad laws regulating corporate conduct tend to protect the public's interest in such situations and make ADR more tenable.

Management Abuse

If ADR does have a dark side, it lies in the opportunities it presents for management to abuse an otherwise good system and take unfair advantage of employees. This can occur in situations such as the following:

- When a system is forced on employees against their will and without their full understanding
- When the system's design or administration violates employees' rights to due process
- When some of the basic processes give management an undue advantage
- When internal ADR is used by management to cover up systemic management problems, irregularities, or abuses

> A system that imposes binding arbitration on employees as a condition of employment and either explicitly or de facto allows management to select the arbitrator can hardly be defended as fair.

Unfortunately, an unfair system can be an albatross around the neck of management. It takes time, costs money, often destroys trust, and creates or escalates disputes rather than solving them.

Costs

Assuming management is not deterred by more general concerns and does not abuse the system or take unfair advantage of it, the final issue to consider is whether the likely costs justify the potential benefits. That subject is discussed in the following section.

Balancing ADR Benefits and Costs

The potential benefits and concerns of ADR provide the context against which management must consider its needs and the type of conflict resolution processes that are likely to add value. Three fundamental issues must be considered.

Size of the Organization

Whether an organization is large enough to justify a dispute resolution system depends on the level of conflict, the type of system being considered, and an assessment of potential benefit as compared to costs. If the organization is small enough that the top decision maker manages the business through her direct personal relationship with employees, a formal conflict management system normally will not be used enough to offset the cost and pay dividends. Further, it could impose a potential barrier between management and employees, limit direct communication, and impede more direct resolution of conflicts. Thus, where a personal relationship drives an organization, management typically should follow good management practices, encourage employees to resolve their own disputes, and adopt an ad hoc approach to ADR, using only practices that are appropriate for individual cases when they arise.

If, on the other hand, an organization is large enough that the top decision maker does not have direct contact with all employees and instead must manage through levels of supervision, policies, and systems, a more comprehensive conflict resolution system may be a cost-effective way to improve communication, surface conflict at an early stage, and resolve it in mutually beneficial ways. When this threshold has been met, management should consider a simple dispute resolution policy or a broader conflict management system, as appropriate.

The Organization's Culture

As previously discussed, the conflict management process is really a subsystem that forms a working part of a larger management system. It is connected to other parts, and it influences and is influenced by them. Its interconnectedness is facilitated by feedback loops through which a change in how conflict is managed influences other parts of the larger management system, which then change in ways that influence how conflict is managed. Thus, for a conflict management process to be effective, it must "fit" with other parts of the management system. This fit must be founded on a common purpose, similar values, and complementary practices.

An effective conflict resolution process must embody characteristics of a collaborative, involved workplace: it must be based on and encourage trust, be open, and facilitate a free flow of information while at the same time respecting the confidentiality of employees and empowering them to resolve many of their own issues. A conflict resolution system will not be effective unless it is part of a broader workplace system with similar characteristics. If a conflict resolution system transmits or receives influences that are fundamentally inconsistent with characteristics of other systems, both management and employees will be confused, and the system may create conflict rather than manage it. Even when individual disputes are resolved, the broad, systemic improvements that make a dispute resolution system more cost-effective are not likely to occur. Thus, a comprehensive system should not be implemented unless it fits the existing corporate culture or is part of a plan to transform the culture so there will be a fit.

> If a workplace is completely devoid of trust, employees will see ADR as manipulative and an effort by management to gain the upper hand. Accordingly, they will resist using it and destroy its effectiveness.

Level of Conflict

Comprehensive conflict management systems take time and commitment and cost money to develop, implement, and maintain. Both costs and benefits are difficult to quantify, and management often faces a chicken-egg dilemma: it cannot assess the cost-benefit relationship without understanding the details of a system for its situation, but it is reluctant to incur the cost and distraction of a detailed needs analysis and preliminary design unless it expects the value to exceed the cost. A logical starting point for dealing with this dilemma is to do a preliminary screen of business need as a prerequisite for further action.

Organizations can do an initial screen of their need for better conflict management by assessing the significance of the following potential concerns:

- Challenges to management actions or policies
- Disputes between employees or groups
- Employee disputes with external stakeholders
- Disputes with major organizational impact
- Employee disciplinary actions
- Employee time involved with conflict issues
- Management time devoted to conflict issues

- Dissatisfaction after conflict settlement
- Recurrence of similar conflicts
- Antagonistic dealings with labor leaders
- Complaints filed with external agencies
- Litigation-handling costs
- Settlement/judgment costs

A preliminary assessment should be done by a small number of informed managers, supervisors, and employees working either individually or in a group. Each potential issue should be considered separately, and a judgment should be made as to whether it is a significant concern. If there is consensus that no factor is an issue, maintaining good management practices and using ad hoc approaches to resolve disputes is probably the best approach. If, on the other hand, there is occasional concern about a large number of factors or even one or a few are considered excessive, further action is probably appropriate. This action should include more extensive organizational diagnosis, a preliminary systems design, an estimate of the expected costs and benefits of an effective system, and a decision as to whether or not to go forward.

KEY POINTS

1. When conflict escalates from disagreement to dispute, management's role shifts from coach or administrator to counselor or advocate.

2. Management should have a thoughtful strategy for handling workplace disputes. Effective strategies often include alternative dispute resolution, which covers a wide range of non-litigious options.

3. Three dispute resolution strategies that span the range of possibilities are

   • Ad hoc alternative dispute resolution

   • Dispute resolution policies

   • Conflict resolution systems

4. There are pros and cons to various ADR strategies. When balancing the benefits and costs in deciding what approach to take, management should consider the following:

   • The size of the organization

   • The organization's culture

   • The level of conflict

5. A needs analysis helps assess the pros and cons of using a dispute resolution system.

CHAPTER 12

Learning from Conflict

"Freedom to learn is the first necessity of guaranteeing that man himself shall be self-reliant enough to be free."

—FRANKLIN D. ROOSEVELT

The unbelievably fast pace of change is perhaps the most striking feature of today's business environment. To thrive—or even remain viable—in this environment, organizations must adapt to the new world and change themselves before change is forced on them. They cannot rely on their current knowledge and static, backward-looking strategies that foster doing old things in old ways. Instead, they must expect all employees to try new things, learn from their experiences, and contribute this learning to the organization so that new challenges can be met with innovative ways of doing things.

Employees and organizations must learn from everything that happens—from their successes, their failures, and their conflicts. Conflict almost always surfaces differing information, beliefs, and ideas; the motivation to try to reconcile them; and the need to either confirm the value of the status quo or initiate needed change. What better environment for learning!

This chapter briefly reviews some important concepts of organizational learning and discusses how managers can use conflict resolution to attain it.

LEARNING IN ORGANIZATIONS

We all understand that individuals can learn, and we have a general idea of how they do it. But how can organizations—groupings of people ranging from a legal entity to just a bunch of individuals with only a tenuous tie— be said to learn? A brief discussion of organizations, learning, and how the two work together explores this question as a context for later discussion of how conflict management and dispute resolution can foster both individual and organizational learning. This discussion draws heavily on the work of Chris Argyris in *On Organizational Learning,*[19] Argyris and Donald Schön in *Organizational Learning II,*[20] Peter Senge in *The Fifth Discipline,*[21] Arie de Geus in *The Living Company,*[22] and the various contributors to the Harvard Business Review's *Knowledge Management.*[23]

Organizations

An organization is a body of persons brought together for some work or for a particular end. It is composed of individuals and has many characteristics of a person but is more than an individual or even a collection of individuals. An organization has its own purpose, interests, reputation, personality, and values, each of which may be different from those of many of the individuals in it. A typical organization usually has more resources and more power than any individual or the aggregate of the individuals it comprises

Most organizations have several supporting layers. Individuals form small groups, small groups aggregate to form larger groups or departments, departments aggregate to form larger groups or divisions, and so on. While all layers are part of the organization, each also forms a separate organization with its own characteristics, interests, values, mental models, and ability to act and learn. Thus, individuals have a dual citizenship in which they are part of both their organizational layer and the larger organization. From the viewpoint of a particular group, the other groups are part of the "they" that comprises the external environment. Each layer in effect becomes its own organization, with an ability to decide, act, and learn that is different from the individuals in it and the larger organization of which it is a part.

A manufacturing facility is one entity, pursuing a clear purpose, and all employees are part of it. Its group of production workers has many interests in common with the facility's management, but it also has many that are different, and it views the management team as a separate entity for many purposes.

Several factors combine to make an organization a holistic entity that has many characteristics of its individual members but also is more than the sum of those characteristics. The following paragraphs discuss three such areas that are critical for organizational learning.

Making Decisions

For a group of individuals to become an organization, they must develop agreeable processes for making decisions that are attributable to the group as a whole and delegate to individuals the authority to make those decisions. Developing decision processes and establishing authority is done in different ways in various organizations. It may be done by direct vote of all the individuals in political organizations, while the owners may select certain individual members to make all the decisions in business organizations. Individuals with power, financial or otherwise, make the decisions in other organizations. Regardless of how the process is developed, however, the organization as an entity separate from its individual members is said to make decisions for itself.

Communication material states, "The company decided to implement a new salary policy." But the decision was actually made by an individual or individuals according to the organization's decision processes.

Taking Actions

When decisions are made, organizations can also act. Although the organization's individual agents actually take the actions, they are attributed to the organization, where they become part of a pattern of activity seen, in the aggregate, as belonging to the organization.

We frequently say, "The company implemented a policy," "Management investigated the dispute," or "The agency responded to an employee's complaint."

Holding Knowledge

Knowledge is an acquaintance with facts, truths, or principles. Individuals can hold knowledge. Organizations can also, and the most important way is in the minds of individual employees through knowledge they bring to their jobs and which they learn throughout their work life. Their knowledge tends to be passed from employee to employee, but they often forget what they know or leave the organization and take it with them. When either happens, knowledge is lost to the organization unless it is held in other, more permanent, ways.

Fortunately, organizations do have other options for holding knowledge. They hold it in their files, which not only reflect history but also record regulations, policies, and decisions that help provide the information and knowledge that tell employees what to do and how to behave. Knowledge also is held in the form of belief systems, rules of thumb, and established practices and routines, written or unwritten, that guide day-to-day action. And finally, organizational knowledge is held in actual physical objects in the workplace that indicate to employees how they should act.

- Closed doors say stay out.
- Office size tells who is considered most important.
- A computer on every desk suggests how decisions should be made.

Some of the knowledge held by organizations, such as written operating policies, is explicit and open for all to see and understand. Other knowledge, like beliefs and values, is tacit or private and often more difficult to discern. All these characteristics combine, however, to make organizations capable of holding knowledge and establishing their own identity over time.

Learning

Learning is a noun as well as a word that expresses the action of a verb. Learning is the process of acquiring knowledge or skill, and the knowledge or skill acquired by that process. When used as part of a verb, we think of experience, reading, listening, training, or other such activities through which our store of knowledge is increased. As a noun we think of the result of such activities; the new understandings, the accumulation of information, or the additional skills attained through the learning process. Learning is of various types and it occurs in various ways.

Individual and Organizational Learning

All of us have experienced individual learning. Our parents teach us and we learn. We go to school and learn, and we have experiences and learn from them. This learning goes into our store of knowledge and helps make us who we are. The same can be said of organizations. They hold knowledge and can be said to learn when their store of knowledge is increased. Individual members of the organization, in the aggregate, can increase the store of knowledge by learning more and staying around to contribute that knowledge. The store of knowledge can also be increased when policies, procedures, practices, and values that form the repositories of knowledge are improved to better reflect current reality and to provide better guidance for individual and organizational actions.

The organization itself does not perform the acts from which it learns. Rather, individuals perform them, usually acting as the organization's agents. Organizational learning occurs when the learning from those individual acts is embedded in the minds of a critical mass of employees, in the organization's policies, procedures, or practices, or in its physical objects. The learning is productive if it leads to improvement in the performance of the organization's tasks or to an informed reassessment of the types of performance and behavior that are needed.

Single-Loop and Double-Loop Learning

Single-loop learning deals primarily with making the current organization more effective. It does not address its underlying principles or values but instead addresses the strategies and actions that are derived from those principles or values.

> Single-loop learning concerns the operation of a machine, but it doesn't address why the machine is being used or why the particular product is being made.

Double-loop learning is more fundamental. It addresses the underlying beliefs, principles, and values of the learning parties, not necessarily those that are espoused, but those that are actually held and may be inferred. Double-loop learning reflects the thinking beneath the surface of employee behavior, which allows fundamental, long-term change to occur in that behavior.[24]

> Two employees are involved in continual arguing and backstabbing. Double-loop learning addresses not only their behavior, but also their different cultural perspectives and underlying values as well as organizational systems that contribute to the behavior.

Both single-loop and double-loop learning are necessary for an effective organization, as it must continually improve its own day-to-day performance while at the same time engaging in the fundamental systemic change necessary to remain viable and grow over the long term.

Synergistic Learning

Learning involves acquiring knowledge, but different kinds of knowledge can work together to create new knowledge that is more than the sum of the parts. This happens through a spiral of knowledge based on the dynamic interaction of tacit and explicit knowledge.[25] Tacit knowledge is private and difficult to communicate in words. It often consists of skills that guide employees in their day-to-day work but also may include the beliefs, perspectives, and mental models that we all hold in our minds. Explicit knowledge, on the other hand, is expressed, easily communicated systemic knowledge, such as that held in product specifications, corporate policies, or safety procedures.

This distinction suggests four basic types of learning. Tacit knowledge, while informal and hard to articulate, can be shared between employees, as where one employee learns a skill by working with another over a period of time. Explicit knowledge can be more directly shared as is or reshaped into new forms and shared, such as when an accountant combines financial numbers and communicates a picture of the organization's financial situation. Both of these types of learning are important because they spread information to more people and expand the organization's ability to use it. Their value is limited, however. Tacit knowledge usually can be transferred only to those in personal contact with the holder of the knowledge. More important, both tacit and explicit knowledge are finite, and their transfer does not create new knowledge.

The interaction of tacit and explicit knowledge fosters the synergy that creates the real power of learning. When tacit knowledge is made explicit, it can be communicated, broadly shared, and leveraged across an organization. Thus, converting tacit knowledge to explicit knowledge expands the number of people who can benefit from it. And when explicit knowledge is shared and employees begin to internalize it, they combine it with their existing tacit knowledge to further enhance their skills and beliefs. This combination allows them to do their jobs better in the future. Their enlarged store of tacit knowledge can then be made explicit, communicated, and further leveraged across the organization in a powerful cycle of synergistic learning.

A teacher has for many years been recognized as the best in the school (tacit knowledge), yet she is able to transfer her teaching skills only to the few team teachers who work directly with her and observe her in action (tacit to tacit). Finally she is given a leave of absence to think deeply about her own success and how she teaches and to prepare written ideas and guidelines for other teachers (tacit to explicit). All the other teachers study these guidelines (explicit to explicit), adopt the ideas that fit for them, and develop new skills and ways of teaching that are even better (explicit to tacit).

Learning Organizations

A learning organization—one that is "skilled at creating, acquiring, and transferring knowledge, and at modifying its behavior to reflect new knowledge and insights"[26]—results when good learning processes and a receptive work environment meet. Individuals engage in both single-hoop and double-loop learning and transfer both tacit and explicit knowledge. And they do so in ways that increase the store of knowledge in the organization as a whole. The increased knowledge is in the aggregate of the knowledge of its individuals: in its policies, procedures, and institutions, and in the physical objects that make up the workplace and affect how people in it act. When this happens, the organization begins to live. It fosters new and expanded ways of thinking, and its people continually expand their capacity to create and learn together.

A river is a helpful metaphor for a living organization.[27] When drops of rain fall from the sky and end up in a hole, they stay where they are and become part of a puddle. As more drops fall, the puddle grows larger, but it stays in the same place and retains its same characteristics until it turns to mud, dries up, and disappears. When drops flow to a river, however, they are continually moving. Some evaporate and others move to the sea, but they are replaced with new drops, which in turn become an integral part of the river and ultimately pass on. Although rivers change continually and are never the same from day to day, they form continuing fixtures of the landscape, and their effects on the landscape are much more than the sum of the drops of water in them. A river is a self-perpetuating community with continuity derived from individual parts entering and leaving.

Effective organizations are like rivers. When individuals learn, they don't act like a puddle and hold the learning to themselves. Instead, they contribute their lessons to the organization like raindrops entering a river. Just as a river is more than the sum of the raindrops in it, an effective organization is more that the sum of its individuals. It is a living, changing, growing entity that continually absorbs new knowledge, uses it effectively, passes it on when it is outdated or no longer of value, and absorbs new knowledge to replace it. The organization continually learns.

To be of value, however, learning must cause positive change in the organization and the behavior of its employees. New knowledge must be translated into new ways of acting and doing that are better than they were in the past. From a conflict perspective, learning is of value when it results in lower levels of counterproductive conflict or better ways of resolving it in the future.

Learning from Conflict

Conflict frequently is a sign that something is wrong in an organization. It suggests an organization or its people may be operating with an ineffective knowledge base, or that the organization has become stagnant, like a puddle, and is not responding to the changing environment. Some approaches to dealing with conflict only exacerbate the situation.

> Management responds to a dispute by repressing it to the extent feasible and then, when repression no longer works, by unilaterally implementing and enforcing new regulations. The result is that nothing is learned, and the level of conflict increases in the future.

Fortunately, addressing conflict can provide new knowledge: knowledge that, like the new raindrops that replenish a river, becomes part of the organization and helps make it a viable, living entity that is more than the sum of its parts. To attain this result, however, management must do more than solve specific problems or make peace between individual disputing parties. Instead, it must view conflict and its resolution as a reciprocal process that both affects and is affected by the larger organization.

Management must ensure that what is learned from conflict does not cause the organization to close in, hunker down, and begin to die but instead causes it to grow, improve, and become more vibrant. It must handle learning—one phase of the "minimize, surface, resolve, and learn" model of conflict management—as a cycle within itself, comprising four phases:

- *Event.* A conflict event is a disagreement or dispute that negatively affects the parties or their organization. It engenders a level of dissatisfaction sufficient to cause one or both parties to surface it and try to get it resolved.

- *Analysis.* In the analysis phase, people investigate the circumstances that may have caused the event. They discuss what happened or is happening, interview witnesses or other third parties, and examine evidence. Someone may research files to determine what the rules are and how such situations were handled in the past, and, in extreme cases, lawyers may be consulted to determine what legal constraints or requirements could affect resolution.

- *Decision.* The parties decide what to do about a conflict event after the analysis is done. Hopefully they are able to use the information from the analysis to collaboratively develop a solution that meets all their needs. In some cases, however, management considers the information available to it, makes its own decision, and enforces it. If the employees involved do not accept the decision, they may refer it to an additional process involving a third party. They may employ mediation, where the parties make their own decision, or arbitration or litigation, where a third party decides what will be done.

- *Implementation.* Someone implements decisions after they are made. In simple disagreements between peers, implementation may be limited to changes in private behavior. But in more significant disputes, or in conflict between employees and management, implementation often is more public and affects more people.

In stagnant organizations, the four phases represent a linear, retrospective process: a clear reinforcement of the fundamental status quo and a strategy to perpetuate it by solving existing disputes without learning from the past to change the future. The process is suggested by Figure 12.

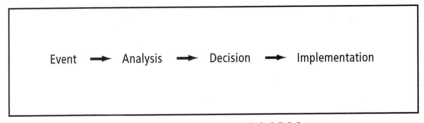

Figure 12 CONFLICT RESOLUTION PROCESS:
STAGNANT ORGANIZATION

In a learning organization, however, conflict causes management to consider changes in practice, new policies, or introduction of new physical objects into the work environment. These changes then become part of the knowledge base that establishes a new context for future relationships, determines whether future conflict grows or doesn't grow, and affects what the new events will be. This cycle of learning from conflict is shown in Figure 13.

The event initiates the other phases and determines how they are handled. In a learning organization, the analysis, decision, and implementation phases are not linear but instead circle back to help define future events. Learning from the resolution cycle helps build a workplace with less conflict. And what future conflict does occur is more substantive than personal, leading to productive synergy and improved organizational performance.

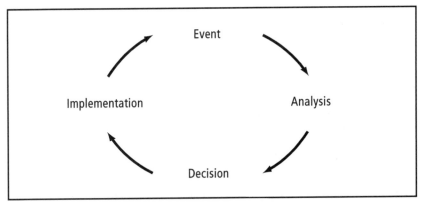

Figure 13 CONFLICT RESOLUTION CYCLE:
LEARNING ORGANIZATION

An effective management uses this cycle to resolve conflict events and to foster organizational learning that works like a river. Doing so requires an appropriate conflict resolution environment: one that both maximizes the opportunities for learning and minimizes the impediments to it.

Learning Environment

Like a seed ready to sprout, the conflict learning cycle is of little value unless it exists in an environment conducive to learning and improvement—one that helps the dispute resolution process acquire new ideas and knowledge and transfer them to the organization and its people so their future behavior changes. This represents the last leg in the "minimize, surface, resolve, learn" conflict management cycle, and without this feedback of new ideas and knowledge, learning does not occur.

Just as there are many opportunities for learning from conflict and its resolution, there are impediments—the most important of which is management itself. Managers are well positioned to stifle learning, and they often are reluctant to resolve conflict in ways that the organization learns and benefits from. Conflict often involves threats or confrontations that engender feelings of embarrassment, vulnerability, fear, or incompetence. Managers often deal with these feelings by becoming defensive, trying to cover up their distress, and talking about only the obvious facts. They keep private their personal feelings, beliefs, inferences, or conclusions that are critical to really understanding conflict and addressing it in the long term. When this happens, only single-loop learning takes place, and it fails to address the underlying causes in ways that could help the organization learn.

Unfortunately, defensive thinking can become a downward cycle. The symptoms of conflict, but not the real causes, are addressed, and the immediate threat goes away. Since the underlying causes were not addressed, however, similar conflict occurs again, and the parties behave even more defensively because they know how to make the immediate threat go away. And the cycle continues.

Argyris has noted that there seems to be a universal human tendency to design one's actions consistently according to the need to

- Remain in unilateral control
- Maximize "winning" and minimize "losing"
- Suppress negative feelings

- Be as "rational" as possible, which means people defining clear objec- ives and evaluating their behavior in terms of whether or not they have achieved their objective[28]

When parties to conflict and its resolution engage in such activities, they may feel they are protecting themselves, but they are instead closing the feedback loop that is necessary for learning. To create an environment conducive to learning, management must prevent conflict from merely being swept under the rug or settled in whatever ways make it conve- niently disappear, only to reappear when time passes, people's behavior reverts to old habits, or circumstances change. Each conflict event—and, more important, patterns of events—must be addressed thoughtfully and with discipline to ensure that both individual and organizational learning actually take place.

INDIVIDUAL LEARNING

Building a learning organization is not simply a matter of introducing objective information directly into an organization's systems. Rather, orga- nizational learning flows from individual learning—from the objective information and the highly subjective insights, intuition, hunches, and skills people acquire and make available to the organization as a whole. Thus, without individual learning there is no organizational learning.

Fortunately, opportunities for individual learning abound. The most obvious are the various training programs that most organizations make available, such as classroom, online, and on-the-job training. Although crit- ically important, these are largely vehicles for spreading existing knowledge (explicit to explicit, or tacit to tacit) rather than for actually learning new knowledge. Therefore, they will not be discussed here. Instead, the follow- ing sections will consider how management can create new knowledge and improve individual learning through its handling of conflict.

Learning Through the Spiral of Knowledge

To create a spiral of knowledge from conflict, management must (1) han- dle conflict events so that tacit knowledge becomes explicit, (2) communi- cate to more employees, and (3) help employees internalize the new ex- plicit knowledge and make it tacit and second nature. There are several ways management can accomplish these objectives.

Surface Conflict

Conflict comes in a variety of forms. As discussed in Chapter 8, some is public and available for all employees to see, know about, and learn from. Some is acknowledged between the parties but is private and hidden from the public. Other conflict is suppressed and never acknowledged. Each party privately knows that a grievance exists but refuses to acknowledge it to the other parties, and others in the organization are not aware of it.

People can learn from all varieties of conflict, but the value and breadth of learning usually increase as the conflict becomes more public. Learning is limited, and often counterproductive, when conflict is suppressed and the participants ignore one another in the hope it will go away. They generally avoid confrontation, tolerate or accommodate the other party, or engage in camouflaged self-help. When this happens, only the disputants learn, and they generally only learn how to be more effective in their counterproductive behavior. They acquire tacit knowledge, which unfortunately may be spread to others in close contact as they observe the behavior and tend to imitate it.

Conversely, when conflict is acknowledged and addressed, productive learning usually takes place. Acknowledging conflict makes it explicit, so disputants can talk about it, address more issues, and create new knowledge. The parties learn how they should behave in the future, and their work in resolving disputes improves their conflict resolution skills.

The most learning occurs when conflict and its resolution are made public. While at times there is a need for confidentiality, it often is quite appropriate to publicize information about conflict to make it explicit and more available to learn from.

- *Suppressed conflict:* A woman feels a man is harassing her. She doesn't acknowledge the situation or confront him but instead avoids contact whenever possible. She learns to tolerate the situation by avoiding it, and the man "learns" that his behavior is acceptable.
- *Acknowledged conflict:* The woman uses the organization's conflict resolution system to privately confront the man. She learns that she has misinterpreted his actions, and he learns that his behavior appears to be harassing. Both behave differently in the future.
- *Public conflict:* Management keeps records of such incidents and periodically discusses them with all employees in general terms that respect the confidentiality of the disputants as part of its harassment training, so the broader organization learns.

Deal with Emotions

Emotions are an important part of most conflict. They represent its often unconscious or spontaneous aspects, which are driven by impulses or feelings such as hate, loneliness, happiness, displeasure, guilt, insecurity, humiliation, disdain, fear, love, or anger. Emotions may be expressed directly and verbally or in nonverbal body language or held inside and not expressed at all.

Emotion represents tacit knowledge. It is private, based on a person's perceptions, beliefs, and mental models, and often is not easily expressed. Often the attitude that feelings are bad and that the display of emotions should be avoided leads to a tendency to be secretive. When pressure must be released, it is often in the form of private venting to similarly situated parties who are not positioned to do anything with the new knowledge.

To foster learning, management must facilitate the transfer of the tacit knowledge inherent in the emotional aspects of conflict to explicit knowledge that can be conveyed to others. The first step in accomplishing this is for management to convey, through how it acts and what it says, that emotions are a normal and acceptable part of human behavior that it accepts and is willing to try to understand. Such attitude and actions by management hopefully will cause disputants to believe at a cognitive level that the potential rewards from discussing their emotions exceed the potential dangers of releasing them because other employees and management itself will listen carefully and without bias and respond appropriately. After their emotions are released, the parties are in a better frame of mind to explore the reasons for their emotions and what should be done to address them. They can deal with the underlying facts that prompted the feelings and take actions that address the true causes of the conflict.

Surfacing and addressing emotions fosters learning in two ways. First, experiencing success in dealing with emotion builds confidence and self-esteem among those directly involved. This can begin a self-reinforcing cycle of learning in which emotion leads to discussion, which leads to learning, which in turn increases the likelihood that future emotion will be a learning experience. And second, the process surfaces facts and information, transforming tacit knowledge to explicit knowledge, which can be expressed, communicated, and made part of the organization's systems. When this happens, the organization learns.

Resolve Conflict Slowly

Management's goals in conflict resolution should be not only to resolve the immediate issues, but also to improve the skills and ability of the disputants, other employees, and the organization. The interaction of tacit and explicit knowledge helps attain this goal, but it requires time—often more than would be necessary to just solve a dispute. Parties to a conflict often possess different information, perceptions, and skills and also are generally aware of some of the same information, but struggling to articulate it. Effective learning requires surfacing and articulating all this tacit knowledge and reconciling differences so that it becomes explicit and transferable to other employees. Two concepts are important in accomplishing this:

- Dialogue allows people to think together in analyzing a shared problem or creating new knowledge. Participants in dialogue are not out to win. Instead, they suspend their assumptions, explore their different perspectives, and attempt to discover an entirely new perspective. Dialogue can be used at all levels of dispute resolution. At the initial, informal level, management can ask questions, listen, be open to various options, and share its views as options and possibilities rather than dictates. If this is not enough, and a formally facilitated dialogue or mediation is required, management can encourage use of a transformative approach.[29] This approach concentrates less on resolving the specific issues and more on encouraging a dialogue that empowers the parties and helps each recognize the perspectives of the other.

- Redundancy contemplates involving more people in the resolution process than are necessary to simply resolve a presenting conflict. Since different people are privy to different information or are able to articulate information that others are struggling to articulate, having more people involved surfaces more information, makes it explicit, and leads to more learning. More employee involvement also spreads new explicit knowledge more broadly across the organization. Redundancy can be accomplished by including representatives of the disputants in the resolution processes, by using large group problem-solving techniques, or by asking several groups to develop competing options. Group processes should, of course, be carefully managed to foster synergy, respect confidentiality needs, and avoid the type of "group think" that only solidifies the status quo.

Dialogue and redundancy require more time than attempts to just solve a particular problem, and they can delay the resolution process. But they contribute to organizational learning and improvement in ways that just solving a presenting problem cannot.

Fostering Double-Loop Learning

Parties resolving conflict as a matter of course usually determine what happened and confirm it or agree to a new and better way. This typically results in single-loop learning for the individuals involved and is necessary for resolving conflict and managing an organization. But considering only the facts of what happened misses the opportunities inherent in double-loop learning, which not only considers what happened but also challenges the disputants' underlying beliefs, principles, and values as well as the systems contributing to their behavior. With single-loop learning, only behavior can change. With double-loop learning, both systems and behavior can change concurrently. Management can do several things to foster double-loop learning in the dispute resolution process.

Address Systems Causes of Conflict

The single-loop learning approach is straightforward and often easy, but it does not address the underlying causes. To really learn from conflict resolution, those involved must be more disciplined and push beyond the superficial, personal symptoms. They must consider the highly interdependent parts of the organization and see both the details and the big picture. With respect to the conflict itself, they must insist on accurate and precise data rather than perceptions and assumptions and continually ask why things happened, the why behind the why, and how one knows his conclusions are true. They must look for answers beyond the usual places and consider how all the organization's systems are allowing or motivating the conflictive behavior.

- *Single-loop learning:* Employees in a small department with a four-shift operation have a high absenteeism rate, causing continuing conflict with their supervisor. The supervisor maintains records, counsels employees, and occasionally administers discipline in an attempt to correct the absence problem.
- *Double-loop learning:* The supervisor looks more deeply into the problem and notes that when an employee is absent, the vacancy is filled by calling out an employee from another shift at a double-time pay rate. Thus, being absent from scheduled work and later working to cover another employee's absence is financially advantageous. The system for covering absences needs correcting.

Minimize Defensive Thinking

Defensive thinking and the behavior that follows are primary impediments to double-loop learning. Defensiveness leads the disputing parties to try to address the symptoms, settle the matter, and get rid of the problem without using the double-loop logic that addresses the more fundamental issues. Management's objective is to foster productive rather than defensive thinking through actions such as the following:

- Create a safe environment for conflict resolution. Threats and perceived vulnerability lead to defensive thinking. Safety encourages deeper thinking and dialogue that leads to double-loop learning. Many factors, such as willingness of supervisors to listen, a history of fair dealing, and the presence of mutual trust, determine whether employees feel safe in dealing with conflict. Perhaps the most important, however, is the presence of a conflict resolution system that ensures employees' right to due process in the resolution of their concerns. This protection against arbitrary actions goes a long way toward eliminating defensiveness.

- Deal in tough reasoning rather than emotion. Emotion tends to be subjective, arbitrary, uncertain, and threatening. Dealing in valid data, analyzing it carefully, and drawing appropriate and defensible inferences removes much of the uncertainty and brings an element of predictability to the process. It allows employees to feel safer when looking beneath the surface and engaging in double-loop learning.

- Lead by revealing management's own vulnerabilities and avoiding its own defensive thinking. Doing so sets an example that employees are likely to follow.

Consider Management's Responsibility

Managers usually see themselves as in charge, able to decide what, how, and when things will be done, and employees often are unable or unwilling to challenge these decisions. Because managers are so rarely questioned, they rarely learn from their mistakes. When disputes arise, they tend to look beyond themselves for the cause. They screen out criticism, assume the blame must belong to someone else, and concentrate on the symptoms they see in others rather than the real cause, which could be in themselves. Their ability to learn is shut down by their own power. The only learning possible is that which addresses the event itself but does not look underneath for the fundamental issues that could bring positive change. This is like looking for a lost ring only where the light is brightest. It may be there, but the fact that this is the easiest place to look doesn't mean it will be.

For double-loop learning to take place, management must also be willing to look at itself, where the light is not so bright. This is not to say that management is responsible for all conflict. But it must be open to the possibility that its agents, processes, or systems are to blame even when the symptoms do not necessarily make its culpability obvious. When it is resolving disputes, management must look underneath the obvious and consider the effect of its behavior, principles, and values. Are they still appropriate and valid in today's changing world of work? Are they causing counterproductive conflict, either directly or indirectly? And if they are no longer valid and are causing problems, what can be done about revising them? Management can learn at two levels only if it honestly considers such fundamental issues about itself.

Separate Personal Conflict from Substantive Conflict

Much conflict is personality based and fueled by emotion. Those involved are not in control of their own lives, believe they are not valued or treated appropriately, and perceive threats to their self-esteem. Dealing with such human aspects of conflict is important, as doing so addresses important issues such as the event, the emotions, how people acted, and how they should act in the future. But dealing with just these aspects generally fosters only single-loop learning.

Conflict usually involves much more than the personality differences that can be seen on the surface. It also involves substantive differences, and addressing them fosters double-loop learning. Effectively addressing substantive issues requires cross-fertilization of ideas and the collaboration of people who receive different messages from the same words, make different observations about the same events, and use their cognitive skills to address ideas, decisions, principles, and directions. This can happen only if the parties separate the personality issues from the substantive issues and concentrate on both types independently on their own merits. Personal conflict can be dealt with by using techniques that foster changes in how individuals think and act. Substantive differences can be addressed with problem-solving or other appropriate approaches.

ORGANIZATIONAL LEARNING

Double-loop learning and the spiral of knowledge are important, but the knowledge they build is of limited value if it is confined to the people involved in a conflict. To be of maximum value, new knowledge must be embedded in the minds of a critical mass of the organization's members and its institutional memory in ways that last a long time and cause smart decisions, rather than mistakes, to be repeated.

Embedding Learning in the Minds of Individuals

Individuals may learn and still work at cross-purposes. When some individuals learn and others do not, a misalignment may be created that causes conflict. Thus, organizational learning requires that knowledge be embedded in the minds of a critical mass of employees so they can begin to function as a whole. When all individuals become more aligned, a common direction emerges, less energy is wasted, synergy occurs, and the organization's performance improves.

Conflict learning may be embedded in a critical mass of people by involving as many individuals as feasible in the resolution process, and by communicating the resulting learning to others who cannot be directly involved. The value of employee involvement in creating new knowledge through the spiral of knowledge was discussed earlier, and it is no less important as a way of spreading knowledge. It keeps recurring because it is so valuable for so many reasons.

Involvement provides actual experiences that teach employees and embeds the learning in their minds in ways that simple telling cannot. It teaches them conflict resolution and problem-solving skills, substantive information about issues of concern, what is expected, and how they should behave in the future. More important, all this combines to teach them that they usually have the ability to resolve their own issues and can do so with appropriate effort. The value of such learning is leveraged by involving as many people as feasible through group processes. The organization learns when enough individuals form a critical mass that learns.

Unfortunately, considerations such as cost, time, and confidentiality must be balanced in the decision process, and they may dictate less rather than more employee involvement. When this happens, learning must be communicated to the extent feasible through normal communication and training channels. While such communication is less effective than the actual experience, it does make a broader group of employees more aware.

> A conflict management point person could communicate appropriately worded explanations (respecting confidentiality) of conflict issues electronically to all supervisors or, if appropriate, all employees, or an intranet bulletin might feature learnings from resolved conflicts.

Ad hoc communication is valuable, but planned, strategic training is key to ensuring a critical mass of employees learn from conflict and its resolution. Such training should address two fundamental issues. First, it should address any job or behavior deficiencies that become apparent through the conflict resolution process. Much conflict results from such deficiencies, and appropriate emphasis on root causes should ferret it out. When it does, training should be considered a primary method of remedying the deficiencies.

Second, after the root causes are addressed, it may be appropriate to provide training on basic conflict management skills. Such training should be customized to benefit the target audience and might include topics ranging from conflict theory to more practical skills for dealing with disagreements and disputes in the day-to-day work environment. Details of the training should be guided by what is learned from the conflict resolution process.

Embedding Learning in Organizational Systems

Organizational learning also occurs when new knowledge is embedded in the organization's systems and processes. This can be done in several ways.

Fix the Root Cause

When only the symptoms of a conflict are addressed, the learning isn't embedded in the organization, and people thus do the same things time and again. But when root causes—the most basic reason or reasons the conflict occurred, which if eliminated would have prevented the occurrence—are addressed, the organization's systems that influence how employees behave are considered and adjusted. When this happens, employees are motivated in a different direction and behave differently in the future.

The process for addressing root cause will depend on the circumstances. Much conflict is relatively limited in scope and organizational impact, so all that is needed is to implicitly consider root cause as a normal part of the resolution process. This means never taking for granted that things are what they appear to be on the surface, and pursuing not only what happened, but also how it happened and, more important, why it happened—at progressively more basic levels.

Experience, intuition, and logic are essential to deciding what "why" questions to ask and to arriving at an answer. Quite often, the circumstances or causes of conflict are veiled; their influence is hidden, and they do not surface readily. Once the underlying whys are discovered, however, this information can be objectively assessed as part of the decision process addressing what to do systemically to reduce future conflict.

> Two employees are continually arguing over their workloads and who does what work. Why? Because one is paid less than the other and feels he is being paid too little in comparison. Why? Because the supervisor never explained the reason for the pay difference to him. Why? Because the pay system is ad hoc, and there is no objective reason for the pay difference that the supervisor can defend.

Other situations have greater impact and justify a more structured approach. This may be the case when a single conflict event has major organizational impact or when patterns of similar conflict persist over time. Situations of these types are likely to have organizational consequences that justify a more disciplined, structured approach to learning: one that explicitly amasses a body of experience, interprets that experience, and changes behavior.

> - A class action lawsuit, a major lawsuit filed by an individual employee, or a strike can have major effects on an organization.
> - A continuing series of "small" sexual harassment complaints or persistent violations of a particular policy set the stage for a major problem.

Analysis techniques often used by the quality, safety, and engineering professions to address workplace accidents or other operating problems provide guidance on addressing such major issues. These "prevention solutions" go beyond fixing things to preventing recurrence of the same or similar problems. A number of techniques are used, many of which are probably not appropriate for conflict resolution. We can, however, use them as a basis for the following steps, which can help get at the root causes of conflict and prevent its continuing recurrence.[30]

- Cause analysis, in which all the causes producing a conflict are identified, recorded, and evaluated. The goal is to accurately identify all the causes of conflict (not just the primary or most obvious ones), record them in a way that provides decision support, and evaluate their relative importance.

- System analysis focuses on the whole causal system and the interrelations of its various parts and processes. To identify the root cause or causes, we need to know if the conflict is a result of several actions or inactions, decisions, or omissions that are part of how an organization does things. This is possible only if the whole, all its parts, and how they work together can be seen and understood.

- System control, which recognizes that root-cause analyses should identify, not only the causes of conflict, but also the points (all of them if there are several) in the causal process where management control exists, and changes can be made to prevent recurrence. Decision makers can then validate the data and make a balanced decision as to whether change is appropriate, considering other organizational priorities such as budgets, discipline, and consistency. Because of this need for balance, all opportunities for intervention must be identified so that management can decide which are in the overall best interests of all those involved.

Explicit root-cause analysis is more structured, is likely to involve more people, and typically would be used to address more significant issues than an implicit approach. It typically involves use of group problem-solving techniques, with an emphasis on how and why conflict developed and what changes can be made to minimize it in the future. Two primary considerations govern the approach.

- Individuals who are able to understand and articulate the causes of the conflict, are familiar with the organizational system and its individual parts, and are able to change the system when it is broken should conduct root-cause analyses.

- The analysis should usually include a factual investigation combined with a facilitated problem-solving effort. With guidance from a facilitator, a group can analyze the facts and see trends, process flows, probabilities, and other issues that point to possible root causes. Nominal group techniques, brainstorming, or other similar processes will ensure that all participants contribute to developing options.

Implement Formal Policies and Procedures

Too many formal rules stifle an organization's creativity and innovation. On the other hand, appropriate policies and procedures provide the maps that tell all employees what is expected and provide the continuity necessary for a living, learning organization. They should be considered when learning from conflict resolution, root-cause analyses, and other sources indicates a need for changes in behavior or more consistency over time. When policies or procedures are needed to meet such needs, they should be clear, concise, and communicated to all affected so they will drive desired behavior. And finally, they should be under continuing review and revised as appropriate based on learning from the conflict resolution process and other sources.

Appoint a Conflict Management Coordinator

This individual would be the focus of management involvement in conflict and could serve as an internal facilitator, ombudsperson, or simply someone to handle the administrative aspects of conflict resolution. Having such a position on a full- or part-time basis provides a focus for an institutional memory of conflict and for leveraging individual learning from it.

Maintain Good Organizational Files

People come and go, and they often have poor or convenient memories. Therefore, good files are necessary for good institutional memory. Maintaining files about conflict and its resolution as well as those reflecting policies, procedures, or other actions that affect or are affected by conflict can be one of the roles of a conflict management coordinator. The files can be used to discern patterns and other information that helps identify root causes and how they need to be addressed, and to guide supervisors and employees over time about how they should behave to minimize counterproductive conflict.

- An employee has been involved in several personal conflicts with other employees. Research of the files shows that several employees in his department also have been involved in conflict—more than in other departments. This leads to further investigation, which shows high stress and poor working conditions as the cause.

- Review of files provides a basic needs analysis for a conflict management training program.

KEY POINTS

1. Effective organizations must learn from conflict and its resolution in order to minimize conflict and enhance performance.

2. Organizations are holistic entities that have many characteristics of their members, including the ability to learn.

3. Organizational learning from conflict involves a cycle that contains an event or happening, analysis of that event, a decision as to what to do about it, and implementation of that decision, all of which circle back to affect future events.

4. Management can foster individual learning by encouraging a synergistic spiral of knowledge and double-loop learning, which addresses both the symptoms and the underlying causes of conflict.

5. Organizational learning occurs when knowledge is embedded in the minds of a critical mass of individuals and in the organization's systems so that it becomes a part of the institutional memory.

Epilogue

Conflict, like death and taxes, will be with us always. As we have mentioned in this book, some counterproductive conflict is natural and inevitable, and any management that thinks it can impose simple solutions or legislate it away is engaging in wishful thinking. The good news is that conflict can be managed in ways that greatly limit its negative effects and take advantage of its unlimited opportunities for both individual and organizational learning and growth. Whether an organization benefits from this good news is up to its management.

Management's challenge is to take those actions that will make the most of this less-than-perfect situation. It must understand why conflict exists, think deeply about the best ways to address it, and work collaboratively with employees to leverage all their energy and talents to minimize the effect of counterproductive conflict to the extent possible. The "minimize, surface, resolve, and learn" cycle introduced in this book provides a framework for a systemic approach to doing that.

One of the beauties of this conflict management cycle is its flexibility. Using it does not require a program or an identified initiative aimed at changing the behavior of employees. Instead, management, managers, and supervisors lead an organization toward its destination by changing the way they behave. They can change employee behavior and minimize the negative effects of workplace conflict by managing themselves: by improving both their personal behavior and how they promulgate and administer the organization's systems and processes.

The basic question seems to be why a management representative should take this journey and make the effort to change her own or management's behavior. Doing so requires effort and risk and often can be done only at considerable cost. The answer lies in whether a manager wants to steward the organization on a journey to optimize its performance or settle for being an observer of an entity floating without direction to an unknown destination. Stewardship involves more rewards for the organization and all its stakeholders and more fun for those willing to devote their time and energy to it.

The conflict management journey can start at any point on the cycle. And it can be traveled by management as a whole or by individual managers and supervisors. Whether they start with actions to minimize conflict by improving systems and processes, to surface that which is being suppressed, to resolve existing conflicts, or to learn from those they are already dealing with, the route is always the same. It is a circle of continuous improvement with no beginning and no end.

Individual managers and supervisors at all organizational levels can do many things, even if management as a whole is reluctant to go along. Individuals can change their own behavior within the scope of their responsibilities. As outlined in Chapter 7, they can foster a mutual-gains climate, maintain a collaborative management style, handle rewards appropriately, communicate effectively, and build on all this through the principle of reciprocity. In addition, individuals can do many of the things discussed elsewhere within their spheres of responsibility. They can properly manage change, effectively administer policy, build trust, and take all the other actions that will minimize conflict in their corner of the organizational world. Doing this will build islands of excellence that will inevitably rub off on other parts of the organization and move it incrementally in the right direction.

In some organizations, however, incremental, bottom-up improvement in conflict management may miss opportunities or be insufficient to meet competitive challenges. In these organizations, management as a whole must use its broader scope and greater power to transform the way conflict is managed across the entire workforce. When senior management leads the aggregate efforts of all managers, supervisors, and employees toward a common vision, the organization benefits from the synergy of ideas and the power of collaboration. Once a critical mass is onboard, an organization troubled by excessive conflict can cross the tipping point to relative peace, productivity, and excellence. Leading a corporate journey such as this requires management to do several things.

First, it must assess the business need for a concerted effort to better manage conflict. The change required to do so can be difficult, expensive, and at times risky, and it must be carried out over a long period of time, through ups and downs in the business cycle. The commitment and continuity necessary for the long haul will not be present unless managers see a real opportunity for payback. Before beginning an improvement initiative, therefore, management must be confident that opportunities for improvement are available, and that pursuing them will further the organization's business purposes. Without such assurance, maintaining support of the critical mass of managers, supervisors, and employees necessary for success will be almost impossible. A process for determining this need was outlined in Chapter 11.

Second, senior managers, the drivers of change, must change themselves. Only individuals can have values, think, act, or decide—so managers must change as individuals if they are to lead a broader change. And they must set the tone for the organization and lead by example if they expect others to follow. Senior managers are supervisors, too, and this means that as individuals they should consider the ideas presented in Chapter 7 and adopt those that will improve their performance. To lead a broader change, however, they must also ensure that management—the aggregate "they" who run the organization—is also perceived as being onboard. This happens when a critical mass of managers and supervisors support, rather than resist, the organization's initiatives. The ideas presented in Chapter 5 for managing change effectively can be helpful to managers implementing a changed approach to conflict management.

Third, managers should not talk about it—they should do it. This doesn't mean not having a plan or not communicating appropriately regarding specific initiatives. It does, however, mean avoiding high-profile, programmatic solutions of the month that are likely to make changes seem bigger than they are and engender more resistance than support. It also means leading with action rather than with words and having success build on success. Building success on success requires working on substantive issues of real importance to the organization. Communication, training, and other such interventions may be helpful, but making progress in real areas important to the business provides the incentive and immediacy for commitment to change, the laboratory conditions for learning from doing, and the clear and immediate feedback necessary for continual learning and development, as discussed in Chapter 12.

And finally, management must follow through. Follow-through is probably the most neglected yet critical aspect of any change effort. The energy and mutuality that exist at the start frequently decline as reality hits and people begin to appreciate the effort required and the competitive pressures in other directions. But just as death, taxes, and conflict never end, efforts to manage conflict also must never end. That's why the conflict management model presented in this book is circular. Minimizing conflict, surfacing that which nevertheless occurs, resolving it, and learning from the process in order to begin the cycle again requires continuity of management attention on a never-ending journey.

Only the people within an organization can decide whether to take this journey. The ideas presented in this book must be filtered through the lens of their own experiences and adapted to the circumstances in their particular workplace. But if they see managing conflict as an opportunity, they are obligated to capitalize on it. Anything less is an abrogation of their responsibility.

Notes

1. *Houston Chronicle, 101* (57), December 9, 2001.

2. The essence of the following section was first published in "How to Make the Most of the Employment ADR Process," by Kirk Blackard, in the May 1999 *Dispute Resolution Journal,* pp. 71–77.

3. O'Connor, J., and McDermott, I. *The Art of Systems Thinking.* San Francisco: Thorsons, 1997, p. 2.

4. Folger, J. P., Poole, M. S., and Stutman, R. K. *Working Through Conflict.* New York: Addison-Wesley, 1997.

5. Ideas in this section rely heavily on J. R. Boatright's *Ethics and the Conduct of Business* (Upper Saddle River, N.J.: Prentice-Hall, 1993).

6. Boatright, J. R., *Ethics and the Conduct of Business,* p. 195.

7. Bush, R. A. B., and Folger, J. P. *The Promise of Mediation.* San Francisco: Jossey-Bass, 1994.

8. Kurt Lewin is generally credited with describing the force-field analysis as the basic dynamic of the change process. See O. G. Mink, P. W. Esterhuysen, B. P. Mink, and K. Q. Owen, *Change at Work* (San Francisco: Jossey-Bass, 1993), for a more complete discussion.

9. Conner, D. R. *Managing at the Speed of Change.* New York: Villard, 1993, p. 132.

10. Blackard, K. *Managing Change in a Unionized Workplace.* Westport, Conn.: Quorum Books, 2000.

11. Grote, D. *Discipline Without Punishment.* New York: Amacom, 1995.

12. Burley-Allen, M. *Listening.* New York: Wiley, 1995, p. 3.

13. Grote, D., *Discipline Without Punishment,* p. 12.

14. Bush, R. A. B., and Folger, J. P. *The Promise of Mediation.* San Francisco: Jossey-Bass, 1994, pp. 85–90.

15. The information contained in this section was first published in "How to Make the Most of the Employment ADR Process," by Kirk Blackard, in the May 1999 *Dispute Resolution Journal,* pp. 71–77.

16. Senge, P. M. *The Fifth Discipline.* New York: Doubleday, 1990, pp. 69–174.

17. Van Slyke, E. J. *Listening to Conflict.* New York: Amacom, 1999, p. 75.

18. The information contained in this section was first published in "Assessing Workplace Conflict Resolution Options," by Kirk Blackard, in the February-April 2001 *Dispute Resolution Journal,* pp. 57–62.

19. Argyris, C. *On Organizational Learning.* Cambridge, Mass.: Blackwell, 1992.

20. Argyris, C., and Schön, D. A. *Organizational Learning II.* Reading, Mass.: Addison-Wesley, 1996.

21. Senge, P. M., *The Fifth Discipline.*

22. De Geus, A. *The Living Company.* London: Nicolas Brealey, 1997.

23. Harvard Business Review. *Knowledge Management.* Boston: Harvard Publishing, 1987.

24. For a more complete discussion of the two types of learning, see C. Argyris, *On Organizational Learning,* p. 8.

25. For a more complete discussion of synergistic learning, see Ikujiro Nonaka, "The Knowledge-Creating Company," Harvard Business Review, *Knowledge Management,* p. 21.

26. Garavin, D. A. "Building a Learning Organization," Harvard Business Review, *Knowledge Management,* p. 47.

27. The idea for this metaphor is from A. de Geus's *The Living Company,* p. 125.

28. Argyris, C., *On Organizational Learning,* p. 26.

29. For a more complete discussion of transformative mediation, see R. A. B. Bush and J. P. Folger, *The Promise of Mediation.*

30. For a more complete discussion of root cause analyses, see P. F. Wilson, *Root Cause Analysis: A Tool for Total Quality Management* (Milwaukee, Wis.: ASQC Quality Press, 1993).

Resources

Alternate Dispute Resolution Systems

Bush, R. A. B., and Folger, J. P. *The Promise of Mediation*. San Francisco: Jossey-Bass, 1994.

Costantino, C. A., and Merchant, C. S. *Designing Conflict Management Systems*. San Francisco: Jossey-Bass, 1996.

Nolan, D. R. *Labor and Employment Arbitration*. St. Paul, Minn.: West, 1998.

Ury, W. L., Brett, J. M., and Goldberg, S. B. *Getting Disputes Resolved*. San Francisco: Jossey-Bass, 1988.

Change

Bridges, W. *Managing Transitions*. Reading, Mass.: Addison-Wesley, 1991.

Conner, D. R. *Managing at the Speed of Change*. New York: Villard, 1993.

Dalziel, M. M., and Schoonover, S. C. *Changing Ways*. New York: Amacom, 1988.

Kanter, R. M. *The Change Masters*. New York: Simon & Schuster, 1983.

Kotter, J. P. *Leading Change*. Boston: Harvard Business School Press, 1996.

Leigh, A. *Effective Change*. London: Institute of Personnel Management, 1988.

McCrimmon, M. *The Change Master*. London: Pitman, 1997.

Mink, O. G., Esterhuysen, P. W., Mink, B. P., and Owen, K. Q. *Change at Work*. New York: Jossey-Bass, 1993.

Plant, R. *Managing Change and Making It Stick*. London: HarperCollins, 1987.

Communication

Alessandra, T., and Hunsaker, P. *Communicating at Work*. New York: Fireside, 1993.
Burley-Allen, M. *Listening*. New York: Wiley, 1995.

Conflict in Organizations

De Dreu, C., and Van De Vliert, E. (eds.). *Using Conflict in Organizations*. London: Sage, 1997.
Folger, J. P., Poole, M. S., and Stutman, R. K. *Working Through Conflict*. New York: Addison-Wesley, 1997.
Kolb, D. M., and Bartunek, J. M. (eds.). *Hidden Conflict in Organizations*. London: Sage, 1992.
Muldoon, B. *The Heart of Conflict*. New York: Perigee, 1993.
Nicotera, A. M. (ed.). *Conflict and Organizations*. Albany, N.Y.: SUNY Press, 1995.
Tjosvold, D. *The Conflict Positive Organization*. Reading, Mass.: Addison-Wesley, 1991.

Conflict Management

Borisoff, D., and Victor, D. A. *Conflict Management*. Boston: Allyn & Bacon, 1989.
Fournies, F. F. *Why Employees Don't Do What They're Supposed to Do*. New York: McGraw-Hill, 1988.
Rahim, M. A. *Managing Conflict in Organizations*. Westport, Conn.: Quorum, 2001.

Dispute Resolution

Cavenagh, T. D. *Dispute Resolution*. Cincinnati, Ohio: West, 2000.
Cloke, K., and Goldsmith, J. *Resolving Conflicts at Work*. San Francisco: Jossey-Bass, 2000.
Eaton, A. E., and Keefe, J. H. (eds.). *Employment Dispute Resolution and Worker Rights in the Changing Workplace*. Champaign, Ill.: IRRA, 1999.
Fisher, Roger, and Ury, William. *Getting to Yes*. Boston: Houghton Mifflin, 1981.
Gill, L. *How to Work with Just About Anyone*. New York: Fireside, 1999.
Hirsh, S. K. *Work It Out*. Palo Alto, Calif.: Davies-Black, 1996.
Kheel, T. W. *The Keys to Conflict Resolution*. New York: Four Walls Eight Windows, 1999.
Lebedun, J. *Managing Workplace Conflict*. West Des Moines, Iowa: American Media, 1998.
Levine, S. *Getting to Resolution*. San Francisco: Berrett-Koehler, 1998.
Pachter, B., and Magee, S. *The Power of Positive Confrontation*. New York: Marlowe & Company, 2000.
Scott, G. G. *Work with Me!* Palo Alto, Calif.: Davies-Black, 2000.
Stone, F. M. *How to Resolve Conflicts at Work*. New York: Amacom, 1999.
Van Slyke, E. J. *Listening to Conflict*. New York: Amacom, 1999.

Learning

Argyris, C. *On Organizational Learning*. Cambridge, Mass.: Blackwell, 1992.

Argyris, C., and Schön, D. A. *Organizational Learning II*. Reading, Mass.: Addison-Wesley, 1996.

Harvard Business Review. *Knowledge Management*. Boston: Harvard Publishing, 1987.

Management

Blackard, K. *Managing Change in a Unionized Workplace*. Westport, Conn.: Quorum Books, 2000.

Boatright, J. R. *Ethics and the Conduct of Business*. Upper Saddle River, N.J.: Prentice-Hall, 1993.

Dana, D. *Managing Differences*. Overland Park, Kans.: MTI, 1989.

Fein, R. *101 Hiring Mistakes Employers Make*. Manassas Park, Va.: Impact, 2000.

Gordon, T. *Leader Effectiveness Training*. New York: Putnam, 1977.

Grote, D. *Discipline Without Punishment*. New York: Amacom, 1995.

Nadler, G., and Hibino, S. *Creative Solution Finding*. Rocklin, Calif.: Prima, 1995.

Power

Dilenschneider, R. L. *On Power*. New York: HarperBusiness, 1994.

Galbraith, J. K. *The Anatomy of Power*. Boston: Houghton Mifflin, 1983.

Lambert, T. *The Power of Influence*. London: Nicholas Brealey, 1996.

Lee, B. *The Power Principle*. New York: Simon & Schuster, 1997.

Systems

Ahl, V., and Allen, T. F. H. *Hierarchy Theory*. New York: Columbia University Press, 1996.

De Geus, A. *The Living Company*. London: Nicolas Brealey, 1997.

Gleick, J. *Chaos*. New York: Penguin, 1987.

O'Connor, J., and McDermott, I. *The Art of Systems Thinking*. San Francisco: Thorsons, 1997.

Senge, P. M. *The Fifth Discipline*. New York: Doubleday, 1990.

Senge, P. M. *The Fifth Discipline Fieldbook*. New York: Doubleday, 1994.

Wilson, P. F. *Root Cause Analysis: A Tool for Total Quality Management*. Milwaukee, Wis.: ASQC Quality Press, 1993.

Trust

Fukuyama, F. *Trust*. New York: Free Press, 1995.

Ryan, K. D., and Oestreich, D. K. *Driving Fear Out of the Workplace*. San Francisco: Jossey-Bass, 1998.

Shaw, B. R. *Trust in the Balance*. San Francisco: Jossey-Bass, 1997.

Index

absenteeism, 117
ad hoc alternative dispute resolution, 224–225
administrator role, 197
ADR. *See* alternative dispute resolution
advocate role, 197
affective conflict. *See* personal conflict
allocation policies, 72–73
alternative dispute resolution: abuse potential of, 230; ad hoc, 224–225; arbitration, 222, 227; benefits of, 227–233; bottom-up communication benefits of, 228; concerns regarding, 229–230; confidentiality benefits of, 228; cost-benefit evaluations, 230–233; cost sharing, 223; definition of, 220; education in, 223–224; facilitation, 221; fact finding, 223; feedback, 224; level of conflict and, 232–233; litigation costs reduced by, 228; mediation, 222; ombudsperson, 168, 222; open-door policy, 220–221; options for, 220–224; peer review, 223; policy statement, 221; selection of, 226–233; strategies for, 224–226; trust-building benefits of, 228
arbitration, 222, 227

attitude, 150–151

behavior: changing of, 65; climate for, 19–20; distrust effects, 49–50; learning of, 83, 88–89; patterns of, 206, 208; self-interest motivations, 20; supervisor, 139–140; trust-building, 52–62; unacceptable, 176; validating, 213–214
behavior policies: description of, 73; learning of, 88–89; punishment for violating, 78–79, 176
beliefs: factors that affect, 22
bonus programs, 74, 79
boundaries, 174

causation: contributing, 17–18; proximate, 17–18; root, 17–18, 254–257; theories of, 19–24
cause analysis, 256
change: acceptance stages, 98; adjusting to, 104–105; communication of, 107–108; conflict caused by, 96, 109–110; employee involvement in, 105–107; feedback regarding, 110; follow-through of, 262; importance of, 235, 261; overview of, 95–96; participants